Gateway to Gettysburg

The Second Battle of Winchester

By
Larry B. Maier

BURD STREET PRESS
SHIPPENSBURG, PENNSYLVANIA

This Burd Street Press publication
was printed by
Beidel Printing House, Inc.
63 West Burd Street
Shippensburg, PA 17257-0708 USA

The acid-free paper used in this book meets the guidelines for permanence and durability of the Committee on Production Guidelines for Book Longevity of the Council on Library Resources.

For a complete list of available publications
please write
Burd Street Press
Division of White Mane Publishing Company, Inc.
P.O. Box 708
Shippensburg, PA 17257-0708 USA

Library of Congress Cataloging-in-Publication Data

Maier, Larry B., 1949-
    Gateway to Gettysburg : the second battle of Winchester / by Larry B. Maier.
       p. cm.
    Includes bibliographical references (p.   ) and index.
    ISBN 1-57249-287-2 (alk. paper)
    1. Winchester, 2nd Battle of, Winchester, Va., 1863. I. Title.

E475.5 .M35 2002
973.7'34--dc21

2002074502

PRINTED IN THE UNITED STATES OF AMERICA

This effort is dedicated to my son, Eric D. Maier, of whom I am enormously proud, and to my loving and patient wife, Janet Joy Maier.

Table of Contents

List of Illustrations vi
List of Maps vii
Preface viii
Acknowledgments xii

1   WINCHESTER   1

2   ROBERT HUSTON MILROY   14

3   UNDER MILROY'S HEEL   59

4   COMING...OR GOING?   101

5   "LET THE REBELS COME"   131

6   WEST FORT   175

7   CARTER'S WOODS   212

8   MILROY'S WEARY BOYS   255

    EPILOGUE   281

    ORDER OF BATTLE   314
    BIBLIOGRAPHY   319
    INDEX   328

List of Illustrations

Winchester Court House 10

Robert H. Milroy 17

A Milroy Patriotic Cover 56

Military Pass 67

Milroy's Accoutrements 82

Milroy's Presentation Sword 82

Milroy and Family 94

Robert H. Milroy 99

Richard S. Ewell 103

Henry W. Halleck 117

Robert C. Schenck 117

Jubal A. Early 187

Milroy Broadside 308

List of Maps

Lower Shenandoah Valley 4

Winchester 61

Kernstown Skirmish 153

Elliott's Counterattack 169

Early's March 189

Assault on West Fort 197

Carter's Woods: Johnson's Advance 219

Carter's Woods: Initial Contact 225

Carter's Woods: Keifer's and Ely's Assaults 235

Carter's Woods: Stonewall Brigade's Attack 240

Carter's Woods: McReynolds' Attack 250

Bloody Run / Cunningham's Crossroads 278

Preface

A perfect tragedy should...excite pity and fear....
[T]the change of fortune...must not be the spectacle of a
virtuous man brought from prosperity to adversity: for
this moves neither pity nor fear; it merely shocks us....
Nor, again, should the downfall of the utter villain be
exhibited...it would inspire neither pity nor fear; for pity
is aroused by unmerited misfortune, fear by the misfortune of a man like ourselves.... There remains, then, the
character between these two extremes—that of a man
who is not eminently good and just, yet whose misfortune
is brought about not by vice or depravity, but by some
error or frailty.

—Aristotle, 350 B.C.

Americans are fascinated by the Civil War for a multitude of
reasons. Personally, that curiosity is driven by a desire to delve into
how and why individuals, with varied personalities and backgrounds,
faced and largely overcame mortal fear, extreme hardship, and crushing
stress. The Civil War holds a unique ability to satisfy that interest
because it was recent enough to leave tens of thousands of pages of
personal history, via letters, diaries, reports, and individual or unit
memoirs, but archaic enough that the human element was still pre-
eminent. That is, unlike most modern wars where technology and
industrial power dominate the field of battle, and where the dead and
crippled are often reduced to markers that tally the success or failure of
machines, Civil War soldiers were primarily responsible for the success

or failure of the engagement.[1] Whether the common men of one side or the other were braver or more tenacious, or their commanders were more or less intelligent, daring or indolent than the opposition, usually determined whether blue or gray held the field after the din of battle drifted off into history. Further, perhaps because of the loftiness of the ideals over which they contended, the personalities that emerge from that river of words somehow glow with a brighter light. The heroes seem more heroic, the common soldiers more stoic, the scoundrels more craven, and the generals either more or less brilliant than in either the impersonal and mechanized slaughter of the great wars in the first half of the twentieth century, or in the vicious but relatively small and anonymous skirmishes that characterized guerrilla wars in its latter half.

There were few if any Civil War battles where the outcome was more influenced by the personality of one man than was the conflict now known as Second Winchester. This is especially true since the second battle at Winchester never should have been fought. Almost from the day that the Union garrison trudged into the isolated and vulnerable town of Winchester, Virginia, on Christmas Eve 1862, Union General in Chief Henry W. Halleck began to fret over the potential fate of Major General Robert H. Milroy's division of occupiers. Ultimately, it was the force and product of Milroy's personality that proved more compelling than Halleck's jitters. And more than any other factor, it was Milroy's single-minded determination that caused the Federal garrison to linger in Winchester while Robert E. Lee's Army of Northern Virginia began to pour into the Shenandoah Valley on June 12, 1863. When the true nature of the threat was revealed to Milroy during the 24 hours following Lee's arrival, common sense would seem to have screamed for Milroy to retreat from a force nearly three times the size of his own. Despite the obvious implications of his division's situation, Milroy held on until disaster was virtually assured.

Milroy didn't cling to the fortifications outside Winchester pursuant to orders that he must hold what amounted to the gateway to Pennsylvania "at all hazard." The Federal high command was virtually

---

[1]It has been estimated that 75 percent of Civil War casualties were caused by rifle fire while only 10 percent were caused by artillery. In World War II, 75 percent of casualties resulted from artillery and bombs dropped from airplanes.

oblivious of Robert E. Lee's plans until the garrison in Winchester had already been smashed. Delaying the Rebel invasion until reinforcements could arrive was not the motivation for the Yankees remaining in Winchester. Rather, they stayed because Milroy, for reasons of his own, decided that they should.

Milroy neither issued the fateful orders because he was stupid nor because of an alcohol induced haze. Prior to the war he obtained several college degrees, practiced law, and served a brief stint on the bench, and by all indications he was a man of strict probity. Although a volunteer rather than a West Point graduate, Milroy was not merely a political general and he did not make the decision to stay as a result of ignorance in the ways of war. By the time his garrison began the occupation of Winchester, Milroy had accumulated a degree in military science, combat experience in the Mexican War, and rank achieved by leading men in numerous smaller engagements and one major battle during the first two years of the war. Although he did not record such thoughts, when the true dimensions of the threat became apparent, he must have at least dimly understood the implications of commanding the only force directly between the Confederates and central Pennsylvania. More than any other factor, this effort was fueled by a desire to understand why a man like Milroy could have been responsible for what was arguably one of the most stupid command decisions made during the Civil War.

Milroy was not just a construct of his I.Q., college degrees, and twin stars, acting upon an empty stage. His military experiences shaped his judgment, while the post he commanded, especially the behavior of the residents of Winchester, manipulated his perceptions and thought processes in compelling, yet subtle, ways. Most importantly, however, this writer believes that Milroy's personality harbored what Aristotle identified, and what has subsequently been labeled, as a "tragic flaw." That flaw warped the Union commander's judgment while simultaneously obscuring its own existence. Milroy became a pawn of his own frailty.

Like a rock tossed into a pond, the impact of Milroy's "tragic flaw" sent ripples of consequences through his own life, the lives of his men, his opponent's lives, and perhaps the ultimate history of our country. Nine thousand Bluecoats suffered various penalties ranging from death, to capture, to exhaustion and humiliation, as a result of their association with Milroy. The Confederate commander who opposed

Milroy, Lieutenant General Richard S. Ewell was new to the duties of leading a corps. The afterglow of a marginally deserved triumph may have carried him further than his talents warranted. One may even legitimately speculate that Milroy's "tragic flaw" influenced the duration or even the outcome of the war.

Many participants in the war believed that God was taking a direct hand in determining their fates. If so, it may be that He prolonged the conflict in order that mutual hatred would melt into exhaustion and respect. Perhaps it was even part of His plan to ensure that the most ardent, or those least inclined toward forgiveness, would not return from the field of battle to poison future reconciliation. Had a different man, or a different personality, been in command at Winchester, the Confederates might have had time to wreak so much havoc in Pennsylvania that a demoralized Union citizenry would have compelled President Lincoln to sue for peace. Or, perhaps Milroy's intact division might in some way have contributed to a crushing Union victory that could have ended the war in the summer of 1863. Speculation aside, Milroy's "tragic flaw" scratched a story across the lives of thousands of Americans. This history attempts to chronicle some of that story.

Acknowledgments

First, I would like to thank Ms. Glenda Brown of the Rensselaer Public Library. Access to the Robert H. Milroy collection was essential to this effort, but travel to Indiana for the necessary length of time would have been extremely difficult. Ms. Brown was kind enough to copy and mail the pertinent portions of the collection to me, so that I could fully utilize the material. In addition, she went out of her way to supply me with copies of photographs from the Milroy collection. She was always courteous and diligent in her assistance—attitudes that were both refreshing and much appreciated.

As in my previous books, Donald Barrett wielded his computer keyboard and produced another group of outstanding maps. This time, however, he had to do so under significant time pressure. I am truly grateful for his help, as well as for the patience of his wife who lost his companionship for many hours.

Without the efforts of my office's talented computer wizard Brenda McDonald, this book would not have been possible. Not only did she transform my raw typing into a camera-ready product, but she did so with cheery enthusiasm. How she managed, despite my repeated demands that interrupted her primary office responsibilities and multiplied her stress, is a mystery to me. I may not understand how she managed, but I am very thankful that she did.

Finally, I would like to thank my wife, Joy. She never complained about the hundreds of times that I woke her as I left for the office in the predawn darkness, so that I could do research or write before the usual activities of the law office began, or about all the Saturday mornings that I spent at the computer rather than at home. Time is the most precious commodity in completing a project such as this, and she helped make that time possible. Thanks, Honey!

1

WINCHESTER

*...[T]he men [of Winchester] are all in the army and
the women are the devil.*

—William H. Seward

A host of factors contributed to making the Shenandoah Valley, except perhaps for Richmond or New Orleans, the most important location in the Confederate States of America. Foremost was its strategic geography. The Valley, wedged between the Blue Ridge Mountains on the east and the Allegheny Mountains on the west, stretched from its northernmost point on the Potomac River to its apex in the south a distance of approximately 150 miles.[1] The lower half of the Valley, from Strasburg, Virginia, to the Potomac, was further north than Washington, D.C., while its upper reaches were south of the Confederate capital in Richmond. Winchester, the heart of the Shenandoah Valley, sat only 60 miles from the Federal capital. Staunton, in the Valley's center, lay only 100 miles from that of the Confederacy.

Those correlations represented more than geographer's trivia. The Blue Ridge Mountains amounted to a huge rampart

---

[1]Tanner, p. 3. The Valley's namesake, the Shenandoah River, runs from south to north. As a result, the northern end of the Valley is commonly referred to as the lower Valley and the southern end is considered to be the upper Valley.

1

standing between the Valley and the balance of the Old Dominion
State. Eleven reasonably passable gaps in the Blue Ridge served
as virtual sally ports from which Union forces, if they held the
Valley, could launch a surprise flank attack that could reach
Richmond in about the same time that it would have taken to
march there from Washington.

The Valley offered an even more significant threat to the
Union. Not only could those same mountain gaps allow Confederate forces to launch a surprise offensive into the rear of an unwary
or lead-footed Union force stationed in the Valley, but its mouth
was 30 miles *behind*, and less than three hard days of marching
from Washington.[2] Nearly as ominous, the level bottomland, of
which the Shenandoah Valley was a part, stretched north all the
way to Harrisburg, Pennsylvania. That city was not only the
capital of the Keystone State, but perhaps more importantly, was
a vital railroad depot located where the mighty Pennsylvania
Railroad crossed the Susquehanna River. If Harrisburg were ever
captured, the main route from the east coast to Pittsburgh and the
western states would have been severed. Even worse, if the
Rebels held an intact bridge across the river, and were bold
enough to make the attempt, gray-coated infantrymen could have
reached Baltimore in three marching days or Philadelphia in four.[3]

Man's handiwork made the lower Shenandoah Valley even
more crucial to the North. The Baltimore and Ohio Railroad was
the second most important railroad in the Union because, along
with the "Pennsy," it connected the industrial northeastern states
with western Virginia's coal, and the markets, grain, and manpower of the fast growing Midwest. Constructed at a time when the
possibility of civil strife was only a fear of the most pessimistic,

---

[2]Armies of that day could consistently cover two miles per hour and 20 miles
per day. When necessary that total could be stretched, under ideal conditions, to
30 miles per day for short periods.

[3]The marching distance assumes about 25 miles per day at a marching rate of
two miles per hour. Both sides accomplished comparable marches during the war.

a portion of the B & O ran through the lower Valley on the south side of the Potomac River, from Harpers Ferry, (then) Virginia, to Cumberland, Maryland. When Virginia seceded, that portion of the line lay within the Confederacy for a short period of time, and perilously close to it thereafter, without any geographic protection such as a river or mountains. Almost as important, and equally vulnerable, was the Chesapeake & Ohio Canal which started at Cumberland and helped to supply Washington, rather than Baltimore, with food and fuel.

Further up the Valley, other rail lines provided vital economic links as well as the potential for rapid troop deployment. Winchester was connected to the B & O by the Winchester and Potomac Railroad; Strasburg was tied to the Piedmont region of Virginia by the Manassas Gap Railroad; and Staunton was tethered to Richmond by the Virginia Central. Lynchburg, just to the east of the upper reaches of the Valley, sat astride the most important railroad in the South, the Virginia and Tennessee Railroad, which was the Confederacy's equivalent of the Pennsy and the B & O rolled into one.

Although not as strategically important as the rail lines, the road network in the Valley was of great tactical significance. Preeminent among those roads, and the literal spine of the Shenandoah Valley, was the Valley Turnpike. The "Pike," as it was generally known, was a fairly straight, macadamized nineteenth-century version of a superhighway. Completed in 1840, the Valley Turnpike connected Staunton with Winchester and then passed through the railroad town of Martinsburg, (then) Virginia, on its way to the Potomac River port of Williamsport, Maryland.[4] In addition to its economic importance to the Valley, the Pike allowed its possessor to move troops, and especially their slow and

---

[4]Tanner, p. 17. North of Winchester the road was known as the Martinsburg or Williamsport Turnpike.

Lower Shenandoah Valley

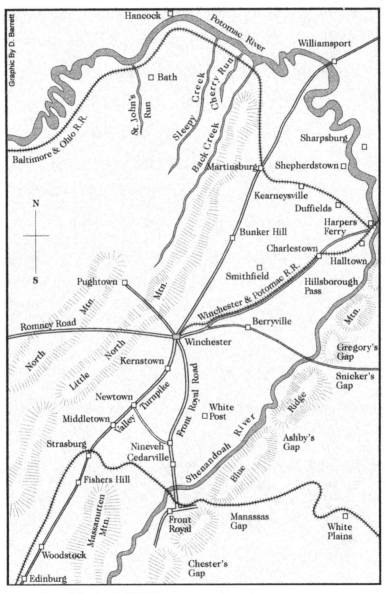

From: O.R. Atlas Pl. CXXXVI

Scale in Miles

0   10   20

cumbersome wagon trains, almost as rapidly, and more conveniently, than would a railroad. If the Bluecoats held the Valley Turnpike, they could use it as a raceway to speed armies to a chosen gap in the Blue Ridge, and from there perhaps to the flank of their opponents. If in Gray hands, the Pike could funnel troops behind the curtain provided by the same Blue Ridge to the rear of the Federal capital—and whoever held Winchester controlled the Pike.

A lesson that the War Between the States would teach to the world was that economics are almost as important to warfare as troops and the ability to move them. To the Confederacy, the Shenandoah Valley was as economically vital as it was strategically and tactically important. Commonly considered to be the breadbasket of Virginia, the limestone-rich bottomland of the Valley produced wheat yields that averaged twice the number of bushels per acre as could be wrung from fields on the other side of the Blue Ridge. When processed through the mills that dotted the banks of its many waterways, huge armies could subsist on the river of flour pouring eastward on its railroads.[5] In addition to food and horse fodder, the Valley also produced an abundance of other vital components of nineteenth-century war-making. The family farmers who tilled most of the Valley had, by the outbreak of the Civil War, become experts at breeding and raising an abundance of the finest horses available to the South. From bottom to top, the Valley spewed products of its numerous forges, woolen factories, tanning mills, flour mills and lumber yards. Its upper reaches also yielded scarce natural resources—lead for bullets and salt for preserving meat. More important than any product, though, the Valley produced that time period's most vital martial resource: strong, active, and spirited young men who

---

[5]Tanner, p. 15.

became some of the Confederacy's most ardent and fearsome warriors.[6]

It was no accident that the young men of the Shenandoah Valley were among the fiercest and most daring of the gray and butternut-clad fighters who became renowned for those traits.[7] Warfare and bloodshed were integral parts of the history and heritage of the Valley. Long before white settlers began to till the Valley's soil, it was a battleground for Native Americans. Although hunted, fished, and traveled by various tribes including Cherokees, Shawnees, Delawares, and Catawbas, it was the latter two tribes who spilled the most blood in the otherwise bucolic wilderness between the mountains. The hit-and-run warfare between the tribes was usually vicious and deadly, as for example when a Delaware raiding party was surrounded and slaughtered at Hanging Rock.[8] Any brave who had the misfortune to be taken alive usually passed from this world in a haze of pain from excruciating torture, while women and children taken in raids spent the remainder of their days as slaves or unwilling wives.

It was not until the 1670s that the first white men viewed the Shenandoah's beautiful battleground, and it was not claimed for England until 1716. The Indians generally ignored the first scattered ethnic and native German and Scotch-Irish settlers who began to sprinkle the Valley. But as fences and fields began to interfere with free travel and hunting, the original inhabitants retaliated with raids on isolated farm families as brutal as any they had inflicted upon each other. By the early 1750s the Valley had become an armed camp where immigrant settlers cowered in their

---

[6]One of the most famous units of the Civil War, the Stonewall Brigade, was raised in the Valley almost entirely from its residents.

[7]Many Confederate soldiers wore uniforms of a tannish color, produced by a dye made from copperas and walnut hulls, which was referred to as butternut. Faust, p. 101. Eventually the Rebels were nicknamed Butternuts because of the color of their uniforms.

[8]Tanner, p. 4.

log cabins at night with their only protection against sudden death, torture, or rape being stout doors, barred shutters, and a loaded and primed flintlock hanging from the mantel.

The hit-and-run war between Indians and settlers accelerated when, at the commencement of the French and Indian War, the French took an active role in encouraging and rewarding atrocities against the farmers in the English-controlled Valley. In an attempt to stem the carnage, the British launched an expedition, led by General Edward Braddock, that was intended to eliminate the French stronghold at Fort Duquesne (present-day Pittsburgh, Pennsylvania). The sortie ended in a disaster for the British, and had it not been for the frontier skills of the young George Washington, who went along as a scout, the entire red-coated army probably would have been annihilated.[9]

Washington was quickly placed in charge of the Valley defenses. With his new authority, the future Founding Father immediately directed the construction of a crude earthen fort on the edge of Winchester, which had only been founded in 1743. Over the next several years, Washington presided over construction of a string of 26 blockhouses and stockades at all of the major gaps in the Allegheny Mountains, which the Indians used to penetrate into the Shenandoah Valley.[10] It soon became apparent, however, that passive defense was inadequate, a fact which prompted Washington to focus upon increasing the potency and aggressiveness of the Valley militia. Years of sorties and firefights culminated with a major battle in 1774 in which 1,000 militiamen from the Valley routed an equal number of Indians in an all-day, stand-up fight that freed the Valley from further significant Indian threats.

---

[9]By the time of the expedition, Washington was already very familiar with the Shenandoah Valley, having surveyed many of its trails as a teenager and having purchased 1,459 Valley acres at the age of 19. Tanner, pp. 6-7.

[10]Tanner, pp. 8-9.

During the Revolutionary War the Valley supplied a host
of battle-hardened sharpshooters to the American cause, as well as
a corridor between the northern and southern colonies that was
sheltered from British infantry and naval power. Over the ensuing
60 years, several generations of Valley men rather actively
participated in local militia units. When at home, those same
weekend warriors nurtured their sons with tales of ancestral
military prowess and heroism. It should not have been a surprise
that by the eve of the Civil War, the Shenandoah Valley harbored
some of the most warlike men in the South.[11]

Fiery spirits did not necessarily translate into a shared
passion with the rest of Virginia, or the ante-bellum South, for
slavery and secession. In fact, the Valley was not particularly
amenable to slavery in either an economic or philosophical sense,
due to the ethnic and religious background of its many Mennonite
German and Scotch-Irish immigrant farmers, and the limited
financial benefit from slave labor on their relatively small family
farms.[12]   Despite its luke-warm attitude toward the "peculiar
institution," the town of Winchester played a key role in the John
Brown uprising—a role that cast the town, in Northern eyes at
least, as a den of rabid slavers.[13] When word arrived that Brown
had seized a building in Harpers Ferry on October 17, 1859, 150
members of Winchester's volunteer militia rushed to the scene.
Even though its volunteers were given only a limited role guarding
a bridge, Winchester's image in the North was further tainted
because Judge Richard Parker, a resident of Winchester, presided
over both Brown's trial and his hanging. The perception of

---

[11]The Virginia Military Academy, perhaps at the time the second most
prominent such institution in the country behind West Point, was located in the
Valley at Lexington, Virginia, and counted many of Winchester's sons among its
roll of cadets.

[12]Colt, p. 5.

[13]"The peculiar institution" was a euphemism for slavery that was commonly
employed by its Southern supporters.

Winchester as a hotbed of slavery was sealed when more militiamen from the town stood guard and watched as Brown choked on
the end of a rope and then swung limply in the breeze.[14]

Although incorrect as to the level of proslavery sentiment
in Winchester, the Northerner perception that the town was the
feisty heart and soul of the Shenandoah Valley was essentially
correct. Because of its railroad connection to the B & O and its
location at the nexus of the Valley Turnpike and at least seven
other significant roads that spanned the lower Valley, Winchester
was able to dominate the economic, political, and military life of
the Valley. At the start of the Civil War, it also held the largest
pool of manpower, as well as a significant proportion of the best
educated young men in the Valley. In 1860, Winchester was home
to about 4,400 persons—3,000 whites, 708 slaves, and 655 free
blacks—and was the seat of Frederick County, which had a total
population of 16,546.[15]

What is somewhat surprising is that as the storm clouds of
war brooded over the Valley, its citizens were initially opposed to
secession despite providing a huge majority in opposition to
Republican Abraham Lincoln in the 1860 election.[16] Two pro-
Union delegates from Winchester represented the Valley at the
Virginia convention that was assembled to debate the issue, and
both voted with the majority against secession on the first ballot.
Despite continuing to support the Union, the Valley delegates fell
into the minority when Virginia's articles of secession were
adopted after the attack on Fort Sumter.[17] Thereafter, allegiance
to their state proved stronger than to their country. Even though
the Shenandoans shared little cultural connection to the large
plantation, slave-owning, ante-bellum South, most of the inhabitants of the Shenandoah Valley gave their support to the

---

[14]Delauter, pp. 3-4.
[15]Tanner, p. 12; Colt, p. 6; Delauter, p. 3.
[16]Delauter, p. 5.
[17]Ibid., p. 7.

Confederate States of America with a vengeance. That allegiance
was so fierce that Federal Secretary of State William H. Seward
was prompted to remark during an early visit to occupied Winchester in 1862 that, "'...the men [of Winchester] are all in the
army and the women are the devil.'"[18]

If its initial pro-Union stance, and then almost fanatical pro-
war response were a surprise, Winchester's key role in the early
phases of the conflict was not. At first, Major General Thomas J.
"Stonewall" Jackson and his Valley army used the town as a
depot, headquarters, and springboard for his assaults against the
B & O Railroad and for a winter campaign against the Yankees in
western Virginia. Eventually, the pressure of vastly superior
Federal forces caused Jackson to abandon Winchester. Shortly
thereafter, on March 12, 1862,
the defenseless town was
seized by the Federals in the
first of many occupations.[19]

After strutting into
town to the cheers of a smattering of pro-Union citizens,
Major General Nathaniel P.
Banks' men found a town of
"...paved and level streets, an
imposing courthouse, a handsome market house, a jail, a
Masonic Hall, lyceum, two
newspapers, at least two
banks, several fire companies
and over fifty stores, not to
mention a dozen churches, one
large hotel, and more than a

Winchester Court House

(James E. Taylor)

---

[18]As quoted in Colt, p. 15.
[19]Delauter, p. 22.

few taverns...."[20] There were even gaslighted wooden sidewalks, from which militant Rebelettes descended into muddy streets in order to avoid the possibility that their skirts might inadvertently brush against the leg of a despised Yankee invader.[21]

The Bluecoats were not permitted to enjoy the comforts of Winchester, or forced to endure the insults of its women, for very long. After two months of near continuous combat in the middle of the Valley, Stonewall Jackson brought the war back to Winchester. On May 25, 1862, Jackson split his Valley army in two parts, sending Major General Richard S. Ewell and his division down the Front Royal Road against the southeastern corner of the town. "Old Jack" led the rest of his army against the southwestern corner in a crucial push to deprive the Federals of control of Apple Pie Ridge, the high ground that sheltered Winchester's western flank. A spirited charge collapsed the Union line posted on Bowers Hill and drove the panic-stricken Bluecoats through the streets of Winchester. As they fled, Rebel civilians fired previously hidden pistols at the backs of the Yankees from second-story windows and even dumped boiling water on a few hapless Federals caught milling about in the pandemonium.[22]

After nearly trapping Banks' army, Jackson turned his attention to the other Federal forces that threatened the Valley and as a result, by mid-June, Winchester was back under the heel of the hated Yankees. Instead of Banks, however, control of the town was placed in the none-too-gentle hands of Major General John Pope, who, thanks to his success on the western front, had just been given command of the Army of Virginia and the district in which Winchester was located. Pope left the town to be garrisoned by a single brigade under the command of Abram S. Piatt. The relatively inexperienced Piatt probably blanched when, along with the assignment, he received the following order: "You are

---

[20]Colt, p. 6.

[21]Ibid., p. 6; Delauter, p. 48.

[22]Delauter, pp. 28-29; Tanner, p. 287.

to understand that your command is posted and entrenched at Winc. to defend that place to the last. It is better to lose your whole force than to make a hasty or discreditable retreat...and if large forces are brought against you be sure that I will assault them in the rear before they can make an impression on you. "[23]

Even though he didn't need an incentive, the possibility of a fight to the last man propelled Piatt and gangs of sweating Bluecoats into a frenzy of fort building. It wasn't long before stone fence rows, parts of local buildings and several farm fields on Apple Pie Ridge were transformed into a series of earthen emplacements and rifle pits. Fort Garibaldi, which bristled with artillery, soon anchored the Union defenses and loomed over Winchester from the town's northwestern quadrant.[24]

Perhaps in recognition of the earlier bushwhacking and dousings with boiling water in the streets of Winchester, the Yankees kept the residents in mind as they made their preparations. The trees between Fort Garibaldi and the town were cut down so that the residents could always look up and see cannon muzzles seemingly pointed directly at them. Piatt's gunners also repeatedly fired wooden cannonballs over Winchester's rooftops in order to both intimidate the locals and accurately gauge the range to various points on the east and south. The townsfolk were undoubtedly angered by the wooden balls that occasionally dropped onto their streets. After a new garrison commander assumed control in August 1862, that emotion evolved from anger into fury when iron was substituted for wood and a Union gunner inadvertently put a shot through a house on Loudoun Street.[25]

On September 2, 1862, as a result of the crushing defeat inflicted on Pope's army at Second Manassas, the Union garrison

[23]*War of the Rebellion: Official Records of the Union and Confederate Armies*, series 1, vol. 12, part 1, p. 483. For convenience, further citations to the *Official Records* will be annotated as, for example, O.R. 1-12-1-483.

[24]Delauter, pp. 37-38.

[25]Ibid., pp. 38-39.

was pulled out of Winchester. It was probably a close question as to which side was the more relieved by the move. To demonstrate how they felt toward the citizens of Winchester, the Yankees torched the train station and several warehouses full of supplies, and detonated the powder magazine in Fort Garibaldi. Despite the Federals' best efforts, though, the fires were contained and the blast only broke a few windows throughout the town. When dawn broke over Winchester on September 3, the town was unoccupied and by that same afternoon gray-coated cavalrymen were meandering through its streets.[26]

The bliss of liberation was dampened when a flood of Southern casualties from the bloodbath at Antietam on September 17, 1862, filled almost every willing home in Winchester. Undoubtedly to the relief of the residents, by mid-October, except for some blood-stained parlor floors and a few severely wounded men who lingered in upstairs bedrooms, Winchester resumed its role as the bustling economic hub of the Valley and as a Confederate forward base. The residents were just becoming readjusted to a normal and agreeable routine when, on December 13, the Rebels were forced to abandon the city in order to contract their lines to a more easily defensible position up the Valley. For two weeks the town remained unoccupied, but on December 24, 1862, 3,000 Federals under the command of Brigadier General Gustav P. Cluseret marched into town. A week behind them rode Major General Robert Huston Milroy. Ironically, although he would become the town's most despised occupier, the citizens of Winchester would eventually have a more detrimental impact upon Milroy than Milroy would have upon Winchester.

---

[26]Delauter, pp. 41-42.

2

ROBERT HUSTON MILROY

Major General Milroy...
    I have never doubted your courage and devotion to the cause...[b]ut...I have scarcely seen anything from you at any time that did not contain imputations against your superiors and a chafing against acting the part they have assigned you. You have constantly urged the idea that you were persecuted because you did not come from West Point, and you repeat it in these letters. This, my dear general, is, I fear, the rock on which you have split....

—Abraham Lincoln[1]

    History has left only a few markers from the early life of Robert Huston Milroy that may be used to chart the development of his personality and character. He was born on June 11, 1816, in the then frontier territory of Indiana.[2] Robert was sired by Samuel Milroy, a man who was renowned for his sense of "honor and probity," and who captained a company of rangers during the War of 1812. Samuel had enough wealth to own at least one farm and a gristmill, and enough political status to have been chosen as a delegate to Indiana's first constitutional convention. Perhaps for

---

[1]Lincoln letter to Milroy, June 29, 1863, as quoted in Beach, p. 245.
[2]Unless otherwise indicated, all material on Milroy's life was obtained from the D. W. Macfie biographical manuscript which is housed at the Jasper County Public Library, along with Milroy's other papers, in Rensselaer, Indiana.

philosophical reasons, Robert's father chose not to provide his son with the more expensive private education that was seemingly within the family's means. Instead, along with what was probably a strict and proper upbringing, Robert was required to attend the local common school and to toil for hours each week in the various family businesses.

Apparently, the young Milroy tired of his rustic, and possibly subservient, life at home. In 1840 he displayed the first significant burst of independence that would later punctuate his military career, and moved to New England to seek his fortune. While there, Milroy enrolled in Captain Partridge's Military Academy of Norwich, Vermont.[3] Through a combination of intelligence and hard work, Milroy garnered three separate degrees in as many years: a bachelor of arts; a master of military science; and a master of civil engineering.

After completing his studies and touring the big cities of New England, the 27-year-old Milroy returned home and immediately commenced the study of law. Before long though, the reservoir of wanderlust that propelled him all the way to New England for schooling began to overwhelm both his ambition and his thirst for knowledge. In the spring of 1845 he pulled his nose out of boring legal tomes and moved to Texas in order to be a part of the excitement and drama of the transformation of Texas from a former Mexican province and independent nation into a newly annexed state. That adventure proved to be short-lived, however, because only a few months later the young adventurer received word that both his father and oldest brother had died. Duty to kin exerted a stronger pull than the thrill of adventure, and as a result Milroy, who may have been the oldest living brother, returned to the family homestead.

Either after he had made the necessary arrangements or after he could stand the boredom no longer, Milroy succumbed to

---

[3]Prowell, p. 63.

the call of patriotism and another adventure. In June of 1846 the untested military scientist raised a company of volunteers to fight in the Mexican War. The effort proved such a success that Milroy was mustered into the service as the captain of Company C, 1st Indiana Volunteer Infantry. Although records are scarce, it seems that Milroy and his regiment performed competently during their nearly two-year tour of duty under General Zachary Taylor.

When the war ended in the summer of 1848, Milroy and his regiment worked their way back to Indiana. When the final paper work was completed and he and his men were mustered out, Milroy resumed the study of law—this time at Indiana University in Bloomington. With the completion of his studies in the spring of 1849, sufficient fees began to flow from his law books to allow the Hoosier to take Mary Jane Armatage as his bride. It is not clear whether his marriage to the daughter of a contractor on the Erie Canal brought wealth and connections along with love and children, but within a year Milroy was elected as a delegate to a convention to revise the Indiana constitution.

In 1853, the governor of Indiana appointed the relatively inexperienced Milroy to a judgeship on the state's circuit court. Possibly because he suffered a pay cut by taking a seat on the bench; because he despised stupefying hours listening to contentious attorneys squabbling in stifling summer courtrooms; because of lonely nights spent in shabby hotels away from his beloved Mary while touring the circuit; or simply because he missed the thrill of competition, Milroy gave up the position in 1854. Not willing to take the easier path of partnering with a mentor though, Milroy moved his family to Rensselaer, Indiana, and hung out his own shingle.

Neither the next six years spent living the life of a quiet country lawyer nor the responsibilities of raising a growing family were sufficient to dampen Milroy's ambition, self-confidence, patriotism, or lust for adventure. As the momentum toward secession and civil war accelerated, the Hoosier's zeal for the twin causes of abolition and republicanism grew proportionately. On

February 7, 1861, slightly more than two months before artillery shells burst over Fort Sumter, Milroy issued a challenge to his fellow residents of Jasper County, Indiana, to join him in preparations to defend the Union. The petition, despite the overheated rhetoric common to the time, clearly displayed the passions and the personality that drove the man. "...Shall the flag of our Country, the glory and honor of which were laid and established by the wisdom of our forefathers, 'to secure the blessings of liberty to ourselves and our posterity,' and

Robert H. Milroy

(Frank Leslie's Illustrations)

before which tyrants have trembled and which has never yet been defied or questioned with impunity, be thus contemosed [probably an antiquated derivative of the word contempt] and set aside within our own borders? Forbid it Almighty God!... Within the next thirty days, the imbecile Administration [of President James Buchanan] whose pusillanimous conduct has given strength and confidence to this impious treason, will have expired and a new Administration, pledged that 'the Union must and shall be preserved,' will have commenced.... All who love their country, and are ready to lay down their lives for the perpetuation of our glorious Union, are requested to come forward and enroll their names. R. H. Milroy."[4]

---

[4]Macfie, pp. 10a-10b. Editorial additions to a quotation will be noted with brackets.

One hundred thirty men were sufficiently moved by Milroy's fervor to join his nascent company. Obviously impressed by Milroy's intelligence, education and war experience, and hoping to benefit from all three, the men also elected him to be their captain. Given that there was an abundance of officers with political pull but a scarcity of men with military credentials equal to Milroy's, the men of the other nine companies who eventually comprised the 9th Indiana Volunteer Infantry were probably satisfied when Milroy was promoted to colonel and given command of their regiment. Within days of his promotion in April 1861, Milroy was teaching his 90-day regiment their formations and evolutions from atop Jasper, the horse given to him by the citizens of his home county.

While the 9th Indiana spent its first month in the service performing drills and inspections, its commander took his first stab at challenging his superiors. All hands agreed that the regiment would be far more lethal if armed with Springfield rifled muskets rather than the antiquated smoothbore weapons that had been issued to them. To remedy the situation, Milroy prepared and forwarded to the United States Congress, a petition demanding those better arms. Indiana Congressman Colfax was so impressed by Milroy's idea that he solicited additional petitions from the other Indiana regiments then in training. At first, the Secretary of War refused all of the requests, claiming a poverty of Springfields. But after Colfax pleaded that he would be humiliated if totally unsuccessful, the secretary relented and authorized a shipment sufficient to arm one regiment—Milroy's 9th Indiana.

Clutching newly unpacked Springfields, the 9th Indiana was shipped to Grafton in western Virginia on May 29, 1861. Upon arrival, the regiment was placed under the command of Colonel Benjamin F. Kelley, an officer with no military experience but with a hefty wallet and a significant amount of political pull garnered through thirty years as a merchant and agent on the

Baltimore and Ohio Railroad.[5] Three days after their arrival, area commander Brigadier General Thomas A. Morris, a West Point graduate, ordered the troops under his command to attack a Confederate force ensconced at Philippi, western Virginia. The Union forces were split into two columns with Colonel Kelley in charge of the left wing. Kelley's own 1st West Virginia, nine companies of Milroy's 9th Indiana, and the 16th Ohio boarded a train at 9:00 a.m. on June 2, ostensibly for a movement to Harpers Ferry. After they had traveled far enough down the line to make the feint credible, the Federals disembarked and slogged 25 miles over rain-soaked country roads in order to reach their assigned jumping-off point at the rear of Philippi. As dusk descended on June 3, Kelley's men, and the right wing under the command of Colonel Ebenezer Dumont, surprised and routed an estimated 1,000 Confederates. As the battle neared conclusion, Colonel Kelley was seriously, but not mortally, wounded by a Confederate prisoner who shot him in the chest with a hidden pistol.[6]

After several weeks at Philippi, overall area commander Major General George B. McClellan led his command, including the 9th Indiana, in pursuit of a Rebel force led by General Morris' West Point classmate, Brigadier General Robert S. Garnett. The Southerners were caught at Rich Mountain, western Virginia, attacked in the rear by McClellan, soundly defeated, and mostly captured. Despite the dimensions of the victory, McClellan made a point of criticizing Morris for belatedly launching what was supposed to be a simultaneous frontal attack and thereby allowing some of Garnett's soldiers to escape.

During the Federal pursuit of the harried Confederates, Colonel Milroy and his commander, General Morris, repeatedly butted heads. On the first occasion, Milroy tried to convince

---

[5]Faust, p. 410.

[6]O.R. 1-2-1-66, 68, Morris; Stephens, pp. 131-132; Faust, p. 581. Although he had no direct role in the triumph, the victory helped to catapult Major General George B. McClellan into national prominence.

Morris to permit placement of a battery on a prominence so that the Southern works could be shelled. In the midst of the discussion one of Milroy's scouts rode up and reported that the Rebels had fled. Morris scoffed at the report, so Milroy led a skirmish line, and Morris' worried adjutant Captain Henry W. Benham, up and into the empty trenches of the enemy. Although Milroy proved his point, the embarrassment inflicted upon his superior officer may have generated more ill will than respect.

A more serious confrontation occurred a few days later. Milroy's 9th Indiana was in the vanguard of the pursuing Federal column when the Hoosier received orders to pause and wait for the balance of the command to catch up. Milroy shrugged off the order and pressed ahead until Adjutant Benham arrived on the scene. When Milroy asserted the necessity to continue forward and refused to halt, Morris' adjutant jumped into the middle of the road and threatened that Milroy would have to ride over Benham's corpse in order to continue. Morris arrived at midnight with a full head of steam over that confrontation, as well as Milroy's insubordinate choice of a different marching route than the one specified by Morris. Rather than stoically accepting the rebuke with dignity, Milroy responded to the criticism with the retort that the road he had chosen was shorter and better than the one specified in his orders. Morris wasn't about to accept such insolence from a mere graduate of Captain Partridge's Military Academy and gave the Hoosier colonel a loud and explicit "blowing up." Milroy was fortunate that his only punishment was the assignment of his regiment to the rear of the column rather than an arrest and court-martial.

The friction continued into the following day after the Federals chanced upon the rear of Garnett's fleeing column and killed the Confederate commander while he was trying to save his wagons. In the aftermath of the skirmish, some of Milroy's boys caught a Confederate captain who had the misfortune to have been a lawyer in civilian life. Milroy rode up to the hapless Rebel and lectured his captive, "'...if you are a lawyer you know what treason is; and in that capacity you also know what is the penalty attached to treason. These dead men over there did not really know what they were doing. They were brought into it by intelligent men like you. So it is time we're commencing to put the penalty in execution. I think you [are] a very good subject to begin with.' He then called out 'bring a rope here and we'll hang this traitor scoundrel.'"[7] Before Milroy could hoist his intended victim, however, General Morris rode up and with a wry chuckle told Milroy, "'...I guess we'll not hang the fellow. I'll take charge of him.'"[8]

The source did not offer an opinion as to whether or not Milroy was serious. Later actions, though, made it is clear that Morris was the much more generous of the two toward their common adversary. After Garnett's body was recovered, Morris had it sent through Union lines under a flag of truce so that it could be returned for a proper burial, and was also observed to have been visibly upset by the death of his former classmate.

Morris was not nearly so solicitous toward the sensibilities of his contentious subordinate from Indiana. The following morning Milroy got his regiment on the road at dawn and began to follow the rest of the Union column in pursuit of the Rebels. Before he could pass by Morris' tent, Milroy was interrogated about exactly what he thought he was doing. When the explanation was offered, Morris curtly ordered the 9th's commander to return his regiment to its former bivouac site and not to move an inch until ordered to do so.

Milroy was shocked and humiliated by another apparent reprimand. Although he had to submit, Milroy couldn't resist the opportunity to get in the last word. As his regiment was reversing its march, Milroy explained to his troops, "'...men, our campaign has come to an inglorious end. We are ordered to go back and not

[7]Macfie, p. 23.
[8]Ibid., p. 24.

to molest the rebels any more.'" Whether Morris' order was intended as an insult, or was merely in recognition of the fact that the 9th Indiana's term of enlistment was about to expire is now an open question, but it certainly wasn't in doubt as far as Milroy was concerned. In either case, within days Milroy and his charges were back in their home state and mustered out of the service.

Predictably, the same zest for killing Rebels that compelled Milroy to risk charges of insubordination rather than let any of them slip away drove him to immediately begin recruiting a new regiment as soon as, and perhaps even before, his old one detrained at Indianapolis. The former attorney was such a persuasive orator that by August 14, he had fully re-recruited the 9th Indiana as a three year regiment. A grateful government rewarded Milroy with a star two weeks later.

On September 14, Milroy and his new command received an urgent order to proceed to Elk Water, western Virginia, to reinforce Brigadier General Joseph J. Reynolds, whose command was being hemmed in by Rebels on several fronts. The arrival of the 9th Indiana (probably along with other blue-coated regiments) allowed Reynolds to reverse roles and begin to pursue his former besiegers in the direction of Cheat Mountain. Milroy was the perfect man to put in the vanguard if one wanted to press the enemy, and press them he did. On October 2, Milroy's infantrymen drove the Graybacks to within 600 yards of their camp after a four-mile running skirmish.[9] Unfortunately for the Yankees, the ensuing four-hour artillery barrage was unable to fracture the Confederate fortifications and, as a result, Reynolds was forced to withdraw.

On October 9, after they were all safely back in camp, Milroy was rewarded for his aggressiveness with command of the Third Brigade of the Cheat Mountain Division, which consisted of

---

[9]The term grayback was a nickname applied both to Confederate soldiers and to body lice.

his own regiment plus three Ohio regiments and an Indiana battery. Not only did the newly minted general receive his first brigade, he also received his first semi-independent command, a deployment to the summit of Cheat Mountain and orders to monitor the surrounding environs. It took Milroy only until November 24 to challenge the Butternuts. With his four regiments and battery, Milroy blew the Rebels away from their line behind Green River and back into their fortifications on top of Allegheny Mountain.

The Hoosier was forced to abandon his first effort to dislodge the Southerners from off their mountaintop, but appointment to command of the Cheat Mountain District on December 1, 1861, apparently supplied some additional men and further stoked the fire in his belly. On December 12, Milroy led 1,500 infantrymen against an estimated 2,000 well-entrenched Confederates under the command of Brigadier General Edward "Old Allegheny" Johnson, who was an 1838 graduate of West Point and a fellow veteran of the Mexican War.[10] Borrowing the plan that he had seen work at Philippi and Rich Mountain, Milroy divided his force into two contingents, reserving the frontal assault to himself and sending a Colonel Moody and two regiments to attack from the rear.

Moody was late in getting started, but rather than wait, Milroy launched an impetuous frontal bayonet assault that carried the enemy entrenchments and drove the Butternuts deep into their campground. For a few, seemingly endless, moments in the midst of the defender's huts, the contending forces dodged, parried, blocked, or were felled by bayonet thrusts, clubbed muskets, and point-blank rifle fire, all while trying to avoid becoming tangled in cook pots, tent ropes, and stray equipment.[11] Numbers quickly

---

[10]Tanner, p. 168.
[11]O.R. 1-5-1-456,457, Milroy.

prevailed though, and a Confederate counterattack drove the Federals almost back to their jumping-off point.

Faced with disaster, Milroy committed his reserves and stabilized the Federal line. Recognizing that his ammunition was all but depleted, Milroy launched one more desperate attack intended merely to recover his wounded. Perhaps to the surprise of everyone, that last-gasp assault carried the Federals all the way back into the Rebel camp.[12] The salient was held until the wounded were scooped up and then the Bluecoats scurried back down the mountain. After four hours of fighting, the Federals in front had traded 20 dead and 107 wounded for 26 Rebel prisoners and an acknowledged Southern loss of 118 killed or wounded.[13]

At 9:00 a.m., an hour after the fighting on Milroy's front had petered out, Moody finally attacked the Confederate rear. He had even less success than his commander and was only saved from further useless slaughter when Milroy rode around the mountain with only a small escort and called off the attack. Almost as soon as the gunfire ended, the Northern and Southern commanders began jousting for bragging rights through conflicting claims of victory in their respective after-action reports. Johnson boasted that his men held the field at the end of the contest and therefore the victors wore gray. Milroy asserted, somewhat less convincingly, that his Bluecoats had twice breached Rebel entrenchments that had been manned by markedly superior numbers while inflicting the majority of casualties.[14] Neither claim probably provided much solace to the bereaved or crippled.

During the balance of the winter of 1861-1862, Milroy kept his steadily growing force busy by dispatching them on small unit patrols and raids through snow-covered passes and over wind-swept mountains. On April 1, 1862, after winter in the mountains had broken, Milroy's brigade abandoned its earlier limited sorties,

---

[12]O.R. 1-5-1-457, Milroy.
[13]Ibid., 1-5-1-456, Milroy; O.R. 1-5-1-468.
[14]Ibid., 1-5-1-456, 460.

broke camp, and as the vanguard of Major General John C. Frémont's army, headed east toward the Shenandoah Valley in a measured pursuit of Allegheny Johnson's tiny command. At the start of the campaign the Bluecoats were able to claim the abandoned Rebel camp on Allegheny Mountain without a fight. Shortly thereafter they captured Monterey, western Virginia, following a small but bitter engagement. After being temporarily delayed in their march toward Staunton, Virginia, by 10 inches of newly fallen snow, Milroy's Federals finally reached the hamlet of McDowell, western Virginia, on May 1, 1862.

On May 4, the head of Milroy's column made contact with Johnson's rear guard about 15 miles west of Staunton at Buffalo Gap, the last pass into the Valley. Simultaneously, orders arrived from Frémont prohibiting a disgusted Milroy from launching an attack. Strung out along the valley and barred from taking the initiative, Milroy posted the men of the 32nd Ohio as an advanced picket and then pulled the balance of his command back into the mountains to marshal their strength. On the same day that the Blue and Gray bumped into each other at Buffalo Gap, Stonewall Jackson's Army of the Valley arrived on the scene and joined forces with Johnson's troops. Three days after that, the combined force of about 14,000 Rebels stormed over the 32nd Ohio "...so suddenly that they had to fall back leaving their tents and most of their baggage...."[15]

Sometime between the 4th and the 7th of May, Milroy received word of the Confederate combination. It is doubtful that he anticipated Jackson's full plan to rush down the Staunton and Parkersburg Turnpike, pummel Frémont before the Pathfinder could unite with the other Union forces lurking in the Valley, and then rush back out before being bottled up in the mountains.[16] But even without perceiving Jackson's entire plan, Milroy certainly

---

[15]Milroy letter, 5/13/1862.
[16]Tanner, p. 183.

recognized the immediate threat to his command created by the
Rebel combination and the ensuing rout of the 32nd Ohio.
Reacting promptly to the drubbing of his Buckeye regiment,
Milroy ordered the bulk of his command to fall back into a
defensive position outside McDowell, while leaving a small
contingent in front of the Southerners in order to maintain contact
and knowledge of their whereabouts. For the balance of May 7,
the gray vanguard and the blue rear guard exchanged sporadic
long-range sniper fire as the numerically superior Confederates
swept the Federal skirmish line down the Turnpike toward
McDowell.

Johnson's men received a rude surprise when their advance
carried them down the western slope of the Shenandoah Mountain.
A masked Federal battery, hidden by Milroy on Shaw's Ridge to
the west, began to "...shell them...with such effect as to cause the
enemy to retire beyond the Shenandoah Mountain."[17] That small
triumph proved to be short-lived. A sharp-eyed Federal scout soon
spied more Southerners crossing the mountain on the Union right
flank two miles to the south, a development that left Milroy with
no choice but to break off contact and pull the battery back to
McDowell.[18]

Fully cognizant that the responsibilities of a rear guard
(which his brigade had suddenly become) were to maintain contact,
delay the enemy, and survive, the Hoosier redeployed his men
during the night along the slight ridge that rose up behind the
western banks of the Bull Pasture River. Even as Milroy made his
dispositions, he must have recognized that this new position was
far weaker than it appeared and that his grip on the approach to
McDowell was tenuous at best. The Hoosier's brigade was too
small to hold his front and simultaneously repulse an attack that
the more numerous, and better situated, Rebels could afford to

---

[17]O.R. 1-12-1-465, Milroy.
[18]Ibid., 1-12-1-465.

launch against his vulnerable southern flank. Equally as ominous, his lines were dominated by the higher Bull Pasture Mountain on the east side of the river. That disparity in height between the two ridges was so great that in order to obtain the required elevation for their shells to have any effect, it was necessary for the Union cannoneers to dig holes under the trails of their guns.[19]

Delaying the enemy would be the easier part of his job. It would take the Confederates the better part of a day to either march a column through the forest to gain his right flank or to manually drag their artillery up the steep, wooded eastern slopes of Bull Pasture Mountain in order to blast the Federals away from the opposite side of the river. Assuring the survival of his command in the event of either possible Confederate maneuver would be Milroy's challenge. If the Hoosier was emotionally capable of doubt, his last fretful thought as he drifted off to sleep that night may have been to wonder whether his command would bed down the next night under his, or Stonewall Jackson's, command.[20]

On the morning of June 8, Johnson, who was undoubtedly confident that the day would bring more easy progress against the grossly outnumbered Federals, pushed his vanguard just over the crest of Bull Pasture Mountain. Rather than the welcoming sight of blue coats hustling into the distance, the first Rebels over the ridge were greeted by exploding shells and case shot. Despite the hail of shrapnel, the leading Butternuts took their positions and then hunkered down under the barrage while their more fortunate

---

[19]Tanner, p. 190.

[20]In Milroy's correspondence to his wife over a period of three years, not one comment was discovered that even hinted at introspection, circumspection, self-doubt, or fear. It is difficult at this point to determine whether Milroy's letters fully and accurately reflected his true self, were merely a stoic front displayed to his wife in hopes of allaying her fears, or if he refrained from such musings because he believed that was what a man of his time should do. Based upon his contemporaneous actions, however, it is this writer's opinion that if Milroy ever questioned himself, the answers always came back positive.

comrades shuffled along the Pike and up the eastern slope of the mountain.

Although the Yankee's artillery fire proved unable to staunch the flow of Rebels up and onto the ridge, the Federal's tactical situation changed from grim to hopeful during the early afternoon, when Brigadier General Robert C. Schenck's force of about 1,500 riflemen began to arrive in McDowell.[21] The reinforcements freed Milroy from the constraints imposed by poor geography and inferior numbers, especially the fear of being flanked and "gobbled up." The extra muskets also allowed his naturally pugnacious instincts to surface. The Hoosier apparently went immediately to meet with Schenck, who, as the senior officer on the field, was thrust into command as soon as he rode into the village. Knowing that Schenck lacked any knowledge about the situation, Milroy pressed the former politician for permission to make a "...reconnaissance for the purpose of obtaining accurate information of [the enemy's] strength and position."[22] With Schenck's consent in hand, Milroy gathered the 3rd West Virginia and the 25th, 32nd, 75th and 82nd Ohio regiments, at least 2,000 men in all, for his "reconnaissance."[23]

Then, undoubtedly to Johnson's amazement, Milroy launched the 25th and 75th Ohio regiments in a sudden and

---

[21]Macfie, p. 34. Prior to the war Schenck was a lawyer, Ohio state legislator, four-term United States congressman, and an ambassador to Brazil. Thanks to political pull, Schenck entered the service as a brigadier general. Prior to joining Frémont, his most significant exposure to combat came while leading a brigade at First Manassas. Faust, p. 660.

[22]O.R. 1-12-1-466, Milroy.

[23]Ibid. Milroy reported that he did not know the strength of the 82nd Ohio, but that the other regiments totalled 1,768. It may be safely assumed that Milroy always intended more than just a reconnaissance-in-force because a force that large would not have been necessary to locate an enemy that was already in plain view and being shelled. Further confirmation for this interpretation is found in his May 13 letter to his wife where he wrote that after observing that the Rebels "...were preparing to plant a battery [on the top of Bull Pasture Mountain], I obtained permission from Gen. Schenck to go up and try to dislodge them."

audacious frontal assault up the mountain. "Numbering less than 1,000 men, unprotected by any natural or artificial shelter, they advanced up a precipitous mountain side upon an adversary protected by entrenchments and the natural formation of the mountain...."[24] Arrayed to meet them, probably wearing incredulous looks on their faces, were four Southern infantry regiments, the 44th, 52nd, and 58th Virginia and the 12th Georgia.[25] The latter regiment, Johnson's former command, held the center, and the keystone, of the Rebel formation. Unfortunately for the Georgians, not only was their position the most important, it was also the most dangerous because they were close enough to the crest so as to be highlighted against the sky behind them.[26]

As the Federal battle line struggled up the slope, the Confederate rifle fire mostly whizzed harmlessly over blue-capped heads. Conversely, the volleys from the Yankees, who apparently wielded their Enfield rifles with uncommon marksmanship for Northerners, tore and shredded the Georgian line, leaving scores of Rebels in crumpled heaps bleeding at the feet of their comrades.[27] Even the scrub bushes were scythed by the attackers' withering fusillades.[28] The blistering fire and uncharacteristic Union aggressiveness were too much for the Butternuts and "...unsupported [the Federals] drove them (being at least twice their numerical strength) over the crest of the mountain, and for one and a half hours maintained unaided, while exposed to a deadly fire, the position from which they had so bravely driven the foe."[29]

"At about 4 o'clock in the afternoon, perceiving that the enemy's force was being constantly increased, I [Milroy] ordered

---

[24]O.R. 1-12-1-466, Milroy.
[25]Tanner, p. 190.
[26]Ibid., p. 191.
[27]Milroy letter, 5/13/1862.
[28]Tanner, pp. 191-192.
[29]O.R. 1-12-1-466, Milroy.

the 82nd [Ohio] regiment, of your [Schenck's] brigade, the 32nd Ohio, and 3rd West Virginia to turn the right flank of the enemy, and, if possible, attack them in the rear."[30] The Yankee reinforcements "...attacked the rebels with great spirit having to get at them by clambering down and up tremendous rocky heights."[31] Johnson must have been stunned to see his outnumbered adversaries, who, according to accepted military wisdom, should have been fleeing down the valley, actually following their temporary success by throwing even more troops across the stream and up into the Southern lair.

To his credit, the Southern commander maintained his composure and fed a newly arrived brigade under the command of Brigadier General William B. Taliaferro into the maelstrom.[32] "The [Union] regiments named, however, attacked them briskly and kept up a destructive fire, causing the enemy to waver several times; but fresh reinforcements being brought up by them, and a portion of the reinforcements coming down the turnpike, the 3rd West Virginia became exposed to their fire in its front and rear. Unable, however to withstand the fire of the 3rd West Virginia, the latter reinforcements joined the main body of the rebels and the contest became general and bloody."[33]

Milroy launched repeated assaults against perceived weak spots in the patchwork Confederate line. Johnson, and then Taliaferro, after the former received a gunshot wound to the ankle and was assisted off the field, countered by shifting reinforcements to each new hot spot. The Federals probably should have been blown back down the mountain by superior Southern numbers but Milroy's aggressive tactics kept the Rebels off balance while the

---

[30]O.R. 1-12-1-466, Milroy.

[31]Milroy letter, 5/13/1863. For the sake of authenticity, all quotations from original sources will be reproduced as found, without editing for grammar, spelling, or punctuation except where absolutely necessary to allow comprehension.

[32]Tanner, p. 192.

[33]O.R. 1-12-1-466, Milroy; Tanner, p. 191.

fearsome Yankee gunfire sent nearly as many Butternut skulkers down the far side of the mountain as could be replaced by new units coming up. Even so, had he been allowed more daylight, Stonewall and his men, who arrived at the base of the mountain in the early evening, would have undoubtedly routed the tenacious Federal brigade. Instead, the onset of twilight, and their nearly empty cartridge boxes, prompted Milroy to pull his boys off the mountain in good order before they could be driven off.[34]

The Hoosier's performance, and that of his men, had been outstanding. Not only had his riflemen delayed the enemy and given Frémont another full day to prepare, but he accomplished the objective by rocking the Confederates back on their heels rather than by fleeing the scene ahead of a flanking movement or a bombardment. In the process, the Yankees struck down 532 Confederates to only an admitted 240 casualties of their own. They even purchased enough time to burn the excess supplies in McDowell.[35] Most importantly, the Union forces remained virtually intact and, emboldened by their success, ready, willing, and able to resume delaying tactics in the morning.

Milroy understood that his job was to buy Frémont as much time to prepare for Stonewall's arrival as possible. Although the Hoosier viewed his role as "...a most painful and bitter trial...to have to fall back before traitors and relinquish to them any portion of the country I had struggled so hard to recover from them...," he performed the job with grit and tenacity.[36] Where advantageous, Milroy left well-protected batteries which barred Confederate progress with doses of grape and canister until the Butternuts shifted from column to battle line and drove them off. At other points, the Federals set fire to the tangled forest that crowded the

---

[34]Tanner, pp. 192-193.

[35]Ibid., p. 194; Milroy letter, 5/13/1863. Milroy's report listed only 199 killed or wounded but that tally did not include losses among Schenck's borrowed regiments.

[36]Milroy letter, 5/13/1862.

steep slopes of the ravines through which the Southerners had to march, thereby choking them with smoke, blurring their vision, and giving many the eerie feeling of taking a stroll through a portal to hell.

Finally, after days of slowing the Rebel advance to nearly a crawl, Milroy's command joined with Frémont's well-emplaced army at Franklin, western Virginia. On May 15, after a day long artillery duel, Jackson concluded that Frémont's position was too strong to carry, and that his army was dangerously far from the Shenandoah Valley. The Butternuts pulled out without having even bruised Frémont's army, thanks in large part to Milroy's efforts at McDowell and along the Pike.[37]

Despite a week of arduous duty, the ever aggressive Milroy "...asked Frémont for the privilege of following them but he refused saying we must rest awhile. He has kindly relieved all my guards and pickets and those of Gen. Schenck and we are taking our ease [and would not begin the pursuit until May 26], but would much prefer being after the rebles. We have a splendid army of infantry artillery and ought to be after the rebles and make them get back quicker than they come."[38]

Had Frémont followed Milroy's advice, he might have been able to delay Jackson in the Allegheny Mountains and ultimately to save his position at the head of his own army. Instead, the Pathfinder meandered along the Pike, probably in hopes of staying far enough behind Jackson so as to avoid giving the Southern predator another opportunity to do what he hoped to do at Franklin. Frémont's promenade was so slow that Jackson was allowed sufficient time to march north and defeat a Union force in Winchester.

---

[37]Tanner; pp. 197-205. Although he failed in his plan to smash Frémont, Jackson was able to freeze him in the mountains and thus prevent a juncture with the other Union forces in the Valley, the ultimate strategic objective.

[38]Milroy letter, 5/13/1862.

When the Pathfinder's army finally emerged into the Shenandoah Valley, Stonewall was faced with the possibility of being trapped between three Union armies. Despite the potential for a decisive Federal victory, Frémont's indolence allowed Jackson's foot cavalry to slip through the trap before it could be slammed shut in his face. It was more by accident than design that Frémont finally made contact with the rear of the fleeing Rebels at the battle of Cross Keys on June 8, 1862.

Milroy's aggressive instincts cost his men dearly during that battle. The day before, while on a reconnaissance, the Hoosier would have pitched into the Rebels but was restrained only by positive orders from Frémont not to precipitate a general engagement. On the morning of the eighth, Milroy hustled his men toward the sound of a battle growing in the east. Upon arrival, the Hoosier's brigade was assigned to a position between Schenck's brigade on the right and Brigadier General Louis Blenker's German division on the left. "Seeing no enemy in sight I [Milroy] asked permission to advance which was granted and I advanced my four Regiments by heads of Regts. about a half mile when I found a fine position for my artillery in full view of 3 reble batteries—I threw my Regts. into a ravine under shelter from their batteries which had again opened on us and sent back [my] aids for my batteries.... As soon as they [the Union artillery] got to work in fine style, I rode forward myself to examine the ground and discover the best way to getting my Regiments up where they could use their Minnie Enfield rifles. After a few hundred yards I discovered a ravine...[and I] brought them up cautiously along the ravine...but as soon as the head of my columns got within 60 or 70 yards of [a] second ravine we discovered it was full of rebles [belonging to the division of Major General Richard S. Ewell] laying behind a fence in the tall grass almost wholly concealed from view.... [T]hey mowed down the head of my column by a deadly fire almost as fast as they appeared, and we could not return their fire with any effect as we could not see them.... I tried to dislodge or raise them by skirmishes but without effect."[39]

Milroy then tried to flank the Butternuts by sending his men through a forest. The Federals "...recd. a perfect storm of bullets from the woods which appeared to be full of rebles, but the folage was so thick we could not see them. I brought up my Regiments and opened a tremendous fire into the woods but a deadly fire come out of it and my boys were dropped by it rapidly—my noble horse Jasper recd. two shots in quick succession...."[40]

Seemingly oblivious to the heavy casualties his command had already suffered, the pugnacious brigadier was in the process of attempting another flanking movement when one of Frémont's Dutch aides galloped onto the scene and ordered Milroy to pull his men back to the original point of departure. Milroy wrote to his wife that "I could not believe what the dutchman said and made him repeat it three times, the balls were whizzing around him like bees and he was dodging his head down behind the horse like a duck dodging thunder while he was repeating the order and as soon as he got through he dashed off at break neck speed. I was standing close behind the center of my Bgd. but felt ashamed to order them to cease firing and file to the rear."[41] One may legitimately wonder whether the rankers were as reluctant to obey the order to withdraw as their general was to give it.

In what was becoming a pattern, Milroy claimed to be highly indignant about receiving orders to disengage, and subsequently vented his frustration over the perceived incompetence that led to the order. "The reason why we were ordered to fall back was that the German Brigades on the left had been partially rebuked and thrown back by the rebles and Frémont fearing for the safety of the right wing ordered us to fall back also, but had he

---

[39]Milroy letter, 6/15/1862.

[40]Ibid.

[41]Ibid. Milroy reported his losses during the battle as 16 killed, 95 wounded, and 4 missing.

ordered the advance of his whole right wing we could have swept around and captured everything.... I have lost confidence in Frémont tremendously and so has his whole army."[42]

Three weeks later Milroy spewed even more bile. "Poor Frémont is 'played out' and down forever. The world has been greatly deceived in that man. He is intellectually a poor thing and if it had not been for his wife 'Jessie' and his father in law...he would [never] have been heard of."[43] Although an impetuous advance without adequate reconnaissance had placed his own brigade in jeopardy, there was some justification for Milroy's assertion that a more vigorous assault on Jackson's rear guard that day might have bagged the entire Confederate force and significantly impacted the outcome of the war.

After Frémont resigned a few weeks later, a Dutchman, Major General Franz Sigel was promoted to command of the Pathfinder's army. Having been impressed with Milroy's aggressiveness, Sigel designated Milroy's regiments as an independent brigade and tapped it to lead the column as it marched to join Major General John Pope's Army of Virginia. This was a perfect placement for both Milroy and Sigel. The former obtained the opportunity to be the first to get at the Rebels and the latter got the former off his back and, as a bonus, obtained a vanguard that was virtually guaranteed to find and retain contact with the enemy.

The only losers in the arrangement seem to have been the secessionist citizens along the line of march, because Milroy had a fairly free hand with them and used his power to the fullest. "I require them to furnish my troops with corn, oats, beef and flour and bacon and give them a certificate that will entitle them to pay after the War is over, provided they can then show that they have

---

[42]Milroy letter, 6/15/1862. The administration should have been added to the list of the disillusioned. At the end of June, Frémont requested to be relieved rather than serve under General John Pope. The request was accepted without protest or reassignment.

[43]Ibid., 7/4/1862.

been loyal to the Government of the U. S.   This grinds them
terribly but they have got to stand it...[s]o that they both fear and
have a high respect for me—and I find that they have heard of me
and know me wherever I go."[44]

Soon after Sigel's column made the connection, Pope's
army tangled with Jackson at Cedar Mountain. At dusk on August
9, as the battle wound down to its bloody conclusion, Milroy
received orders to lead his brigade toward the sound of the
artillery. Way out in front of his brigade as usual, Milroy and a
few of his aides tried to stem a flood of nearly panic-stricken
Federal soldiers retreating from the fighting. Although personally
only marginally successful, when the Hoosier rejoined his unit he
found that they, acting as a provost line, had rounded up a huge
number of stragglers and skulkers.

The next day, Milroy's seeming compulsion to be in the
lead could have gotten him killed or captured. At first light, the
Hoosier rode out alone to get a look at the enemy dispositions.
"When I had gone a few hundred yards and saw six horsemen
coming around the point to the grove. I could not distinguish in
the haze of the morning who they were. They were riding along
carelessly in a walk [and] I seen they were dressed in the common
'Butternut' of the country...so I supposed that they were citizens.... When the foremost one got near me I asked him in a
stern manner 'Who are you sir' they all stoped and eyed me for a
moment—then wheeled as quick as thought and went off like a
deer. I put spurs to my horse after them and jerked out one of my
pistols. I cocked it as I pulled it out and as I raised it in a hurry
the muzzle caught my bridle rain which jerked it down and it went
off slightly wounding my horse in the neck, but I kept on trying
to shoot the fellow for a few hundred yards, when it occurred to
me that they were the advance guards of the reble army advancing
to attack us and fearing I might run into a large force I wheeled

---

[44]Milroy letter, 7/14/1862.

my horse and hurried back to rouse up my Regts and get my battery into position. The hindmost fellow's horse fell dead a short distance from where I left him and his leg was broken by the ball that killed his horse...."[45]

Shortly thereafter, Milroy's Independent Brigade was ordered to reconnoiter the enemy lines. Disappointed with only catching a few dozen stragglers and deserters, the Hoosier had his men press ahead to find and attack the main body of the enemy. Just before they reached the Rapidan River, Milroy was summoned back by Pope—an order that provoked the type of bitter tirade that was becoming almost a ritual. "According to West Point Science...I was getting along too fast, The rebles must be given time to fortify and prepare to receive us as they did McClellan at Richmond. If our Govt. fails to put down this rebellion, so called West Point Science will be the cause of it. If the Devil had swallowed that institution 40 years ago, this rebellion would have been crushed Months ago—our Genls. would now have been Governed by common sense instead of West Point Slavery."[46]

Following the Battle at Cedar Mountain, Pope's army began to feel its way back toward the northernmost part of Virginia. Milroy's Independent Brigade was repeatedly given the opportunity and honor of manning the point. So that she would not miss the full significance of his assignment to the vanguard, Milroy bragged to his wife about being "...in the hotest furnace of the fighting first and last all the time when death [and] destruction reigned around...."[47] Despite Pope's giving him the chance to repeatedly ride into the "furnace," Milroy took a nearly instant dislike of his overall commander, calling him "...[o]ur miserable humbug-bag of gas Genl. Pope...," an opinion that was probably instigated by Pope, a West Pointer, occasionally tugging on Milroy's leash.

---

[45]Milroy letter, 8/15/1862.
[46]Ibid., emphasis in original.
[47]Ibid., 9/4/1862.

Pope relaxed his grip on that leash on the morning of August 22, perhaps because he needed the Independent Brigade to quickly secure Freeman's Ford for the balance of the army. Upon arrival at the ford, almost a mile and a half ahead of his men, the Hoosier galloped to the top of a hill overlooking the ford, which elicited a blizzard of canister from a Confederate battery on the other side. Milroy summoned a battery of his own, and what was to become a multihour artillery duel was quickly initiated. As the gunners hammered away at each other, some errant Rebel shells mangled two of Milroy's foot soldiers who were plodding onto the scene.

At 3 p.m., the Southern guns suddenly and inexplicably fell silent. "…[W]ishing to ascertain the cause of the enemy's silence, I determined to cross the river, and accordingly sent for my cavalry, numbering about 150 effective men. I then crossed the ford, sending a company of sharpshooters across and deploying them, ordering their advance up the hill occupied in the morning by the enemy's batteries, myself with my cavalry in the mean while going around by the road…. I discovered the greater part of the enemy's wagon train, accompanied by their rear guard, moving up the river in the direction of Sulphur Springs."[48]

Physical courage under fire did not necessarily guarantee the moral courage to disclose details about embarrassing command results. Milroy left out of his report that upon discovery of the Rebel wagon train, his cavalry swooped down and seized a goodly number of wagons, ambulances, and horses. Undoubtedly this minor success was omitted because the audacious general and his troopers were quickly driven back across the river sans wagons and with 10 empty saddles.[49]

If he sensed any latitude, Milroy was not above disregarding orders that limited his discretion or that attempted to hold him

---

[48]O.R. 1-12-1-316-317, Milroy.
[49]Allen, pp. 187-188; Milroy letter, 9/4/1862.

back. "I wished to cross with my Brigade but Sigel refused to let me do so, but I slipped over [another river] with my 3 cavalry companies and two companies of sharp shooters and pursued them a Mile and amused Myself pitching into them some, but found them in great force...and receiving a peremptory order from Sigel to return I did so - The rebles dared not follow."[50]

Several days later another ill-advised sortie almost put the Hoosier and a host of his men on the casualty rolls. After having forced a crossing over one river on August 23, the Independent Brigade faced the daunting task of storming a bridge across the Hedgeman's River on the following morning. Upon approaching the bridge, Milroy's Bluecoats were assailed by canister from a Rebel battery on a bluff across the creek. After being rocked by counterbattery fire from newly arrived Federal ordnance, the Butternut gunners uncharacteristically appeared to abandon their guns and flee. Without any apparent forethought, Milroy "...moved down with my Bgd. and I thought I would take one of my Rgts. and run across and get the abandoned reble batteries. I galloped across...and ordered the 5th West Virginia to follow. A few moments after I had got onto the opposite Bank of the river I observed the rebles rapidly coming out of the woods and remanning the abandoned batteries and other batteries coming out of the woods on the edge of the forests around in Semi Circle for over a mile in front and they commenced rapidly to pour [a] storm of shot and shell and canister.... I saw at a glance that my Regt. would be torn to pieces if they attempted to cross.... I shouted back to them to fall behind a large Mill close by and lay down...[and] I seen that it would not do for me to cross back for awhile...so I galloped to the pike a short distance and turned off some 30 or 40 yds and waited for the storm to abate."[51]

---

[50]Milroy letter, 9/4/1862.
[51]Ibid., 9/4/1862, emphasis in original.

Milroy's good fortune, bravery, and brashness seemed endless, but each would receive its severest test in a little less than a week.

On August 25, Stonewall Jackson and his corps commenced a dash around the Federal far right flank. Late the next day his men captured the huge Union supply dump at Manassas Junction and on August 27 they pillaged it. When word of the incursion reached Pope, he drove his army northward in hopes of catching and crushing Jackson before reinforcements from the balance of Lee's army could arrive. Milroy's brigade remained in the vanguard of the pursuing Federals but about a day behind Jackson.

Outside of Gainesville, Virginia, the Hoosier's penchant for being as far out front as possible placed him in another situation where he was incredibly fortunate to have escaped from personal disaster. "I sent my cavalry on into Gainsville and dashed over the R. R. at a major point with one of my aids—an artillery Lieutenant and 5 of my orderlies. I reached the R. R. in a little grove of timber just as I got to the edge of the woods I observed a squad of reble soldiers on the other side of the woods who started off on seeing me. I ordered them to halt and dashed around ahead of them and they surrendered. There was 11 of them and they all had loaded guns but they were stragglers worn out with fatigue and said they did not want to fight any more."[52] Milroy rode away unscathed.

While the men of the Independent Brigade paused to survey the wreckage that the Rebels left at Manassas Junction the day before, another segment of Pope's army finally uncovered Jackson's location in what developed into the battle of Groveton. At 3 p.m., Milroy received orders to move in the direction of New Market and there to connect with the balance of the Army of Virginia. The Hoosier's brigade arrived to the sounds of skirmishing in the distance and immediately commenced struggling through tangled underbrush in an effort to reach the continually

---

[52]Milroy letter, 9/14/1862.

receding thunder and clatter of battle. Before making contact though, the gunfire suddenly stopped and distant shouting, possibly indicating a victory by one side or the other, drifted out of the deepening gloom. Rather than continue farther and risk either stumbling into a victorious enemy or becoming lost in the dark, Milroy pulled his men back into closer proximity to Sigel's First Corps and allowed them to go into bivouac for the night.[53]

At dawn on August 29, the Independent Brigade received orders to press forward and reacquire the enemy. But after advancing about 500 yards and shaking out a skirmish line in response to a few potshots from Rebel sharpshooters, Milroy received new orders from Sigel to halt and allow his men to cook breakfast. At that point the Hoosier and his brigade were located approximately in the center of Sigel's corps, with Brigadier General Carl Schurz's Third Division on the right and Schenck's First Division on the left. While the entire First Corps' battle line ate breakfast, "...Gen. Schenck rode up and he started to ride up to an eminence some 500 or 600 yds to the front to reconnoiter the country but had not proceeded but a short distance before we recd. a volley of musketry which brought the balls whistling around us on all sides. Luckily neither of us were touched and two genls. about that time were observed making a handsome and rapid retreat."[54]

When a third set of orders arrived from Sigel, Milroy's brigade resumed its advance along with the rest of the First Corps. Schurz's division on the right was the first to encounter serious opposition and quickly became embroiled in a nasty gunfight with Jackson's men, who enjoyed the protection of a railroad embankment that served as an effective breastwork. Milroy, not yet in small arms contact, and lacking a clear grasp of what was transpiring in the woods to his right, dispatched the 82nd Ohio and 5th

---

[53]O.R. 1-12-1-319, Milroy.
[54]Milroy letter, 9/4/1862.

West Virginia toward the sound and smoke in order to support Schurz's embattled Dutchmen.[55] The two regiments, under the command of Colonels Cantwell and Ziegler respectively, angled toward a portion of the Confederate line known as the "dump," that was only scantily manned due to the uncomfortable heaps of rocks and dirt that littered the hundred yard strip. A blistering fusillade from behind the railroad embankment to their right stopped the Mountaineers in their tracks but the smattering of musketry from the defenders in the dump was insufficient to deter the Buckeyes. Within moments Cantwell's Ohioans stormed into and over the dump, sending Butternuts fleeing pell-mell toward the rear.[56]

Although Milroy's regiment had accidently achieved one of the few penetrations of the Confederate line that would occur that day, the breach could not be exploited due to lack of support on either flank. When this fact became obvious, and his regiment began to be flailed by volleys from Confederate reinforcements advancing on their flank, Cantwell ordered his men to fall back shooting. The Buckeyes sprinted for cover but many of them, including Cantwell who was killed instantly by a bullet in the brain, never reached the shelter of the trees from which they had emerged only a few minutes earlier.

The Rebel counterattack rolled forward, forcing Milroy to commit his two reserve regiments to relieve the others. Closest to the action, and the first into the fray, was the 2nd West Virginia. They were pummeled by Butternut gunfire and fell back in disorder. Next to get the order to advance was the 3rd West Virginia's commander, Major Theodore Lang, who heard Milroy shout over the din, "'Major Lang, now is the opportunity to distinguish yourself. I want you to charge the railroad

---

[55]O.R. 1-12-1-319, Milroy.

[56]About the decision to launch this sortie, one of Milroy's staffers wrote, "[t]hese circumstances should have suggested caution, to say the least, but that was a virtue not known to Milroy." As quoted in Hennessy, pp. 209-210.

embankment...and see what is behind it.'"[57] Lang knew full well what was out there and although he probably didn't view the assignment as a career builder, he led his men forward anyway. The Mountaineers were promptly smashed by a hail of lead and practically sprinted back to the shelter of the woods, offering only a few retaliatory running shots from over their shoulders.[58]

At least some of the Johnnies couldn't resist the sight of flapping blue coattails.[59] Filled with battle fury, they clambered over the embankment and rushed towards the woods where the Federals kneeled, gasping for breath. Whatever his other faults, Milroy was quick to recognize the threat to his disorganized command and possibly to the entire Union line. First, he rode among his men on his white horse trying both to rally them and steel their nerves for the blow that was coming.[60] Apparently not satisfied with the effect of his efforts, the Hoosier summoned his reserve battery and requested reinforcements from General Schenck.[61]

Milroy was pleased with the work of his gunners who raced up to his teetering line and quickly unlimbered. "...[Five] of them [cannons] got into position and commenced mowing the rebles with grape and canister most beautifully but before the 6th gun could back to where I pointed one of their wheel horses were droped dead. The boys were greatly confused and scared. I dashed up and made them unlimber and commenced pouring in the grape and canister from where they were, which they did upon the masses of rebles with splendid effect."[62]

---

[57]Milroy as quoted in Hennessy, p. 212.

[58]Hennessy, pp. 212-213.

[59]Johnny or Johnnie was another nickname the Federals pinned on the Confederates, as in Johnny Reb and Billy Yank.

[60]Milroy couldn't resist trying to impress his wife, writing, "The balls fell thick and fast around me...." Milroy letter, 9/4/1862.

[61]Hennessy, p. 213. In his letter to his wife, Milroy did not mention that he requested help—only that they were sent.

[62]Milroy letter, 9/4/1862.

The Hoosier was not nearly as impressed with the commander who shortly thereafter led the sought-after reinforcements onto the field. "Gen. Stahl came to me and reported.... I saw by the little man's terrified and anxious countenance that I could not depend on him for much. He asked me what he should do—I told him to draw up his Brigade of dutchmen on my left and help support my battery and drive back the rebles...and I soon afterwards saw him and his dutchmen double quicking it down to a ravine towards our rear and that was the last I seen of them that day...."[63]

About this time Milroy's sense of personal responsibility for the outcome of the entire battle seems to have become significantly inflated, a result, perhaps, of the effects of months of semiautonomy, the enormous stresses of personal danger and command under fire, and probably sleep deprivation, all imposed upon an already hefty ego. After holding the line with the assistance of a nearby Pennsylvania regiment, Milroy observed Brigadier General Cuvier Grover and his brigade coming through the woods in the general direction of the Independent Brigade. "I saw him forming his Bgd. for the attack and being deeply interested in his success I road up along his lines to where he was and told him how I had wrecked on that position and what he had to expect. He asked me how he had best do. I told him the only way he could drive them was to go forwards with fixed bayonetts and loaded guns, fire when they got close and dash over the R. R. embankment with a yell and drive them at a point of a bayonet. He adopted my suggestion and started his bgd. in line of battle toward the terrible R. R. through the woods."[64]

Even though the Johnnies who rocked Grover's advancing line with a deadly volley were sheltered behind the relative security of the railroad embankment, some of them began to skulk

---

[63]Milroy letter, 9/4/1862.
[64]Ibid.

away from their line rather than stand and reload. Milroy seized what seemed to him to be a golden opportunity to do some good execution and sent the 3rd West Virginia out to fire into the exposed flank of the enemy. "I dashed ahead cheering my boys, but before I got near across the meadow I noticed heavy masses of rebles in front and as far down the R.R. as I could see...."[65]

The rallying Confederates blasted Grover's brigade again and sent them scurrying for cover in the forest, leaving Milroy's men exposed and grossly outnumbered for the second time that day. Milroy tried to order his men to run for cover but claimed his voice could not be heard over the roar of battle. Apparently, the rankers quickly got the message implicit in seeing their general's headlong dash back into the woods. All dignity was abandoned as the Independent Brigade's officers and riflemen sprinted toward shelter amidst dust geysers kicked up by errant Minié balls and the not-so-occasional thud from bullets that weren't.

Even though he put them in harm's way, the Hoosier did manage some compassion for the plight of his men. "The greater part of my unlucky 3rd Va. started pell mell for the grove, but had to run the gauntlet of a deadly shower of reble bullits for over 200 yds before getting there.... Oh! what an agonizing sight it was to me on looking back to see my boys running and rapidly dropping before the terrible fire of the yelling rebles and no power with me or near me to relieve them."[66]

Not one to be stunned into inactivity, Milroy rushed to the rear and brought up another battery, then a stray cannon, and then some of his own men to bolster the gunners. The Confederates quickly overwhelmed both Milroy's cannoneers and his infantry and sent the whole bunch, including the Hoosier, fleeing to the rear for their lives. "I too dashed through them woods at no very

---

[65]Milroy letter, 9/4/1862.

[66]Ibid. Milroy did not even hint at having had second thoughts about the advisability of ordering the advance.

slow speed—the balls rattling like hail and cutting the bark off the trees and twigs of the bushes around me as I went.... I felt so bad and mad that I did not get away as fast as the rest, and the rebs kept the balls from their long range rifles whistling around me till I got back to our batteries on the hill near ¾ of a mile distant where I had shelled them from in the morning. "[67]

When that battery also came under artillery fire, Milroy galloped all the way back to Pope's headquarters and "...reported to him [Pope] how matters were in front and that if he did not send forward fresh troops and batteries soon the rebles would be on him.... He ordered up a Bgd. of infantry there with other batteries."[68] This would not be the last time that Milroy would offer advice to a superior officer whom he believed had blundered, through adherence to "...West Point Tactics...," by not sending reinforcements well before they had to be requested.

Fortunately for the nearly overwrought Hoosier, the day's fighting, that had cost many of his brigade's eventual 495 casualties, was over. After locating the shaken remnants of his command another half mile to the rear, Milroy probably spent much of the night trying to get them organized, fed, and their cartridge boxes replenished. It is also likely that as he reviewed the day's events over and over in his mind, the significance of his own role, the importance of the next day's fight, and the likelihood that Pope would botch it thanks to his West Point tactics, all expanded geometrically.

Milroy was up early on August 30, 1862, for what would prove to be one of the most important days of his life. After completing preparations, the Independent Brigade received orders to move out at 8 a.m. and occupy a reserve position on a ridge that gave the Hoosier a panoramic view of much of the battlefield. Filled with nervous energy, and the nagging sense that the day's

---

[67]Milroy letter, 9/4/1862.
[68]Ibid.

fate rested on his shoulders, Milroy "...became very impatient and road over to the extreme front of our line to an eminence in rear of our line of skirmishers which afforded a fine view of the country for miles in advance. From this position I could see distinctly with my spy glasses large columns of the rebles passing toward our left rear two miles to the front. Gen. Schenck and Col. McLean come to the same place while I was there and I showed the movement to them, which was reported to Gen. Sigel who reported it to Gen. Pope, but Pope gave very little attention to the report...."[69]

If the foregoing was accurate, rather than post-battle aggrandizement intended for home consumption, Milroy had probably sighted the corps of Major General James Longstreet on its way toward flanking and collapsing the Union left flank. In the same sentence where he highlighted Pope's alleged failure to act upon critical intelligence, Milroy also penned words that would be prophetically significant for his own career and, if remembered, must have haunted him for the rest of his postwar days. "...[H]e [Pope] gave very little attention to the report, he seemed to think that the disposition he had made of his forces and arrangements made to receive the rebles, was so very perfect and scientific that nothing more was necessary."[70] Pope was just as wrong in 1862 as Milroy would be a little less than a year later.

Within hours, Longstreet fell on the exposed and unprepared Federal left flank and literally blew the Bluecoats off their line and toward the rear in a panic. From his reserve position, Milroy recognized a disaster in progress and grandiosely wrote, "I saw that a Second Bull Run was commencing and thought I would stop the great tide of cowardly runaways. I tried this awhile alone with my sword but soon found I could not stay the tide. I then ordered my Bgd. to deploy into line...and ordered my Regts. to

---

[69]Milroy letter, 9/4/1862.
[70]Ibid.

face the front and fix bayonets and stop every man whether officer or private who was not wounded, we soon had a great multitude...."[71]

Before he could organize the skulkers and refugees into companies, Milroy was summoned by Sigel and shown where the Independent Brigade was to form a battle line that would hopefully help the Union First Corps to blunt the Confederate advance. On the way, new orders came directly from Pope that sent the Hoosier's brigade to a different location. Upon their arrival, though, it was discovered that the designated position was already occupied by another unit. At that point one of Pope's frazzled staff officers told Milroy he could position his men anywhere the brigadier thought would be advantageous. Milroy claimed that he "...observed the track of the old road [the Sudley Road on Henry Hill] a short distance in front of the forest which had been worn and washed...and was from 3 to 6 feet deep.... I immediately threw my Bgd. into this road...[and when the retreating Yankees had cleared the woods in front and Southerners began to emerge from the foliage]...I ordered my boys to open on them and they did it with splendid effect. The way the reble column tumbled and melted away was most beautiful and cheering...."[72]

Milroy's exultation was cut short when another Butternut column appeared and renewed the assault. When that one was driven back into the woods, an even larger contingent broke out of the forest with rifles blazing—and after they were repulsed it became apparent that a still larger force was coiling for another strike. Despairing for his line, and without artillery of his own, Milroy galloped a short distance to the rear and commandeered a battery of brass Napoleons and began directing their fire over the heads of his men into the Rebel-infested forest. When case shot

---

[71]Milroy letter, 9/4/1862.
[72]Ibid.; Hennessy, p. 410.

and shells failed to disperse the enemy, the Hoosier ordered the gunners to switch to canister.

While the cannons roared, the Confederate riflemen in the woods and their Federal counterparts in the sunken road tried to blast each other into oblivion. "The scene about this time was awfully grand and terrific. The vast quantity of artillery and small arms on both sides that were belching forth their sulphurous streams of death, raised vast columns of dense smoke above the wide field of combat, the thunder and din of battle made the earth fairly tremble and the air groaned and shrieked with the vast quantity of deadly missels that were passing through it and the horror of the scene was increased by the trembling and groaning of mangled and bleeding men and horses...." One of those horses belonged to Milroy. After the animal expired, the Hoosier leaped onto its still warm side, swirled his sword over his head and screamed encouragement to the skittish gunners around him.[73] Within minutes the gunners fled anyway.

Mortal peril, the responsibility of command, the red rage of battle, and the belief that "...the crises of the nation was on hand, and that the happiness of unborn millions and the progress of the world depended upon our success..." all sent a flood of adrenalin into the Hoosier's already heavily taxed nervous system. That hormonal overload, and the certainty that he was the most competent general on the field, either propelled Milroy into acts of uncommon leadership and courage—or caused him to become somewhat unhinged.[74] First, Milroy rushed over to a regiment that was starting to crumble on his left flank "...and by the use of the most energetic exertion, language and gesture I got the men back into line and to reopen their fire."[75]

---

[73]Hennessy, p. 416.

[74]Ibid.; Milroy letter, 9/4/1862.

[75]Milroy letter, 9/4/1862. The 73rd Ohio apparently responded to the commands of a foreign officer because they knew him, having been previously in one of Milroy's brigades.

Next, the Hoosier latched onto a regiment of Regulars he
spotted passing by and "...got the Regts. to form in rear of my
Bgd. near where the battery had stood and they opened on the
reble columns like a clap of thunder which added to that of my
boys from their <u>road entrenchment</u>, rapidly thined the reble
columns, but they stood their ground with great pertinacity." Not
all the Regulars were impressed by the exhortations from Captain
Partridge's star pupil, prompting a wag in their regiment to yell at
Milroy, "'...clear out and go away from here.'"[76]
Soon after the attack on Milroy's immediate front was
finally blunted, the Confederates shifted their pressure to the left
flank of what had become the last Union line of defense, providing
the Independent Brigade with a desperately needed respite. The
Hoosier was incapable of resting with his weary foot soldiers. "I
[Milroy] did not remain with my own Bgd. a minute after the
fighting ceased there, but followed along our line where the
fighting raged fiercest to sustain our wavering men."[77] One may
legitimately question why Milroy took the highly unusual course
of abandoning his command and its relative safety in order to
pursue additional danger. His explanation was: "...I had seen with
pain that our army needed <u>leaders</u> worse than <u>men</u>, and that much
the greater portion of the time and attention of a large portion of
our higher officers, in the field of battle is taken up in looking out
for the safest places, and in taking care of themselves, instead of
watching the movements of the enemy and directing the movements of their own men...."[78]
Despite all his efforts, the Union resistance continued to
crumble, threatening a total collapse of the entire line. "I [Milroy]

---

[76]As quoted in Hennessy, p. 419. Milroy may have become confused about
when during the battle the Regulars arrived. John Hennessy, the leading authority
on the battle, placed their arrival after Milroy confronted General McDowell
(discussed later) while Milroy had them arriving before then.

[77]Milroy letter, 9/4/1862.

[78]Ibid., emphasis in original.

saw that we must have fresh troops soon or all would be lost. I galloped rapidly back to where McDowell was and found him setting calmly on his horse amidst his numerous staff and body guard, surrounded by the columns of his Corps. I appealed to him in the most energetic Manner for a Bgd. telling him that the crises of the battle and of the nation was at hand and that not a moment was to be lost.... [He] answered me coldly and insultingly that he was not bound to help every body and that he was not going to help Gen. Sigel (whom he with all other West Pointers Mortally hate) [presumably the statement in parentheses was Milroy's editorial comment rather than a quote]."[79]

McDowell, perhaps in furtherance of his own agenda, had a markedly different recollection of the exchange. "When he [Milroy] spoke to me he was in a frenzy, not accountable scarcely for what he said...[and] his manner, his dealing in generalities, which gave no information whatever, and which in the way he uttered them, only showed him as being in a state of mind as unfit to judge of events...."[80] Staff officer Washington Roebling seconded that description. "He was in a very excited state of mind. He spoke at the top of his voice. He was waving his sword and

---

[79]Milroy letter, 9/4/1862.

[80]O.R. 1-12-1-320, McDowell; McDowell as quoted in Hennessy, p. 418. Although he was the only source to do so, Colonel (later general) J. Warren Keifer recorded that Milroy had a speech impediment of some sort that prevented him from getting his words out when he was excited. Perhaps McDowell misinterpreted Milroy's desperate attempts to explain the situation. Keifer, vol. 1, p. 316. If the Hoosier did lose his composure, he had good company. Two eminent Confederate generals, Second Corps commander Lieutenant General Richard S. Ewell, and division commander Brigadier General John B. Gordon both purportedly acted oddly during the battle of Spotsylvania. The former became so excited that Lee was forced to admonish him, with, "'General Ewell, you must restrain yourself; how can you expect to control these men when you have lost control of yourself?'" Gordon at one point was "'talking rapidly and literally foaming at the mouth.'" As quoted in Pfanz, pp. 386-389. Regarding a motive to spin the event, McDowell faced enormous amounts of criticism for his conduct in the battle, which might explain why he might have wished to diminish Milroy's pleas for reinforcements.

his hat was off."[81]   But, after hearing Milroy manage to blurt out "'For God's sake general, send a few regiments into these woods, my poor men are being cut to pieces,'" and after receiving independent confirmation of the situation (from a fellow West Pointer), McDowell finally deigned to send help.[82]

When McDowell's relief column began to deploy for action Milroy "...dashed in front and told the boys to come on.   The noble fellows were eager for the fight—they gave three rousing cheers and started after me on the double quick.... [T]here was a stern work ahead for the 2500 men I was leading [the new brigade].   I pointed out to them the position they were to occupy and the sharp and rapid cracking of their 2500 Minies soon turned the tale against the rebles again, but they soon afterwards came around on our flank further to the left through a thicket of pine bushes."   Still not satisfied, the frantic Hoosier saw another brigade advancing and "...went out to meet them and upon inquiring learned it was one of Burnsides veteran brigades....   I was so delighted that I waved my sword and shouted a welcome to them...[and] pointed [to their commander] where he had best plant his battery and form his line of battle which he promptly did and their fire soon completely silenced the rebles."[83]   Like McDowell and his staff, Burnside's officer saw Milroy's behavior in a somewhat different light, "...as we dressed our lines, [he] rode along our front, shouting like a crazyman."[84]

By then it was around 8 p.m. and the weight of saving the Union had finally slipped from Milroy's shoulders.   Upon returning to where he expected to find his men, the Hoosier

---

[81]O.R. 1-12-1-268.
[82]Ibid., 1-12-1-268, Roebling; Hennessy, p. 418.
[83]Milroy letter, 9/4/1862.
[84]As quoted in Hennessy, p. 422.

discovered that they were gone.[85]   When he learned that his
command had joined in a general withdrawal across the Bull Run
pursuant to Pope's orders, Milroy was personally devastated. "I
felt that not only had the good...labor and suffering of our Govt.
and people since the beginning of the war been thrown away and
made a useless waste by that miserable cowardly order, but that it
had also rendered all that was gained by the American Revolution
a nullity by completing the destruction of the Union."[86]

Undoubtedly, Milroy suffered from adrenalin burnout
immediately after the pressure was lifted, but he also seems to
have fallen into a rather severe depression over the outcome of the
battle, and probably over what he perceived to have been a waste
of his heroic efforts. As he plodded back to the rear to find his
men, Milroy allowed that "...I never received such a stunning
blow and felt so entirely miserable in all my life—but remembering
I must look after the health, comfort and safety of my own worn
out brigade...I moved back in the darkness [and]...found the larger
fragment of them about midnight."[87]

Although he had never "...had the blues so bad in my
life..." and apparently remained in despair and depression well
into the month of September, it didn't take long for Milroy's more
than ample ego to at least reestablish his military equilibrium.[88]
It is likely that after the passage of time revealed that the Union
cause was not lost, he was bolstered by the interpretation that he
almost certainly placed upon his own performance. With some
justification and some rationalization, the Hoosier very likely took

---

[85]Milroy is fortunate that during his wanderings that disaster did not befall his
own brigade, because if it had he might very well have been court-martialed and
cashiered.

[86]Milroy letter, 9/4/1862.

[87]Ibid.

[88]In addition to the quoted material which illuminates Milroy's substantial self-
esteem, his 1862 letters were also sprinkled with references to expressions of
respect, affection, and loyalty received from both officers and men in his brigade.

pride in: his personal courage and audacity; the fact that his brigade was one of the few to have penetrated Stonewall Jackson's line (albeit unintentionally and very briefly); and that his command, and from his prospective his own aggressive leadership, had been instrumental in blunting the Confederate assault and saving the Union army on the last day of the battle.[89] Undoubtedly, Milroy viewed his brief stint as head of the First Corps, while Sigel was incapacitated by a short illness, as an appropriate acknowledgement of his own self-assessment.

Even more inflating was the audience granted to the brigadier from Indiana by President Lincoln, Secretary of War Edwin W. Stanton, and army Chief Henry W. Halleck sometime between September 2 and 12. "They treated me with the most marked respect and friendship and flattered me so much about my fighting and bravery that it made me blush and feel awkward. I told them in the strongest terms that a splendid victory had been lost and thrown away by Pope's cowardly order to retreat. I told them how we held the field till we had completely checked the rebles—They had not heard these things and were greatly surprised. I told Old Abe, privately, that if he continued to let West Point rule in our armies that it would ensure the destruction of the Union beyond a doubt. He looked grave at me but made no reply. They all shook me warmly by the hands when I left and asked me to call again."[90] It is no wonder that Lincoln wore a grave look as Milroy shared his insights about West Point, and even less so

---

[89]An impartial assessment of his performance leads to a mixed assessment. Milroy was a fearless leader, who boldly fought his men when others shrank from the fray, and his stand in the sunken road on Henry Hill undoubtedly help save Pope's army from being entirely "gobbled up." On the other hand his brigade suffered unnecessary casualties because of his rash decisions and poor reconnaissance, just as they had at the battle of Cross Keys. Although the risk he took by confronting McDowell when searching for reinforcements may have helped save the line, the desertion of his command under fire, especially when he was cheerleading other units, could have led to an even greater disaster.

[90]Milroy letter, 9/4/1862, emphasis in original.

that West Point graduate Halleck would thereafter refuse all future requested meetings with his officious subordinate.

To Milroy's satisfaction, it took only until the end of September for his connection with the Army of the Potomac to be permanently severed. With a reconstituted brigade comprised of the 2nd, 3rd, 4th, 5th and 8th West Virginia Infantry regiments, the Hoosier was soon back in the home territory of his troops.[91] On October 9, Milroy moved to Point Pleasant, western Virginia, and took charge of a force of about 12,000 soldiers and immediately began to make preparations for an offensive that he predicted would clear the entire future state within 40 days.[92]   Before he could get started, however, overall command of the territory was awarded to newly promoted Major General Jacob D. Cox, who halted the offensive and dispatched the Hoosier to the mountains with 10 regiments and four batteries.

Those regiments, which would form the core of Milroy's division for the next nine months were the 2nd, 3rd, 9th, 10th and 12th West Virginia; the 87th Pennsylvania; and the 110th, 116th, 122nd, and 123rd Ohio Infantry regiments. The force was divided into three brigades.   The First Brigade was commanded by Brigadier General Gustave P. Cluseret, a French soldier of fortune who had won the Legion of Honor in Algiers.   Colonel G. R. Latham of the 2nd West Virginia led the Second Brigade, and

---

[91]Milroy letter, 9/4/1862. According to Milroy, the men of his brigade were returned home, thanks to a petition they all submitted to the president and secretary of war. Also, according to Milroy, because "the Va. troops in our army think me the greatest Gen. Living...," the petition contained a request that he be promoted to major general. It may legitimately be surmised that the meeting with Lincoln, Stanton, and Halleck was an informal job interview intended to determine if Milroy was a good candidate for promotion within the Army of the Potomac. If so, the Hoosier apparently failed.

[92]Ibid., 9/28/1862, 10/19/1862.

A Milroy Patriotic Cover

Colonel James Washburn of the 116th Ohio headed the Third Brigade.[93]

Until the middle of December, Milroy occupied himself with two tasks, fulminating over the apparent incompetence of generals from West Point and trying to protect Unionist in his area by suppressing their secessionist neighbors and the guerrillas they abetted.   The following is a sampler of some of the Hoosiers thoughts about the Union's professional generals: "...all this has been brought about by <u>West Pointers</u>—Souless, brainless—selfish Villians who having made their <u>Profession</u>—care nothing for the country, so they can be hoisted into high places...; [a]ll military power is in the hands of <u>West Pointers</u> mear <u>Military Gamblers</u> who have ruined the country and wrecked and lost the noble institution bequeathed us by our forefathers...; in the hands of such

---

[93]Milroy letter, 11/7/1862.

selfish, biggoted, supercellious, incompetent West Pointers [at that moment he was fuming over West Pointer Halleck's refusal to grant another audience] the destiny of our Great Country has been mistakenly placed and the lives of a million volunteers staked and 200,000 uselessly sacrificed...I consider West Point next to slavery the great bane of our country...; Halleck had him [Cox] made a Majr. Genl. and sent back to Western Va. to hold everything in check as usual...therefore I am snubbed and put down by Halleck and Cox put over me to keep me in check...."[94]

Milroy was no more tolerant of the secessionists and partisans who plagued the loyal citizens of mountainous western Virginia than he was of graduates from West Point. "The rebles hate and fear me as they do the Devil. I reciprocate their reason to fear me, for I have sent out troops to clear out the guerrillas and active traitors and to bring in no prisoners.... I am doing all I can while laying here [Petersburg, western Virginia] to straighten up the wrongs of [to] the Union citizens who have all suffered, many of them very greatly at the hands of the secessionists, in being robed of their property, imprisoned and in some instances murdered.... I require the amount of each Union man's loss to be ascertained and have the amount in each case assessed upon the active secessionists of the neighborhood and require prompt payment upon penalty of being shot or burning the houses when the man is off in the reb army, which is often the case....

"I directed that all be <u>invited</u> to take the oath of allegiance and when any male or female of adult age refused to do so, that their house and property should be marked and no longer considered under the protection of my troops and that the houses of persons so refusing should be taken for hospitals or barracks for my troops without regard to their inhabitants, and that when any portion of the family become insulting to my troops their house should be filled full of troops and the family crowded out until

---

[94]Milroy letters, 9/--/1862, emphasis in original; 10/19/1862.

they begged pardon, take the oath and promised reformation. This order seemed to have operated like enchantment upon the hitherto stiff necked and rebellious natives. The ladies have quit turning up their noses and calling my boys 'Nasty Yankees,' 'Hessians,' 'abolitionists,' etc. and my Provost Martials office has been crowded with males and females anxious to take the oath of allegiance to the 'Lincoln Government' and get certificates. I am curing traitors rapidly and no treasonable talk is heard among the people any more."[95] Ten days after those words were penned, Milroy would undertake the task of trying to "straighten up" the even more "stiff-necked" secessionists and Yankee haters who populated Winchester and the lower Shenandoah Valley.

---

[95]Milroy letters, 11/7/1862 and 12/20/1862, emphasis in original. In her brief biography which accompanied her transcription of Milroy's papers, Margaret B. Paulus reported that the Confederate government placed a $1,000 bounty on Milroy's head because of his perceived brutality toward Southern sympathizers and partisans.

3

UNDER MILROY'S HEEL

*In this city [Winchester] of about 6,000 inhabitants
...my <u>will</u> is absolute law—none dare contradict or dispute my
slightest word or wish. The secesh here have heard many
terrible stories about me before I came and supposed me to be
a perfect Nero for cruelty and blood, and many of them both
male and female tremble when they come into my presence to
ask for small privileges, but the favors I grant them are slight
and few for I confess I feel a strong disposition to play the
tyrant among these traitors.*

—Robert H. Milroy[1]

For both the occupied and the occupiers, the return of the
Bluecoats to Winchester on December 24, 1862, was welcomed
with the same enthusiasm as a lump of coal left in a naughty
child's Christmas stocking. General Cluseret's First Brigade
arrived after a grueling tramp through six inches of snow that
covered his route through Petersburg, Moorfield, Strasburg,
Newtown, Kernstown, and finally into Winchester. At the sound
of thousands of shuffling feet, the residents closed their shutters,
huddled around stoves and fireplaces that seemed to offer less
warmth, and turned up gas jets and lampwicks that were suddenly

---

[1]Milroy letter, 1/18/1863, emphasis in original.

unable to dispel the shadows. There would be no carols, celebrations, or even peaceful gatherings around warming campfires for the Federals that night, either. Instead, after a detachment of Rebel cavalry drove in the Union pickets, Cluseret's men spent the balance of the night braced for an attack while spending more than an hour pondering the implications of the sounds of the nasty little cavalry spat.[2] Nothing of consequence resulted from the altercation, but the newly arrived Bluecoats nevertheless spent the last week of 1862 hunkered down outside Winchester wondering if Milroy and the balance of their division, or the Confederates, would reach them first.

Most of the ardent secessionists in Winchester were just as apprehensive about what the future would bring as were the Federals who nervously manned picket posts on the edge of town. Due in large part to the multitude of horror stories that they had heard about the Hoosier's suppression of guerrillas and Southern sympathizers in western Virginia, the residents expected the second coming of Attila the Hun rather than a Union general. Further, most of the town's residents genuinely believed that as grandchildren of the American Revolution, they had the God-given right to secede, and despised and resented their Union occupiers as tyrants and oppressors for disagreeing. Perhaps most importantly, the ante-bellum social and economic elites of the town were accustomed to having their own way. Despite what they believed to be their own self-importance, each successive Yankee garrison forced them into the humiliating position of subjects rather than rulers, a transition that they never willingly accepted. Because almost every family in town had by then lost a son, husband, father, or close relative to a Yankee bullet or shell, they were not disposed to suspend judgment until Milroy had a chance to reveal his methods.

Short of going somewhere else, or dropping dead, there probably was little that Milroy could have done to placate

---

[2]Prowell, pp. 49-55.

Winchester
June 1863

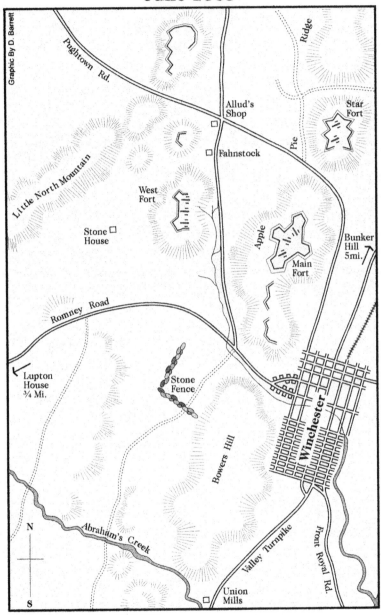

Graphic By D. Barrett

Pughtown Rd.

Ridge

Allud's
Shop

Star
Fort

Pike

Fahnstock

Little North Mountain

West
Fort

Stone
House

Apple

Bunker
Hill
5mi.

Main
Fort

Romney Road

Lupton
House
¾ Mi.

Stone
Fence

Winchester

Bowers Hill

N

S

Abraham's Creek

Valley Turnpike

Front Royal Rd.

Union
Mills

From: O.R. Atlas Pl. XLIII #3

Scale in Miles

0   1   2

Winchester's anti-Union citizens. Unfortunately, his personality, and his hatred of the Rebels and their "peculiar institution" were inimical to the role of conciliator, which could have been part of his duties. As shown in one letter to his wife, those abolitionist beliefs were deeply held and of long-standing. "But our ill success still confirms me more and more in the opinion that Providence is not with us in the War and will not be until the 'Powers that be' removes and abolishes the great and mighty curse and cause of the War, Slavery. I have very great doubts of any permanent success in the Union cause until this is done. I look forward with hope for something to be done in the right way after Jan 1/63 [the day the Emancipation Proclamation was scheduled to take effect]."[3]

Milroy, almost in a messianic way, sensed that destiny was leading him to a position of power in Winchester, the home town of the judge who presided over the trial of John Brown. "Plainly these events are directed and controlled by the Infinite Being who holds the nations of Earth in the hollow of His hand, and who delivered Israels' host from slavery. 'The spirit of Old John Brown Is Marching, Marching, Marching, On.'"[4] If not managed from on High, the impending difficulties between Milroy and the people of Winchester seem to have been at least preordained.

The dreaded event arrived on January 1, 1863, when Milroy rode into Winchester at the head of the balance of his division. Because of the rigors of the journey, Milroy's Federals plodded rather than strutted into town. On the night of December 31, the Federals were forced to endure a bivouac on a desolate peak in a raging snowstorm. On New Year's morning, after burrowing out from under soaked and frozen blankets and a layer of snow, the Hoosier's troops gingerly commenced their descent, while "...the chilling winter blasts...caused the lowest ebb of human enthusiasm to be reached...."[5] Miles of snowy roads and

---

[3]Milroy letter, 12/20/1862, emphasis in original.
[4]Ibid., 1/18/1863.
[5]Keifer, vol. 1, p. 315.

gusts of bone-chilling wind left the Yankees totally drained by the end of the day's ordeal.

Colonel J. Warren Keifer, who shared in that misery while at the head of the 110th Ohio, recorded an episode that occurred at the beginning of the New Year's Day tramp that demonstrated the depths of Milroy's convictions about slavery—as well as one of his peculiarities. From the rear of the column, Keifer heard a series of cheers from the men up ahead, who moments before seemed to have only enough energy to maintain their balance and put one nearly frostbitten foot in front of the other. Compelled by curiosity, Keifer rode toward the front, where he encountered Milroy, whom he described as having "...his hat and sword in his right hand, and with the other guided his horse at a reckless gallop through the snow, his tall form, shocky white hair fluttering in the storm, and evident agitation making a figure most picturesque and striking."

As Keifer approached, it became apparent that the Hoosier was instigating the ruckus. In response to a question about the cause of his behavior, Milroy supposedly responded, "Colonel, don't you know that this is Emancipation Day, when all slaves will be made free?" Milroy then supplemented his mounted cheer-leading about the glory of their mission with exhortations to march faster so that the ordained task could commence sooner. The men, amidst billows of frosty breath, continued to respond with the volume demanded by their commander. Given that Union soldiers were generally ambivalent about blacks and decidedly opposed to having to suffer or die solely for the purpose of freeing them, one may consider the possibility that the most enthusiastic yells erupted when Milroy rode closest to the edge of a cliff.[6]

After his command finally arrived in Winchester, Milroy commenced the process of subjugating the town almost as soon as

---

[6]Keifer, vol. 1, pp. 315-316. The Emancipation Proclamation that was issued on September 22, 1862, was scheduled to become effective on January 1, 1863. Faust, p. 242.

he climbed down from his horse. "...I keep patrols of soldiers on the streets and have given orders that if any officer or soldier is insulted by a traitor, male or female, he or she should be at once arrested and taken to the guard house. An aristocratic femine insulted Gen Closeret a few days ago—her fine mansion was immediately taken for a hospital."[7]

Milroy was concerned about the safety of his men as well as their dignity. In order to curtail the hemorrhage of intelligence about his troop strength and dispositions, the Hoosier quickly banned contact between the people of Winchester and Confederate sympathizers beyond the Yankee lines. The first defiant resident to try to penetrate that curtain was a Miss Dinkle, who spent a night in the guardhouse after being caught with contraband letters.[8] After the Dinkle incident, the Federals began to search the women's belongings as they passed back and forth through the Union lines. Chivalry, and the reasonable fear that body searches would ultimately cause more problems that spying, restrained the Bluecoats from looking in all the places where messages could be hidden, thus dooming the effort. Aware of how porous his lines really were, Milroy also hired several professional detectives to try to ferret out women who were smuggling mail through the lines.[9]

On January 4, Milroy received a copy of the anticipated Emancipation Proclamation that became effective on January 1. He wasted no time in imposing it upon the people of Winchester. The next day, the town was papered with announcements of the proclamation as well as renewed demands for submission. "I expect all citizens to yield a ready compliance with the Proclamation of the Chief Executive, and all persons disposed to resist its peaceful enforcement...upon manifesting such [contrary]

---

[7]Milroy letter, 1/5/1863. Despite the harsh tone of his letter, the order also barred his men from entering private homes and sent them out of town by 6 p.m. Delauter, p. 47.

[8]Delauter, p. 47.

[9]Colt, p. 16.

disposition by acts, they will be regarded as rebels in arms against the lawful authority of the Federal Government, and dealt with accordingly. All persons liberated by said Proclamation, are admonished to abstain from all violence, and immediately to betake themselves to useful occupations."[10]

Milroy was somewhat awestruck by the twist of fate that placed him in charge of enforcing the proclamation in Winchester. "Judge Parker who presided at the trial of old John Brown resides here and it is very remarkable in this theatre of old John's operations 3 years ago that I am enforcing the proclamation of the President of the U. S. freeing the very slaves that old John so insanely attempted to free. Who could have dreamed of such an event then.... Plainly these events are directed and controlled by the Infinite Being who holds the nations of Earth in the hollow of His hand...."[11]

Many of the town's former slaves leaped at the opportunity offered by the Hoosier and, with his permission, piled onto empty army supply wagons heading north to be refilled.[12] Others, despite Lincoln's proclamation and Milroy's edict, remained bound to their masters out of fear or force of habit. Although the tangible results were mixed, Milroy nevertheless thought that at least God was pleased with the effort. "The last day of the year was stormy but New Years morning was a bright clear, pleasant glourious morning...[a] sure augery that President Lincoln's immortal Proclamation has enlisted God Almighty on our side and that he will soon clear away the storms and tempests of war occasioned by that mighty curse slavery."[13]

Since the local elites did not share Milroy's conviction that God favored emancipation, the Hoosier attempted to use the rhetorical skills polished in the courtroom to try to win their hearts

---

[10]Macfie, chap. 4, pp. 8-9.
[11]Milroy letter, 1/18/1863.
[12]Keifer, vol. 1, p. 319.
[13]Milroy letter, 1/5/1863.

and minds. "I have frequent conflabs with the male and female F. F. Vs. [First Families of Virginia] about their peculiar Institution and the War. It does me good to [bring] Heavens anathemas upon them especially the preachers, Methodist and Presbyterian, who call upon me for passes and other favors and I have had several bouts with them. I tell them that in ancient times the cry of a nation of slaves went up to a God out of Egypt and He heard them and sent Moses and Aaron to reason with the slave holders and try to get them to emancipate their slaves and abolish slavery, but all the arguments and reasoning of Moses and Aaron were received by the slave holders with scorn and ridicule. God then commenced sending plagues on them, one after another with terrible effect.... A long bitter cry has went up to that same God from a nation of Slaves in America. He has heard that cry...Gods patience became exhausted and He commenced pouring out his plague on them...war, devestation, want, misery, disease, terror and death...until like Pharoah and his host, they will [be] over-whelm[ed] in total destruction."[14]

Although it must have been painfully obvious that he was not producing many new abolitionists, Milroy thought that at least the preachers and the rest of the better people of Winchester approved of how he managed his garrison, especially in regard to demon rum. "...[A]ll say there never was better order in this city under any General, Union or Secesh that have preceeded me. The principle reason [is] that I have caused the destruction of all intoxicating liquors found in this town and country for miles around, except a little in the hands of physicians and surgeons for medical purposes. I have put the Main Law 'Search seizure and confiscation' in force in my dominions with the utmost rigor."[15] Strict control of his men, as well as the scarcity of ardent spirits, seem to have prevented the serious offenses of murder, rape, and

---

[14]Milroy letter, 2/10/1863.
[15]Ibid.

Military Pass

(Author's Collection)

mayhem that often accompany an army of occupation, but if the residents actually did appreciate Milroy's handling of his troops, they avoided leaving a written record of that approval.[16]

In addition to maintaining strict control over his soldiers, Milroy was also responsible to maintain civil order, a duty which he attempted to perform fairly, if not to the complete satisfaction of the residents. All civilian crimes, as well as offenses against his troops, that ranged from insults to bushwhacking, were tried before a three-member military commission. Each defendant received a semblance of due process along with the right to be

_____

[16]Only one positive Southern comment about Milroy was located. In February of 1863, town notable David W. Barton requested and received permission to farm some of his land south of Winchester and also obtained an order protecting his crops from confiscation. In April his son Randolph wrote, "...Pa said Milroy was the most gentlemanly commander (Yankee) ever been in Winchester...." Colt, pp. 227, 239.

represented by defense counsel. Although of questionable constitu-
tional authority, the sentences, which ran the gamut from prison
to the firing squad, were generally approved by the War Department and the president. A number of miscreants spent time in
Northern prisons as a result of punishments meted out by Milroy's
commission, but Lincoln commuted the few death sentences that
crossed his desk.[17]

Even though the residents would not concede an ounce of
credit to Milroy, his treatment of what he justifiably believed to be
a nest of slave-holding traitors was rather mild compared to
historical precedents. Although he clearly delighted in tweaking
the tails of the leading secessionists of the town, there are no
reports of atrocities or summary executions of noncombatants, and
even property, with some broad exceptions such as the tearing
down of public buildings for construction material and firewood,
was generally respected.[18] Mostly, Milroy talked tough but
limited his repressions to subsisting his troops at Winchester's
expense and annoying the town's elite when they provoked him.

More aggravating to Milroy than the lack of appreciation
for his skills as an administrator was the townsfolks' continued
flaunting of their loyalty to the Confederacy. So, toward the end
of January, when a severe cold snap seemed to offer a golden
opportunity for some effective coercion, Milroy restricted the
purchase of key supplies such as firewood to only those persons
who would take an oath of allegiance to the United States. The
idea that people would actually believe themselves obligated by

[17]Keifer, vol. 1, pp. 323-324.

[18]Delauter, p. 47. A sample of the overblown and disproportionate rhetoric
concerning Milroy's occupation of Winchester is found in the following dispatch
from a member of the Virginia House of Delegates sent on February 2, 1863: "I
have just learned that the brute Milroy has made another requisition upon the people
of Winchester for 2,000 pounds more of bacon.... Will not the administration send
some commanding officer to the Valley that will...chastise the insolent raider?"
O.R. 1-51-2-678.

making such a promise may sound quaint to present-day cynics, who have become calloused by the relentless disregard of solemn oaths taken by high government officials. Most of Winchester's citizens were apparently so impressed by the significance of raising their right hand and swearing on a Bible, however, that they refused to take the oath despite the consequences.

Instead of knuckling under and surrendering principle to necessity, the recalcitrant secessionist first tried to obtain their necessities by appealing to Milroy's sympathies. "...[A] large number of the F. F. [perhaps first family] ladies have come to me to beg the priveledge of going to Baltimore now that the way is open to get necessary supplies for themselves and families. I tell them that it will afford me much pleasure to grant them passes, but before doing so they must take the oath of allegieance to the good old Govt.... This shocks them, they say that the Union Generals who held this place at different times last summer never required them to take the oath to get a pass—I tell them that if our other generals who have been in command here chose to act the fool and get driven away from this place—then they...commence coaxing and perhaps weeping, appealing to their old calico dresses and their old patches and perhaps borrowed shoes—and plead that to take the oath would bring on them the scorn and contempt of their...relatives and friends...and drive them from...society.... I tell them they are proving that 'The way of the transgressor is hard' and that if they could not afford to renounce treason they must suffer on as they need expect no favor."[19]

Rebuffed by their nemesis, the citizens turned to a thriving black market to obtain, at profiteer prices, the proscribed goods. Then, to underscore their disdain for the Federals and their government, Winchester's Rebelettes expanded their already well-practiced rudeness towards Yankee soldiers by choosing to walk

---

[19]Milroy letter, 1/18/1863.

70   **Gateway to Gettysburg**

in muddy and manure-fouled streets rather that risk a sidewalk encounter between a hooped skirt and a faded blue trouser leg.[20]

For a while, the fiery Southern belles were able, under the protection of Victorian chivalry, to verbally tweak and torture their bluecoated victims with relative impunity. When their invective was turned directly upon Milroy, it became inevitable that the cycle of provocation and reprisal would have unwelcomed consequences for the shapely provocateurs. The Hoosier reported the steadily deteriorating situation in a letter to his wife. "The young ladies, most of whom have brothers and lovers in the Reb Army are especially bitter against me, but I have given orders that any male or female Reb who utters a disrespectful word against or to an officer or soldier shall be instantly trotted into the guard house. Enclosed I send you a valentine recd. from one of those amiable creatures."[21]

The referenced valentine was the work of a woman named Cornelia McDonald, who drew an elaborate sketch of a seated Milroy directing a comely young white woman toward the door while two rotund slave women remained in his room for an audience. So that he would not miss the point, the artist included in the valentine a painting on his office wall that depicted a slave woman wearing a liberty cap and a United States flag for a dress.

That caricature was intended to scold the Hoosier for a confrontation that occurred in his office a few days earlier and that was recorded by the extremely prolix diarist, Mary Lee. "I [Lee] went over to see the result of Mrs. B's [Portia Baldwin] last visit to Milroy [about fences being converted to firewood], & Dickens himself could not have pictured a richer scene. She told him John Brown was the cause of the war; he said it was a lie; she drew up close to him & looked, as only Mrs. B. can look & said in a vicious tone, 'don't you say I lie' whereupon he got into such a

[20]Delauter, p. 48.
[21]Milroy letter, 2/27/1863.

rage, that he danced about the room & ordered her out in the most insolent manner."[22]

Milroy neglected to inform his wife of what had prompted the barbed valentine but added, in an effort to convince her that he was above the intended insult, "It [the valentine] is pretty well got up and has made considerable fun for my staff.... How do you like my looks? Ain't I getting Handsome? 'Mrs Sambo and Caffy' as poor specimens...."[23] Probably he was not as impervious as his letter indicated because he was also reported to have said to someone else, "'Hell is not full enough, there must be more of these Secession women of Winchester to fill it up.'"[24]

A few weeks later Milroy issued a directive to the effect that any resident who provoked him would be exiled from town. Within days a Mrs. Logan and her children were removed from their home and sent to Southern-occupied Newtown for allegedly holding an illegal prayer meeting and insulting a soldier. The locals attributed the action not to Milroy's ill humor or wounded pride, but to his desire to obtain a suitable residence for his visiting wife and children. A week later one of the Hoosier's detectives intercepted a letter addressed to New Jersey that related that theory as well as details of the earlier incident. The next day the writer, Mary Magill, joined Mrs. Logan in exile.[25]

The bickering between the blue coats and the gray petticoats reached an absurd level shortly after the nearly deified

---

[22] As quoted in Colt, pp. 217-218. Randolf Barton reported the same confrontation with some interesting differences. "Mrs. Baldwin went to Milroy complaining about horses being picketed in her yard; Milroy—Is your husband loyal; Mrs. B.—Yes, loyal to the South. M. commenced accusing our people of bringing on the war. Mrs. B.—It commenced at the John Brown raid. Milroy—Madam you are a lion, sergeant take this woman off. Mrs. B—Sir, I refuse to go till I am ready; she sat down and continued sitting for some time, she then arose, I am ready to go now, and off she went." Colt, p. 239.

[23] Milroy letter, 2/27/1863.

[24] Milroy as quoted in Delauter, p. 49.

[25] Delauter, pp. 49-50.

Stonewall Jackson was accidentally and mortally wounded in the darkness of the Wilderness on May 2, 1863. Within days of his death, Winchester's Rebelettes began sporting mourning badges bearing Stonewall's picture encircled by a black crepe border. At first the Union soldiers merely demanded the removal of the emblems. When ignored, the Federals began tearing the pins off outraged and heaving Victorian bosoms. When that unchivalrous abuse failed to halt their defiant display of dissension, at least one Stonewall-clad woman was driven out of town. Rather than concede the point to the damned Yankees, the ladies substituted George Washington's likeness for Stonewall's, and then paraded their taunt through the town.[26]

It appears, though, that the combined effect of several of their number having been exiled, while others were physically accosted in the streets, finally convinced the secessionist women of Winchester that they had pushed the Yankees to the limit of their patience and self-restraint. With decidedly unpleasant consequences having been added to the game of invective and provocation, no further serious confrontations between the military and civilians were recorded during the balance of Milroy's occupation of the town. Although they did not know it, the Rebelette's five-month long powder-puff war of insults would soon pay handsome dividends. Because of the repeated wounds to his pride and dignity, Milroy's judgement would soon be influenced by the loathsome thought of giving the harridans of Winchester the satisfaction of seeing the backs of his men in retreat.

-----

[26]Delauter, p. 50.

During their occupation, the soldiers of Milroy's division had more serious duty than merely dealing with political agitation and sexual tension. Although confronted for most of his stay in the lower Valley by relatively small contingents of Confederate cavalry, the motley assortment of Butternuts carried a sting disproportionate to their numbers. Milroy was repeatedly reminded of that latter fact, commencing on his march to Winchester.

By orders of "...poor old (Mother) Gen. Kelly...," Milroy had divided his division between several posts including the disposition of Cluseret's brigade at Winchester. Five hundred Rebel horsemen tried to swallow one of those contingents posted at Moorfield but were driven off when Milroy sent reinforcements from Petersburg. The Hoosier was not so lucky a few days later when he moved the balance of his command toward Winchester. "We had to cross the south branch of the Potomic 3 miles below Moorfield on the road to Romney. It was easy fordable and I had a tree cut and a rough crossing made to prevent the boys wetting their feet. All had crossed but the detachment of the 12th [W.] Va. some 300 strong who were a little slow about crossing and let the forage train...get near a mile ahead of them when a squad of 50 Reb cavalry which was concealed in a thick pine wood...suddenly dashed down on the forage train and unhitched 52 horses from 13 wagons and put the teamsters and some half dozen soldiers that happened to be straggling along there on the horses and lead and drove them back to the mountain at a furious rate. They were not more than ten minutes in doing up the job.... [A]s soon as word came to me I dashed back ordering two pieces of artillery and 100 infantry to follow—when I got in sight of my wagons...the rebs were out of sight in the woods but left a cloud of dust along the road over which they dashed—I set my two pieces of artillery throwing shells after them.... I sent troops to guard all the mountain passes to prevent them from getting out, but they sliped out about ten o'clock that night, between two of my companies...." The Yankees vented their frustration on some hapless bushwhackers encountered further down the road. "My boys capture some and some they did not capture."[27]

Except for Cluseret's skirmish on Christmas Eve, the situation in Winchester remained relatively quiet during the first half of January. The most significant military activity involved the evolving composition of Milroy's division. On January 9, the 1st New York (Lincoln) Cavalry arrived, providing Milroy with his first significant force of troopers, an invaluable commodity when trying to occupy and control a large and porous territory.[28]

Although spared from dueling with the Rebels, Milroy became heavily engaged with his own side during that same period. General Kelley ordered Milroy to desist from all offensive action so as to avoid provoking a counterattack that might endanger the B & O Railroad. About that order the Hoosier groused, "...I recd. a cowardly order...to lay still...act on the defensive and strongly fortify this place...[s]o I must...practice the McClellan practices and drop the sword and musket and take up the spade and pick and may have to remain at this place till spring which is horribly anoying and disheartening to me, as I am getting very anxious to hurry on the suppression of the rebellion and get home."[29]

Compelled to swallow his orders, Milroy apparently spit the acid they generated onto General Cluseret. On January 16, after the Frenchmen stumbled in some way, Milroy had him placed in arrest, and in a few days, shipped out of Winchester. In order to resolve what could have been an ugly situation, with possible international implications, Cluseret was permitted to resign on March 2, 1863. After the departure of the stunned

[27]Presumably, Milroy meant by his emphasis that some were killed either before they could surrender or afterwards. Milroy letter, 1/5/1863, emphasis in original.

[28]Stevenson, p. 152.

[29]Milroy letter, 1/18/1863.

brigadier, Colonel Hay assumed command of the division's First Brigade.[30]

Starting the day after Cluseret's arrest, the Federals began to pay a price, albeit limited at first, for their possession of Winchester. On that day, some of Brigadier General William E. "Grumble" Jones' cavalry slipped behind the Union picket line and nabbed two sentries. The two captives stalled by walking as slowly, and stopping as frequently, as possible without getting shot. The delaying tactics allowed Company K of the 1st New York Cavalry to mount, intercept the raiders, and free the prisoners.

Refusing to concede to the bitter weather of the season, the next day the Hoosier sent the New Yorkers, six companies of the 87th Pennsylvania, and contingents from both the 9th and 12th West Virginia in pursuit all the way to Front Royal—but the raiders had escaped.[31] Although denied retaliation against the Rebel cavalry, nine days later the New Yorkers were able to round up "...a dozen villainous-looking 'bushwhackers' and a large number of cattle, sheep and horses..." from the bandit's/partisan's lair at "Devil's Hole" in the North Mountain.[32]

Despite a foot of newly fallen snow and the doubling of the number of blue-coated troopers, thanks to the arrival of the 13th Pennsylvania Cavalry on February 5, butternut partisans were able to strike Milroy's garrison the next day.[33] A force, supposedly belonging to the Partisan Rangers under Colonel John Singleton Mosby, snatched a stagecoach crammed with officers, men, and the division's mail, that was toiling up the Turnpike from Martinsburg. Word of the raid arrived by way of one of the officer

---

[30]Prowell, p. 56; Keifer, vol. 1, p. 321. Cluseret became an opposition newspaper reporter in New York and eventually a member of the Chamber of Deputies in France.

[31]Milroy letter, 1/18/1863; Beach, p. 209; Prowell, p. 58.

[32]Stevenson, p. 154.

[33]Milroy letter, 2/10/1863.

passengers who escaped while the trunks were being plundered. The story was hardly out of the mouth of the thoroughly chilled officer when Milroy dispatched Captain Abram Jones and 50 troopers from the 1st New York Cavalry to try to intercept the guerrillas before they could escape.[34]

Thanks to tracks in the snow and some hard riding through the dark of the night, the coach was finally overtaken near Millwood. "Revolvers were used by pursuers and pursued, but our men had to be very careful about firing on account of the prisoners [who were made to ride bareback on the coach team]. At last the revolvers were emptied, and Jones' men drew their sabres and dashed in among the retreating enemy, sabring them right and left.... All of the prisoners [who were nearly frozen because the Rebels had taken their coats] were re-captured, together with...half a dozen of the guerrillas as well. Several of the enemy had been killed, and it was found, upon inquiring of the prisoners, that one of the killed was named Jones."[35]

The Federal momentum continued to February 9. Based upon a freed slave's entreaties that Rebels were rounding up his kinsmen for shipment south, Milroy dispatched a contingent from the 13th Pennsylvania Cavalry to abort the outrage. The Pennsylvanians freed the blacks, wounded one Johnnie, captured another, and liberated four horses in the process. Milroy added a touching postscript, "It would do you good to see the poor creatures rejoice when they find they have liberty and their scattered families unite."[36] That same day, while the Keystone troopers were conducting their mission of mercy, a patrol under Captain Robert

---

[34]Milroy letter, 2/10/1863.
[35]Stevenson, p. 156; Beach, p. 211. The New Yorkers also claimed two prisoners. Macfie, p. 77. A review of the Mosby literature did not reveal a reference to this incident. The Union sources may have misidentified their victims either by mistake or to inflate their accomplishment, or perhaps the Rangers chose to ignore one of their few failures.
[36]Milroy letter, 2/10/1863.

H. Hertzog of the 1st New York Cavalry had a spat with a Rebel scouting party. Two Butternuts were killed and one of their lieutenants was taken prisoner.[37]

The delay in his anticipated promotion to major general deflated Milroy's pleasure over his command's two modest triumphs. With typical understatement, Milroy informed his wife about the difficulty he was having obtaining his second star. "This promotion was justly due me five months ago, and the Presdt. and Secy. of War were then in favor of giving it to me, but it has been baffled and kept back by the vindictive malice and little souled jealousy of Halleck, and it has now been so long and so unjustly witheld from me, and so many others, with little or no merit, have been promoted over me, that I attach no honor to it, and look upon it as valuless, and were it not that it unshackles me and gives me wider field of action, I would reject it with scorn. Another reason that reconciles me to the acceptance of the promotion is that it is a complete triumph over old Halleck, and is the first appointment ever made over his protest since he disecrated the office of Genl. in chief."[38]

The Hoosier was fortunate that he was recommended for promotion before word reached Washington of the debacle that befell his Keystone cavalry on February 26. Very early on that bleak winter day a small force of Rebel horsemen slipped behind the Union picket line and captured eight out of the 15 Bluecoats who were shivering at their reserve picket post. After breaking through the perimeter, the audacious raiders headed toward Winchester on the "Back Road" and dispersed a group of riflemen guarding its intersection with the Valley Turnpike. Deciding not to press their luck, the butternut troopers headed back up the Valley, but not in such haste that they neglected to scoop up a few stray Yankees that they encountered along the way.

---

[37]Stevenson, p. 157.
[38]Milroy letter, 2/10/1863.

After an excited aide dragged him out of his warm, cozy bed, Milroy dispatched a goodly portion of his cavalry, first a company of the 1st New York and then the entire, unbloodied 13th Pennsylvania Cavalry, to try to punish the intruders and reclaim the captives. Upon receiving their orders, 50 New Yorkers under the command of Captain Franz Passegger galloped up the Pike in pursuit. "This mounted force proceeded to Strasburg, where they overtook the enemy and charged them at once, driving them through the town and beyond Fisher's Hill in its rear, where a squadron of the enemy's cavalry were on picket. This force was also put to flight and driven some distance, and all of our men recaptured [along with eleven Confederate prisoners]."[39]

What happened next, had men not died, resembled a scene in a Max Sennett *Keystone Cops'* episode. After freeing the hostages, the Empire Staters returned by the Back Road pursuant to orders and arrived in town at 9 a.m. with their dejected gray-backed prisoners in tow.[40] Just after Passegger's men turned off the Valley Turnpike on their way back to Winchester, Major Michael Kerwin, whose battalion of the 13th Pennsylvania Cavalry was able to get on the road first, thundered up the Pike without seeing the New Yorkers heading back. In the white heat of their first opportunity to engage the enemy, the Pennsylvanians galloped to within two miles of Woodstock despite having received orders from their commander not to go past Strasburg.[41] On the outskirts of Woodstock, Kerwin's vanguard discovered that a large force of Confederate cavalry barred further progress up the Valley. The 13th's major was immediately informed of this development, which apparently reminded him of his orders. Kerwin halted his

---

[39]Stevenson, p. 157; O.R. 1-25-1-27, Milroy.

[40]Ibid., p. 157.

[41]Milroy reported such an order in his report, as did his biographer, but no such order was referenced in his letter to his wife that discussed the same incident. O.R. 1-25-1-27, Milroy; Macfie, p. 78; Milroy letter 2/27/1863.

battalion of novice warriors and commenced a slow amble back to base.[42]

On their way back, at a point in the road that was too constricted to allow either to pass, Kerwin's battalion nearly collided with the hard-charging Second Battalion of Pennsylvanians under the command of Major Edward Byrne. The two contingents reined their mounts to a halt and then stood in columns facing each other while their majors debated whether to attack or retreat. "While in this position, firing was heard in the direction of Fisher's Hill [to the south], and the next instant Kerwin's rear guard were observed galloping in with the enemy yelling and firing close at their heels. Kerwin gave the command to his battalion: 'By fours, left about wheel!' and they soon were facing the enemy; but unfortunately the other battalion wheeled also, at the word of command, which was not intended for them, and faced in the opposite direction. Kerwin then gave the command: 'Forward!' supposing that both battalions were facing the enemy, and the result was that each battalion set out in an opposite direction...." At the worst possible moment, the fleeing Yankee rear guard burst into Kerwin's column, accompanied by screams, at the top of their lungs, that the Rebels were coming—a fact which was already painfully obvious to the rest of the rookie troopers. Worse, when those who were headed toward danger glanced over their shoulders for the reassurance of numbers, they saw their sister battalion heading back toward Winchester at an undignified gait.[43]

Tragedy quickly replaced farce. "The Rebs [of the 7th and 11th Virginia Cavalry, Colonel O. R. Funsten commanding] come charging down on them sounding their bugles and yelling and the Pa. Cav. did not wait to receive them but wheeled back in confusion and commenced a pel-mel hasty retreat, the rebs charging into them firing with pistols and carbines, and cutting and

---

[42]Macfie, p. 79.
[43]Stevenson, pp. 157-158.

slashing with their swords upon the poor cowardly Pennsyl-vaninites who were as helpless as sheep, and thus they run them for about 20 miles by which time they [the Rebels] had killed and captured 170 of them including 12 commissioned officers [includ-ing Major Byrne who was wounded]. The New York Co. had dashed off the pike towards the right of Woodstock before the fight, or rather the event commenced, and finding themselves surrounded they cut their way through and got back to a back road and got in with the loss of 17 killed and captured, thus making the whole total loss of 197, besides two of my best scouts. This is horribly mortifying to me...."[44] The surviving Pennsylvanians, who straggled sheepishly into town coated from stirrup to crossed saber emblem in mud, suffered worse than their commander—as the butt of New York scorn and ridicule that continued for months.[45]

      March proved to be as positive for Milroy and his division as February was negative. On the tenth of the month, Brigadier General Washington L. Elliott, a regular army officer, arrived along with the 12th Pennsylvania Cavalry. The 12th, originally named the Curtin Hussars, was a marginally experienced unit. By the time they arrived in Winchester, the Hussars already claimed nearly a year of service patrolling contested territory, including a few months in the Shenandoah Valley, and a sniff of serious combat thanks to provost duty on the fringes of the battlefield at Antietam.[46] Their most extensive exposure to gunfire, as well as a slightly tarnished reputation, came by way of a disastrous night-time encounter with Stonewall Jackson's troops at Manassas Junction in August of 1862, where a few of them were killed, nearly a dozen more were wounded, and half the regiment was

---

[44]Milroy letter, 2/27/1863; O.R. 1-25-1-30, Milroy; O.R. 1-25-1-32, Jones.

[45]Macfie, p. 99.

[46]For variety, the 12th Pennsylvania Cavalry will occasionally be referred to hereafter as the Hussars.

captured.[47] Within days of the arrival of the Hussars, the size of Milroy's Second Division of the Eighth Corps was nearly doubled by the addition of Battery L of the United States Artillery, the 67th Pennsylvania, and the 116th and 123rd Ohio infantry regiments.

Mindful of the increasing size of their division, and perhaps the fate of Cluseret, Milroy's officers apparently decided that the Hoosier's apple was in need of some polishing. They chipped in and purchased their genuinely esteemed leader a $1,000 sash and presentation sword that bore the engraved name of each of his battles. The tribute was presented to Milroy at a grand review of his division that was attended by many notables and their ladies.[48] Even more gratifying than the pomp and sentiment was the arrival of word that on March 31 (retroactive to November 29, 1862) Milroy had been awarded his coveted promotion to major general.[49]

Bolstered by additional troops, a promotion, and adulation from his officers, Milroy surely began to dream about a grand spring offensive in the Valley. General Schenck in Baltimore took some of the powder out of the Hoosier's cannon though, when he reduced the division's offensive punch by ordering that one brigade be sent to occupy Berryville, a defensive deployment intended both to interdict guerrillas crossing over the Blue Ridge and to provide early warning of a Confederate invasion down the Valley.[50] The assignment, which fell to Colonel Andrew T. McReynolds and his Third Brigade, was particularly galling to the troopers of the 1st

---

[47]The 12th Pennsylvania Cavalry, as well as the 1st New York, contained a sizeable contingent of Dutchmen which, due to the prejudice against men of German birth or background prevalent at the time, detracted somewhat from the respect both units might otherwise have enjoyed.

[48]Hartley, p. 30. Hereafter quotations from Hartley's letters will be annotated as here, for example, Hartley letter, 4/1/1863.

[49]Macfie, p. 81.

[50]Ibid., p. 82.

Milroy's Accoutrements   Milroy's Presentation Sword
(Courtesy Rensselaer Public Library)   (Courtesy Rensselaer Public Library)

New York Cavalry, who were forced to surrender the cabins they had perfected over the winter to the newly arrived Hussars.[51]

As anticipated, longer and warmer days brought more vigorous enemy activity. On April 8, Federal cavalry videttes were attacked on the Millwood Road at 10 p.m., with the loss of one wounded, two immediately paroled Yankee prisoners, and five commandeered horses.[52] Five days later, Lieutenant Charles Woodruff and 10 of his troopers from Company K, 1st New York Cavalry, were ambushed near Snicker's Ferry by 37 Butternut horsemen from the 4th Virginia Cavalry. The first Rebel volley

---

[51]Stevenson, p. 161; Beach p. 214. At that point the Third Brigade was comprised of the 67th Pennsylvania, 12th West Virginia, 6th Maryland, Alexander's Baltimore Light Battery, and the 1st New York Cavalry.

[52]O.R. 1-25-1-143. Videttes, also spelled vedettes, were troopers who stood picket duty while mounted. Under the parole system a captured soldier could be released after he promised not to participate in combat until released from his oath by the release of a Confederate prisoner.

killed Private Charles Young. After the initial shock passed, Woodruff rallied his squad and then "...called upon his men to charge, which they did most gallantly, driving the enemy from their ambush...." The effort was successful but at least one New Yorker ended the day as a prisoner because of the encounter.[53]

The next day the New Yorkers retaliated with an ambush of their own near Berry's Ferry. Perhaps suspecting a trap, Yankee Lieutenant Franklin G. Martindale sent a couple of his men across the river to reconnoiter and hid the rest behind a stone wall that ran parallel to the shore. "On reaching the other side they were attacked by Mosby's men, who dashed down to the bank and fired at them as they swam back. At that moment the boys behind the wall fired, dropping one of the 'Johnnies,' and the rest retreated."[54]

The Empire State troopers were not the only ones to come under Rebel fire during early April. On the twelfth of that month Lieutenant John H. Black of the 12th Pennsylvania Cavalry wrote to his fiancée about his own regiment's encounter with the enemy. "Since I wrote you a squad of our regiment was on a scout and on their way home about 13 miles from camp they was fired on by a squad of rebels who were concealed by the roadside in a thicket of low pines, which resulted in one man from Co. E. by the name of Charles Shaw being killed. The rest after giving the 'rebs' a few minutes of a fight, come to the conclusion to return to camp. The 'rebs' were four to one of ours and had the advantage of being in the bushes where our 'chaps' could not get to them.... A large squad went out in search of the rascals but did not find them, we returned by 12 o'clock at night and felt for going to bed, for we had done some fast riding."

---

[53]Stevenson, p. 165; O.R. 1-25-1-143. The prisoner was paroled the same day. As far as the Confederate assailants, Milroy attributed the attack to the 4th Virginia in a contemporaneous report whereas Stevenson credited Mosby's Rangers with the ambush.

[54]Stevenson, p. 165.

"This morning 1500 infantry & some cavalry went out with the orders not to return for several days without they found the 'chaps' sooner, and if they come across them they may catch fits in general."[55] The designated soldiers, the 110th Ohio and a battalion of the 13th Pennsylvania Cavalry, completed a 50-mile tramp (80 for the troopers) up the Cedar Creek Valley but apparently failed to locate any enemy upon who they could "catch a fit." Five days later, the 122nd Ohio and a two-gun section of artillery marched a total of 40 miles to and from Stump's tannery in order to confiscate a load of leather which otherwise would have been bound for the feet of the Army of Northern Virginia.[56]

Although the infantrymen were working harder, the 1st New York Cavalry stole the limelight again a few days later. A gray-haired slave, who came into their camp to buy some sugar, reported that the guerrilla Leopold was in the habit of using his master's house on the other side of the Shenandoah River as a rendezvous. Captain Ezra H. Bailey and 40 New Yorkers were given the assignment to capture the partisan leader.

"The 'darkey' agreed to be on the opposite bank of the river at midnight [on April 21], to strike three matches in quick succession as a signal that all was right, or only one in case a problem had arisen. Our boys were 'standing to horse,' at the appointed hour, peering through the darkness for the signal. At last they observed three distinct flashes and were soon in the saddle swimming for the opposite shore.... On crossing they found the old 'darkey' all excitement, who informed them that Leopold was in bed at the house, and then led them to a point from which they could distinguish the outlines of the buildings. They then surrounded the house quietly, and rapped at the door. There was great commotion within, but the officers sung out that the house was surrounded, and would be burned, and everybody

---

[55]Black letter, 4/12/1863.
[56]O.R. 1-25-1-142, Milroy.

in it put to death, if a single shot were fired. After a good deal of parleying the door was opened and the boys walked in, pistol in hand, and captured Mr. Leopold and seven of his gang, all villainous looking scoundrels. Leopold was quite young looking, but he was a notorious bushwhacker."[57]

The small triumphs of his cavalry undoubtedly further stoked the new major general's lust for combat, even though the Hoosier hardly needed any inducement to get after the Rebels. On April 22, Brigadier General Elliott was sent up the Valley with the 116th and 123rd Ohio Infantry regiments, the 12th and 13th Pennsylvania Cavalry, and two guns of Battery D, First West Virginia Artillery, with orders to go to Woodstock and harry the Confederates. After traveling approximately 18 miles, the foot-weary infantry halted at Strasburg, Virginia, and then watched as their mounted comrades trotted toward Woodstock, Virginia, 12 miles farther.[58]

The Hussars, and perhaps some of the 13th Pennsylvania Cavalry, encountered Major S. B. Myers and a contingent of his troopers from the 7th Virginia Cavalry late in the afternoon. The Southern horsemen were in the process of burying a fallen comrade when the Pennsylvanians "...fell on them with a yell. They [the Rebels] show no quarter when they catch any of our men, nor did we give any on this occasion. They ran in every direction, but did not get far till they were met by some of our men and were shot down. Afterwards our men took the corpse out

---

[57]Stevenson, pp. 165-166; O.R. 1-25-1-143, Milroy; Hewitt, pp. 31-32; Beach, p. 218. There were significant differences between Stevenson's version, as one of the historians for the 1st New York, and the other sources. Milroy reported that the troopers crossed the river in a rowboat in pairs, while Hewitt claimed that the slave was offered $50 for his assistance by the New Yorkers and that Milroy upped the pot to $80 to insure cooperation. Hewitt, the historian for the 12th West Virginia which was not involved, also alleged that the troopers smashed in the door and surprised the bushwhackers in their beds. The burning threat was confirmed by Beach, the other historian for the 1st New York.

[58]O.R. 1-25-1-142.

of the house and put a match to the house and burned it to the ground."[59]

The Confederate version of the skirmish was markedly different. "His [Myer's] loss was 1 killed, 2 wounded, and 12 taken prisoners, of whom 2 were afterward killed by the enemy in cold blood after they had been several hours in their hands as prisoners of war. The conduct of the enemy during this expedition was marked by acts of brutality and fiendishness unknown in civilized warfare, such as the murder of prisoners of war, firing into a funeral procession, and burning the dwellings of unoffending citizens."[60] It is probably beyond knowing which version was the more accurate. Given the comment concerning "no quarter" being offered, and the bitter hatred which many Federals came to harbor against irregulars and partisan guerrillas who were considered to be little better than murderers, it is entirely possible that the truth is to be found in a blend of both.

Breaking up the Rebel funeral did not end the day's action, and the 12th Pennsylvania Cavalry's 2nd Lieutenant Henry E. Gutelius provided an account of the balance of the afternoon. "After the house was burnt down, our men started toward the Rappahannock. We did not go far till we saw a regiment of rebel cavalry just in the act of charging on our men with revolvers. As soon as the Colonel [Lieutenant Colonel Joseph L. Moss] saw them, he ordered our boys to draw their sabers and charge. The word was scarcely spoken till they started, each man trying to get before the other so as to have the first chance at the rebels. Lieutenant Irwin says he never heard such a yelling before. As soon as the rebels heard the yells of our men they did not wait to see how many were coming, but skedaddled every way. Our fellows killed thirty, and captured ninety-one prisoners and about

---

[59]Gutelius, *Mifflinburg Telegraph*, 5/5/1863. Second Lieutenant Henry E. Gutelius, of the 12th Pennsylvania Cavalry, referred to the Confederates as "bushwhackers" in the article he sent home to the local newspaper.

[60]O.R. 1-25-1-144.

forty horses. The loss on our side was one killed and one wounded."[61] Undoubtedly with a more jaunty demeanor, the Hussars and the rest of the contingent sauntered the 34 miles back down the valley to Winchester.

Allowed one day's rest, Elliott and his brigade were dispatched on another foray into disputed territory. This time, in addition to the 116th and 123rd Ohio Infantry and the 12th and 13th Pennsylvania Cavalry, Elliott's brigade was enhanced with detachments from the 87th Pennsylvania Infantry and the 9th West Virginia Infantry. The Yankee column headed towards the southwest with the horsemen plodding along while the ground-pounders ate their dust and struggled to keep up. Twenty-eight hard miles later, the Federals were permitted to bivouac in a woods near Wardensville. Up again at dawn, the blue column reached Sand Ridge at 10 a.m., where they rested before wending their way down the mountain into the valley of the Lost River. Finding the river too high to ford, the Yankees trudged back up the mountain and returned to Wardensville for the night.[62]

Determined to follow the assigned route, on the morning of April 27, Elliott again led his command back to the Lost River, presumably toward what he hoped would be a fordable point. The depth of the river continued to make fording impossible, so on Elliott's orders, "...the wagons were driven into the stream, in line, and planks laid on top of them. A temporary bridge was thus formed and the infantry in that way slowly crossed the river."[63]

The next day the Federals commenced a forced march eastward toward Strasburg with the cavalry on the point. Around 3 p.m. the weary soldiers pulled up near Fisher's Hill, a short

---

[61]Gutelius, *Mifflinburg Telegraph*, 5/5/1863. It may be assumed that the Rebel casualty figures were inflated for the benefit of the readers back home. The official after-action report, and an account included in the history of the 116th Ohio, listed only 30 prisoners taken.

[62]Prowell, p. 60.

[63]Ibid.

distance from Strasburg, and began to set up camp for what they hoped would be a well-deserved rest. The Confederates had other plans.

Accounts of what happened next vary slightly depending upon the side of the observer. According to Private Thomas Crowl with the 87th Pennsylvania, "...there happened to be a force of rebels lying at Strawsburg [Strasburg] of which they showed battle and wanted us to surrender but that was not the aim."[64] Instead, Elliott dispatched his cavalry to disperse the line of Butternuts that had suddenly appeared on the brow of the hill. Pursuant to their orders, "Our cavalry [the 13th Pennsylvania] charged on them but got the worst of the bargain, eight of them was killed in that charge and two or three of the Rebs."[65]

The Confederates claimed that their success was the result of an ambush laid by 150 dismounted and well-hidden carbineers. In the butternut-tinted version, when the Federals came within 30 or 40 yards, the Southerners unleashed an unexpected and deadly volley which drove the Union troopers back down the hill in a rout.[66] The Rebel commander claimed that his snare claimed at least 70 casualties, while the Union leader conceded 27, all from the 13th Pennsylvania Cavalry.

Both sides agreed that the Federals ended the day in possession of the field, although there was also a disagreement over the reason. The Northern version claimed that "...our regt. [the 87th Pennsylvania] and the 9th Va. was ordered to charge up the hill at them but it was of poor account, they run like fine fellows, but we killed eleven of them and none of ours...."[67] From the Southern perspective, "...our handful of men were moved back in perfect order to a position of safety across the

[64]Crowl letter, 5/3/1863.
[65]Ibid. Milroy reported eight killed and six wounded. O.R. 1-25-1-138.
[66]O.R. 1-25-1-144, Funston.
[67]Crowl letter, 5/3/1863.

river...."[68] Both sides seem to have been satisfied with the results of the encounter, so the next day the Blue column returned to Winchester and the Butternuts resumed their duty on the picket line.

While Elliott was probing the central Valley, Confederate Brigadier Generals John D. Imboden and William E. "Grumble" Jones were rampaging through western Virginia in an effort to pry the soon-to-be new state away from the Union and to break the B & O Railroad. In the process the Southerners managed to generate enormous amounts of anxiety in Washington and to seize hundreds of cattle. Terrified that not only might the Confederates succeed in reclaiming the breakaway territory, but also might actually invade Ohio or western Pennsylvania, the Federal high command began to draw troops from all over the surrounding area in order to abort the invasion. Included in that redeployment were Milroy's Second Brigade and the 12th Pennsylvania Cavalry, all of whom departed by train during the first 10 days of May.[69]

The Hussars, who seem to have been the only unit from Milroy's command who saw any action in western Virginia, did not roll into Clarksburg, until late in the day on May 3, 30 hours after their departure.[70] The Union commander at that town, Brigadier General Benjamin S. Roberts, was not impressed with his newly arrived cavalry reinforcements, writing: "The Twelfth Pennsylvania Cavalry, 320 strong, reaches me today, broken down."[71] Regardless of the Pennsylvanians' condition, Roberts needed information about the possible approach into his area of three separate Confederate columns totaling around 8,000 rifles.

---

[68]O.R. 1-25-1-144, Funston.

[69]O.R. 1-25-1-142, 1011; Gutelius, *Mifflinburg Telegraph*, 5/26/1863; Black letter, 5/9/1863; Prowell, p. 61. According to Gutelius, in his letter intended for publication, only a portion of his regiment made the trip, indicating that some of the 12th was retained to continue routine duty at various points in the lower Valley.

[70]Black letter, 5/9/1863.

[71]O.R. 1-25-2-399, Roberts.

He immediately dispatched six companies from the 12th "...some 12 miles farther over an awful muddy road, into hollows and over hills and mountains."[72]

From their new advanced post, the troopers from Pennsylvania and their jaded mounts began an immediate sweep of the area. "...On the 4th, our company [F] and several others were ordered on a scout to Lost Creek, where we arrived at noon of the same day. In the afternoon we went three or four miles farther to reconnoiter, but saw no 'grey-backs.'"[73]

The next day, an expeditionary force consisting of the 12th Pennsylvania Cavalry, one company of the 1st West Virginia Cavalry, two companies of the 28th Ohio Infantry, and a small contingent from the 3rd West Virginia Cavalry were sent out to conduct another reconnaissance.[74] "On the morning of the 5th we started out again in the direction of Janelew [a village near Weston, West Virginia]. When we arrived within a mile and a half of the place we halted while the officers held a council of war. They soon concluded to go into the place on a charge and make the 'grey-backs' skedaddle. At 12 o'clock we began to move forward as noiselessly as possible until we were within four or five hundred yards of their pickets. The command was then given to charge. Company G was in the advance, Company F second, Company K third, Company L fourth, and Company B the rear-guard. As soon as the command was given every man put spurs to his horse and drew his revolver; a yell from every throat was next in order, and away we went through mud two feet deep. We had not gone more than three hundred yards until we saw the 'grey-backs' running as fast as their horses could carry them. Near the middle of the town was a large covered bridge which we had to cross in order to get at the rebels. They rallied on the other side but did not stand long. We fired on them, and away they

---

[72]Black letter, 5/9/1863.
[73]Gutelius, *Mifflinburg Telegraph*, 5/26/1863.
[74]O.R. 1-25-2-496, Moor.

went as fast they could, without firing half a dozen shots. A great many of them threw away their arms without even firing them off. After going about a mile they turned to the left, which gave us a cross-fire on them—if we did not make the bark fly then, I am mistaken. We followed them to the mountain, when the officer in command ordered us to halt. Lieutenant [David A.] Irwin and six or eight others followed them across the first mountain. They had the fastest horses and did not hear the command to halt. Eight rebels were killed, nine wounded and four captured.... Not a man was hurt on our side."[75]

While the 12th Pennsylvania Cavalry was scouting the wilds of western Virginia and scattering Butternuts at Janelew, Milroy sat chafing in Winchester under the twin irritants of neither having been allotted any part in thwarting the Confederate invasion of western Virginia nor a role in Major General Joseph Hooker's offensive at Chancellorsville. Perhaps in an effort to play some part in the events boiling around him, and in spite of his manpower deficiencies, on the night of May 5 the Hoosier sent a squadron of troopers from the 1st New York Cavalry and about 400 novice riflemen from the 67th Pennsylvania, under the command of Colonel F. J. Staunton, to Snicker's Gap in the Blue Ridge in hopes of setting a trap for Mosby's Rangers. After crossing the river, the riflemen took a position along the road while the troopers rode ahead in hopes of making contact, feigning flight, and drawing Mosby's men into an ambush.

About 3 p.m. on May 6, seventeen New Yorkers assaulted the Rangers' picket post near Upperville and drove Mosby's men back on their reserve. When the Confederates in the reserve wouldn't counterattack, the Federals sat on their horses and took long-range potshots at the Partisans in hopes of inciting a charge. "Finally they [the New Yorkers] rode out into the middle of the

---

[75]Gutelius, *Mifflinburg Telegraph*, 5/26/1863. Sergeant Black, also a Hussar, reported that the Rebel force totaled 48 riders. Black letter, 5/9/1863.

highway, so that the enemy could see the paucity of their numbers, and began to yell and fire their pistols, but made no attempt to advance."

Possibly because they already knew the script for this performance by heart, the Rangers continued to refuse to charge, choosing instead to knock two Yankee riders out of their saddles with some sharpshooting of their own. But Southern pride could only stand the Yankee antics so long. Despite probably knowing what the Federals were up to, the Rangers charged anyway, "...firing rapidly, cheering and yelling as only rebels could yell." With the enemy finally in pursuit, the New Yorkers turned and galloped toward the waiting infantry.

Tragically, the scheme failed to anticipate that the 400 rookie officers and infantrymen who lined the road would be filled with fear, excitement, and an overload of adrenalin. "Our retreating cavalry had just got in front of our infantry, when the whole line poured a withering volley into them; which, had the infantry not been so frightened, must have killed every man and horse in the party. As it was, they killed two men and two horses, and wounded several others of our own men and nearly all the rest of the horses. It was dreadful."[76] Or, from the Rangers' perspective as they rode away unscathed, it was dreadfully funny.

Milroy was undaunted by the snafu at Upperville. When he received a report that Grumble Jones had left all his camp equipment, reserve artillery, wagons, jaded horses, and a goodly amount of supplies in the central Valley under the protection of 400 or 500 broken-down troops, the habitually pugnacious Hoosier launched General Elliott and most of the remaining Winchester garrison on an expedition to gobble them up.[77] About the time that Elliott reached New Market, word of the sortie filtered back to Washington. "Halleck heard of it and reprimanded me severely

---

[76]Stevenson, pp. 167-168; Beach, pp. 222-223.
[77]Macfie, p. 83; Milroy letter, 5/17/1863; O.R. 1-25-1-143.

and ordered me to send after them and bring them back at once and lay still—S C I E N T I F I C L Y—I could have taken Harrisonburg and Staunton with ease...[and] their baggage...but this would have been unscientific and hurrying on the war too fast for Halleck, who wants the war to last 4 or 5 years longer."[78] Perhaps Halleck was also worried that Jones might reverse course, capture Winchester, and trap Elliott's brigade. Such a possibility apparently never occurred to Milroy. Compelled to submit, but unwilling to concede the last word, Milroy ordered Elliott to "stop troubling the Rebels," a sarcastic order which brought the First Brigade back to Winchester with nine Johnnies under guard and only five Bluecoats in ambulances.[79]

The first part of May was a decidedly gloomy period for the general from Indiana. His troops had embarrassed themselves at Upperville and he was personally humiliated by Halleck. Just as demoralizing, the Confederate invasion of western Virginia petered out due to the combined deleterious effects of: swarms of Bluecoats, inclement weather, short rations, and many miles of arduous travel—but not even partially because of anything Milroy had done. Even worse, his wife and four children left Winchester around May 3 after a visit of several weeks, leaving the genuinely devoted father and husband so depressed that he expressed sentiments to his wife that were markedly inconsistent with his normal machismo. "My room was painfully lonely after you all left and I kept out of it and absorbed in business as much as possible. Your visit was a bright beam amid the darkened gloom of the war, a delightful oasis amid the darkened gloom of the desert of virtual widowhood and banishment from home."[80]

---

[78] Milroy letter, 5/17/1863, emphasis, capitals and spacing in original. The distance from Staunton to Winchester is about 80 miles. Milroy's railings against West Point and its graduates never included any musing as to why a similar matriculation didn't seem to hobble Lee or Jackson.

[79] Macfie, p. 83; O.R. 1-25-1-143.

[80] Milroy letter, 5/17/1863.

Despite a rebuke from Halleck that might have convinced most men to adopt pacifism just for spite, Milroy continued to wield his cavalry as aggressively as ever. On May 12, the Hoosier sent Major Kerwin and 140 troopers from the 13th Pennsylvania Cavalry to reconnoiter the area of Buck's Ford on the Shenandoah River. Practice did not seem to improve the performance of the 13th, perhaps because they had been intimidated by the drubbing administered in February and the ambush at Strasburg in April. On the way, Kerwin received word that 40 or 50 Rebel troopers had just crossed the river and were bivouacked

Milroy and Family

on the opposite shore. In hopes of capturing the lot, Kerwin took his troopers across the river and then moved behind the Butternuts by way of a back road. Assuming that their prey were trapped by the river, the Yankee commander divided his command into two parts so that the Rebels could be isolated from the fords that bracketed their camp-site, and mashed against the river. After driving a short distance through the woods, the Federals "…met and drove in their pickets, following them up rapidly; they had just time enough to get 'to horse' and take to the woods, after an ineffectual attempt to drive back our advance guard."

Kerwin managed to overplan while ignoring the obvious. "I immediately sent a party through the woods to force them on the detachment I had sent to the upper ford, while I placed another party on a road that led inland, which the guides told me they would take in case both fords were cut off. The balance of my command I deployed around the woods, thus completely hemming them in the smallest possible space.…" The major was certain of success, "…[b]ut much to my disappointment, when they found all avenues of escape closed against them, they made direct for the river and swam their horses over. When I was informed of their crossing, I dashed to the river, but found all had crossed except 1, whom we captured." Whether the fault was to be found in too complex a plan, too cautious an attack, or in the rookie commander's failure to anticipate that horses could swim, Kerwin placed the blame on the guides.[81]

Another detachment of troopers from the 13th Pennsylvania Cavalry fared better thanks to the leadership of Captain James R. Utt of the 3rd West Virginia Cavalry and the steadying influence of two companies of his more experienced Mountaineers. On May 15, Utt's blended unit went on a scout to Front Royal and on the following day they discovered and routed a party of the 2nd Maryland Cavalry (C.S.A.) at Piedmont, Virginia. Forty

---

[81]O.R. 1-25-1-140, 141, Kerwin.

Confederates were captured, but at the cost of the life of Captain Utt and a sergeant from the 13th Pennsylvania Cavalry.[82]

The 1st New York Cavalry was even more successful. Riding out of Berryville, Captain William H. Boyd and 100 of his horsemen crossed the Shenandoah and Blue Ridge for a sortie into "Mosby's Confederacy."[83] At the fringe of Upperville on May 13, the Bluecoats spied 50 Rangers ambling into the village. In an attempt to surround their quarry, Boyd sent Captain Abram Jones and 50 troopers around the flank while he prepared to charge down the main street. Jones got lost in a pine thicket but Boyd charged anyway, surprising the Rangers and capturing 10 or 12 Partisans before they had a chance to mount up. "He [Boyd] then pursued Mosby and the balance of his force for several miles. During the chase, an officer, supposed to have been Mosby, would halt far in rear of his men, fire upon our advance, and then dash away at speed, bidding defiance to his pursuers. He was mounted upon a magnificent gray horse, whose speed seemed to our men almost miraculous. In this way he played with Boyd's advance for several miles, narrowly escaping the bullets from their carbines on several occasions."[84]

Despite, or perhaps because of, his allegedly narrow escape, Mosby retaliated on May 16 by capturing a company of Maryland cavalry (U.S.A.) stationed at Charlestown. Major Alonzo W. Adams and a contingent of the 1st New York Cavalry were dispatched to intercept the raiders. Hoping to intercept the guerrillas by passing through Berry's Ferry, but always cautious when dealing with the Rangers, Lieutenant Isaac D. Vermylia and 25 troopers were sent across to reconnoiter the woods on the far side. The scouting party had hardly gotten into the woods when

[82]O.R. 1-25-1-138, 143.

[83]"Mosby's Confederacy" was a nickname given to an area in Loudoun and Fauquier Counties, Virginia, where Mosby and his Rangers reigned with relative impunity.

[84]Stevenson, pp. 169-170.

twice their number of Rangers, who were apparently laying in wait for a target of opportunity, pounced on the rear of the small Yankee column.[85]

"Vermylia turned on them, and there was a pretty little fight going on when the main column, under Major Adams, having heard the firing in front, dashed up and turned the scales against the enemy; who, finding themselves between two fires, were compelled to fight, run or surrender. They fought desperately...."[86] About half the Butternuts escaped, two were killed, including one Confederate officer who was sabered to death in a ferocious duel in the middle of the river, five were wounded, and 10 were captured. The New Yorkers only suffered a few wounded, including one trooper who was allegedly shot from behind by a Rebel officer who had surrendered but used a pocket pistol when his captor's attention was diverted.[87]

The balance of the month passed in relative tranquility with little to note other than the changing composition of the Union forces in Winchester. Shortly after his cavalry finished sparring with Mosby, the balance of the Hoosier's division returned from

---

[85]Stevenson, pp. 170-171. Brigade commander McReynolds reported that Vermylia led 16 men and was accosted by 22 Confederates. O.R. 1-25-1-141. There is some question about whether the Southerners in the foregoing actions all belonged to Mosby's Partisan Ranger Battalion. Noted historian Jeffry Wert attributed the incident involving the 67th Pennsylvania and the one in Upperville to the Rangers but did not mention Vermylia's fight. None of the Ranger sources mention any of the engagements except the disaster on May 6 at Snicker's Ferry. Wert, *Mosby's Rangers...* pp. 61-62, 327.

[86]Ibid., pp. 170-171.

[87]Beach, pp. 225-226; Stevenson, p. 171. There was apparently quite a schism in the 1st New York Cavalry between the supporters and detractors of Major Adams, who assumed command of the regiment when Colonel McReynolds took over Milroy's Third Brigade. Beach, a member of the latter faction attributed the triumph at Berry's Ferry to Major Quinn, while Stevenson, one of the former, gave Adams the credit. In general this writer has found Stevenson to have been the more credible of the two historians. Stevenson noted that Adams complimented Quinn in the official report, but Beach refused to mention Adams at all.

western Virginia. On May 21 Milroy lost the services of the 9th and 10th West Virginia, but four days later the rookie 18th Connecticut rolled into Winchester with nearly a thousand brightly shining rifles.[88]

During this period, the enemy seemed content to concede the lower Valley to the Federals, even fleeing over the Shenandoah River at Front Royal rather than challenge a patrol from the 12th Pennsylvania Cavalry.[89] Rather than further fighting, the Federal division's soldiers spent most of their time in drilling and preparing for inspections, a circumstance that prompted Private Wierick, of the 12th Pennsylvania Cavalry, to grumble that Winchester had become little more than a glorified camp of instruction.[90]

Despite their best efforts, all the annoying duty the officers could invent was insufficient to prevent a little mischief, as a member of the 122nd Ohio described. "The alarm guns began to fire all around us and at last the old cannon boomed forth its melodious voice and we had to spring out in line on quick time. The word soon came that the alarm was caused by a cavalryman that attempted to pass the pickets without giving the countersign and they fired on him. He was drunk."[91]

May ended with the Connecticut boys engaged in some peculiar duty. Earlier in the month the Confederates designated May 30 as the day that Valley families who wished to switch allegiance could migrate to Northern lines. To ensure their safety, the entire 18th Connecticut, along with a squad of cavalry, marched to Strasburg under a flag of truce to collect Unionists and the families of Confederate soldiers who had deserted to the Federals. After four or five hours in hostile territory, the Yankees returned with a dozen families who were, "...poorly dressed, had little or no furniture, and looked the picture of want and

---

[88]O.R. 1-25-1-143, 144.
[89]Weirick letter, 5/26/1863.
[90]Ibid., 5/26/1863.
[91]Hartley letter, 5/25/1863.

starvation. The boys collected what food they could for them, and it was pleasant to see the appetite with which these poor creatures ate hard tack and pork. The whole party returned to Winchester about six P. M., tired and hungry."[92] It is not clear whether the repatriation was an act of mercy on the part of the Confederates or an emulation of the tactics Milroy had been inflicting upon recalcitrant secessionists for the past several months.

Robert H. Milroy

(Courtesy of Rensselaer Public Library)

Given May's course of events, it can safely be assumed that the Hoosier eagerly awaited the arrival of June. With a full division again under his command, he certainly expected that he would be able to assail, with good effect, the motley Confederate forces that populated the central Valley. Perhaps he even fantasized, with some justification, that a shake-up in the Army of the

[92]Walker, pp. 99-100.

Potomac after the debacle at Chancellorsville might bring him to the main theatre of the war and, along with a transfer, the chance for glory and advancement. The only scenario he definitely did not envision was that his military career would be virtually ended in the next two weeks.

4

COMING...OR GOING?

> *The Rebs are in considerable force at Strasburg and*
> *I have been skirmishing with them daily, and am looking for*
> *an attack hourly and will doubtless have it soon. Am ready*
> *for them and will give them a warm reception.*
>
> —Robert H. Milroy[1]

At about the same time during the first week of May that General Milroy was kissing his four children on the cheek and giving his wife an appropriately reserved Victorian farewell, events were unfolding 75 miles to the southeast that would precipitate a drastic redirection of the trajectory of his military career. On May 1, Major General Joseph "Fighting Joe" Hooker led the Army of the Potomac on a two-pronged assault against Robert E. Lee's defensive line behind the Rappahannock and Rapidan Rivers. On Hooker's left, his First and Sixth Corps crossed the river at Fredericksburg in a daring predawn amphibious landing while the Second, Fifth, Eleventh and Twelfth Corps stormed over the Rappahannock and Rapidan fords to take a position in the Wilderness. From those gloomy thickets Fighting Joe began to squeeze the left flank of the Army of Northern Virginia in a blue vise.

---

[1]Milroy letter, 6/4/1863.

Seriously outnumbered and assailed on both flanks, Lee responded like a heroic swordsman in a swashbuckler, first parrying at Fredericksburg and then thrusting in the Wilderness.[2] On May 2, Stonewall Jackson led his Second Corps on a circuitous march to a position on the right flank of the Union Eleventh Corps and then crushed Major General Oliver O. Howard's Dutchmen in a surprise attack. On May 3, Lee pounded the Federals into a defensive shell in the Wilderness, then shifted his forces and nearly obliterated the Union Sixth Corps at Salem Church. With his right secured, the Southern leader finished the job by shoving Hooker back to the point from where he had embarked four days earlier. Chancellorsville was arguably Lee's masterpiece.

There were two outcomes from the battle of Chancellorsville that would directly impact Milroy and his division at Winchester. Most significantly, Lee became convinced that if he and his men could defeat a double envelopment by twice their number, that they could beat the Federals anytime and anywhere. Almost immediately after it became clear that the Yankees were content to cower behind the Rappahannock River, Lee began to actively lobby Confederate President Jefferson Davis for permission to invade the North.

The idea of moving the war into the bountiful farm country of Pennsylvania came to Lee during the winter as he struggled to wring from war-blighted Virginia enough food for his hungry and ill-clad troops and adequate forage for his army's nearly starving horses. In furtherance of the concept of forcing the Yankees to subsist his army for the summer, Lee even went so far as to request his chief mapmaker, Jedediah Hotchkiss, to draw maps which covered the lower Shenandoah and Cumberland Valleys all the way to Harrisburg, Pennsylvania. Then, after Chancellorsville, Lee became so confident of his army, and so scornful of the

---

[2]At the time of the battle, two divisions of Lieutenant General James Longstreet's First Corps were with him in southeastern Virginia.

Army of the Potomac, that he came to believe that he could probably gain a decisive victory in Federal territory that would end the war.[3]

The second event that would be relevant to the Federals in Winchester was the accidental wounding of Stonewall Jackson on the night of May 2 as he was inspecting the Yankee dispositions in the darkness of the Wilderness. Spooked by suspicious sounds, Jackson's own edgy riflemen unleashed a volley that hit their commander at three different places, most seriously in the left arm. Several days later the arm was amputated and several more after that the revered Stonewall was dead.[4]

In the heat of battle, Lee turned command of his Second Corps over to cavalry chieftain J.E.B. Stuart, who led his men in the gritty assaults on May 3 that facilitated the movement of reinforcements against the Union Sixth Corps at Salem Church. After the battle was over, Lee decided that Stuart was too important an asset to waste on infantry. As the Southern commander considered his options for a replacement, he began to focus on Major General Richard Stoddert Ewell, one of Jackson's division commanders. Despite the fact that Ewell missed Chancellorsville because he had not fully recovered from

Richard S. Ewell

(Frank Leslie's Illustrations)

---

[3]Coddington, pp. 5-8.

[4]Furgurson, *Chancellorsville 1863...*, pp. 202-203, 325-329.

the amputation of a leg after Second Manassas, on May 23, 1863, Ewell was promoted to lieutenant general. Two days later Lee gave him command of Stonewall's Second Corps.[5]

The backgrounds of Robert H. Milroy and Richard S. Ewell could hardly have been more dissimilar. Ewell was born into the fringes of American nobility. His father, Thomas Ewell, a noted and published physician, grew wealthy through his medical practice but dissipated much of that wealth through alcohol. Elizabeth Stoddert, Ewell's mother, was the daughter of Benjamin Stoddert, who had been a major of cavalry in the Continental army, fought and was wounded at Brandywine, became wealthy as a tobacco exporter, and served as his country's first Secretary of the Navy.[6]

Born on February 18, 1817, Ewell's early life was more difficult than it should have been thanks to his father's alcoholism and bouts of depression. The family was land rich but cash poor, a situation that was exacerbated by the death of Ewell's father in 1820. Before Richard turned five, the family moved to one of their holdings, a 1,300-acre farm in northern Virginia which they named Stoney Lonesome due to the poor quality of the soil. During Richard's formative years, life was such a struggle that his older siblings were virtually driven off the homestead as soon as they were economically viable so as to lessen the financial burden on their widowed mother.

At the commencement of his teen years, Ewell began to assume some of the responsibilities of the man of the house. It is probably during these hard times that Ewell developed most of his significant personality traits: courage, a honed and substantial intelligence, a violent temper, a taste for alcohol, and a strong character inculcated by an even stronger mother. He also

---

[5]Pfanz, *Richard S. Ewell*, p. 275. Hereafter all cites to Pfanz's biography of Ewell will be cited simply as Pfanz.

[6]Ibid., pp. 4-8.

developed eccentricities such as a lisp that would mark him for the rest of his life as someone who was just a trifle odd.[7]

When it became clear in 1836 that the family could not afford a proper, formal education for the young man, his mother used her considerable connections to send Ewell and his eccentricities to West Point for a free one. Ewell was not quite as keen a student at West Point as his older brother Benjamin had been. Although he couldn't match his brother's position of eighth in his class, Richard's time at West Point was productive and set a positive course for his future. He showed an aptitude for the military and finished thirteenth out of a class of 42 that included Joseph Hooker, John Sedgwick, Henry Halleck, and his best friend, William T. Sherman. Although Ewell's grades were insufficient to obtain a coveted assignment as an army engineer, he had enough status to have his pick among the other branches, and he finally chose the dragoons.[8]

Following his cavalry training at Carlisle barracks in Pennsylvania, the prematurely balding novice lieutenant was assigned to duty with the 1st United States Dragoons in the Cherokee country of the Oklahoma Territory. Several years filled with hot, dusty, and monotonous garrison duty followed his arrival at Fort Wayne. News of the outbreak of war with Mexico was probably met by rejoicing among the professional officers of the 1st Dragoons and undoubtedly their departure in November of 1846 for the Mexican border was heartily welcomed.[9]

Upon arrival, Ewell's dragoons were assigned to Zachary Taylor's command. Whether or not Ewell and Milroy ever crossed paths in Mexico went unrecorded, but Lieutenant Ewell, after weathering a bout of yellow fever, certainly obtained as much combat experience during the Mexican War as did the volunteer from Indiana. Although not involved at Cerro Gordo, the first

---

[7]Pfanz, pp. 6-11.
[8]Ibid., pp. 11-26.
[9]Ibid., pp. 28-49.

battle fought after his regiment's arrival, Ewell experienced the bitter repercussions of battle as he shared the last moments in the life of his mortally wounded older brother Thomas.[10]

Perhaps that experience cooled the younger Ewell's ardor for combat but it did not dampen his courage. After several weeks spent guarding wagon trains, Ewell got his first whiff of gun smoke on August 18, 1847, in a skirmish that erupted during a mounted reconnaissance mission. Not long after that violent inauguration, Ewell, along with five other officers and a dozen rankers, followed their commander in a charge into an enemy emplacement at Churubusco. When his leader was cut down, command devolved to Ewell, who performed his duties under fire so impressively that he received a brevet promotion to captain for "gallant and meritorious service." After participating in the capture of Mexico City, the young Virginian closed out the war suffering nothing more serious than a severe case of neuralgia.[11]

In October of 1850, after a long and well-deserved leave, Ewell reported for duty in the freshly acquired territory of New Mexico. During the next nine years of frontier garrison duty, Ewell employed his combat experience with good effect against the hostile Indians in the territory, including a significant victory in 1857 at Gila River. Two years after that, the leather-tough captain held his own in several firefights with Cochise, the infamous leader of the Chiricahua Apaches.[12]

Like so many other West Point graduates, when the South seceded, Ewell had to make a choice between the country for which he had fought for 15 years and his home state. Ewell chose Virginia and resigned from the United States Army on April 24, 1861. Curiously, despite his experience and a reputation as an aggressive and skilled fighter, Ewell only received an initial rank of colonel and a position as the commandant of a cavalry camp of

[10]Pfanz, p. 52.
[11]Ibid., pp. 54-59.
[12]Ibid., pp. 66-109.

instruction north of Richmond. That oversight did not continue for long. Following a flesh wound in the neck received in one of the earliest skirmishes of the war, on June 17, 1861, Ewell was awarded a promotion to brigadier general as well as command of a small brigade that consisted of two Alabama and one Louisiana infantry regiments.[13]

Old Bald Head, as his men quickly and affectionately tagged him, was denied a chance to justify his new promotion in the war's first major battle, First Manassas, due to his brigade's position on the flank opposite from where most of the fighting occurred. The chance to shine was not long in coming, however. Promoted to major general in January 1862, Ewell was quickly given command of a division and assigned to a location in northern Virginia between Stonewall Jackson's army in the Shenandoah Valley and Johnston's army in front of McClellan. At first, Ewell and his men were mostly spectators to the beginning of the Valley Campaign that made Jackson a legend, because Richmond kept them hanging on the eastern side of the Blue Ridge so as to be able to lend support to either flank. When Jackson plunged into the Allegheny Mountains after Frémont though, Ewell was summoned into the Valley to guard Jackson's back.[14]

Although only about 20 miles apart at the end of April while the tussle at McDowell was raging, Ewell left Milroy behind when he followed Jackson north toward Winchester. Jackson, the mentor, gave Ewell, the protégé, a lesson in command when they reached that town. The two of them, Jackson from the southwest along the Valley Turnpike and Ewell from the southeast down the Front Royal Road, smashed Banks' army and chased the Bluecoats out of town in a rout. Ewell's orders limited his division to mostly watching Jackson's men storm Bowers Hill and the lower portion of Apple Pie Ridge on the western side of Winchester, but

[13]Pfanz, pp. 121-129.
[14]Tanner, pp. 204-211.

Ewell's independent actions in the early morning fog limited Banks' options and contributed to the eventual Federal defeat.[15]

After their triumph, Ewell's division and the Stonewall Brigade pursued the Yankees all the way to the outskirts of Harpers Ferry. Then, at the end of May, it was learned that the Federals were attempting to surround Jackson's little army from three sides. Ewell and his men turned and practically sprinted up the Valley. The race ended when, after finally catching up with their comrades, Ewell's command drew the assignment of trying to contain Frémont in the mountains before he could seal the Valley Turnpike and trap the Rebels. Thanks to Frémont's timidity, and Ewell's keen eye for good ground, the Yankees were bluffed out of closing Jackson's escape route. Instead of attacking Ewell's much smaller force, the Federals cringed in a mountain pass rather than challenge Ewell's men who were brazenly arrayed on an imposing ridge. With its right flank secured, Jackson's army temporarily slipped out of the blue noose.[16]

The Confederate situation became critical on June 8, 1862. As Jackson's army lay at the base of the Massanutten Mountain, Banks' army pressed up the Valley from Winchester, Frémont lurked to the west threatening the Southern rear, and Major General James Shield's army pushed southward along Massanutten's eastern side in hopes of slicing the Rebels off from access to the gaps in the Blue Ridge. Old Bald Head again drew the assignment to block Frémont, and along with him, Milroy. The Pathfinder opened the battle with a tentative thrust at the Confederate right by one of Brigadier General Louis Blenker's German brigades. The sortie accomplished little more than creating a number of widows and orphans up North. Later in the day, Generals Schenck and Milroy led a somewhat more aggressive assault against the opposite Rebel flank, which Ewell was able to

---

[15]Tanner, pp. 273-281.
[16]Ibid., pp. 339-357.

blunt thanks to the terrain and the timely deployment of a portion of his Louisiana Brigade.[17]

With Frémont beaten into submission and the sounds of battle swelling in the east, on June 9, Ewell rushed his division to Jackson's aid. It is possible that the Virginian's timely arrival at a critical moment during the battle of Port Republic saved his mentor's army and career. Seeing that the Confederate right flank was on the verge of collapse, Ewell launched the leading part of his command in a counterattack that diverted enough Union attention to allow Jackson's army to stabilize. Ewell then dispatched the Louisiana Brigade to take a Federal battery on a commanding promontory that overlooked the battlefield. After the "Tigers" swamped the blue-coated gunners, Ewell led reinforcements in support. Despite being close enough to an exploding shell to lose his horse, the Virginian and his men held the position. Without the benefit of that battery the Federals were forced to withdraw and Jackson's army escaped through the Blue Ridge.[18]

For a short time the bone-weary Johnnies in Jackson's foot cavalry were permitted to rest in the afternoon shadows of the Blue Ridge. Within a few days though, Jackson and Ewell were summoned east after McClellan began to make significant progress up the Peninsula toward Richmond. The normally aggressive Jackson was uncharacteristically slow in getting his forces into position to assist Robert E. Lee's offensive against the Army of the Potomac, perhaps as a result of near overwhelming fatigue accumulated in the Valley. The lack of involvement of Jackson's men in the Seven Days' Campaign changed radically at the battle of Gaines' Mill on June 27, 1862.

At first, while James Longstreet's troops were making repeated, bloody and fruitless assaults against the Union line drawn up behind a swamp, Jackson's Valley Army labored to reach the

---

[17]Tanner, pp. 386-389.
[18]Ibid., pp. 403-406.

fighting. As they neared the battlefield, Ewell, whose division led the column, was approached by one of Lee's aides, who pleaded for help. Rather than wait for his entire command, Ewell shoved his column-leading Louisiana Tigers into the roiling caldron of fire and lead. The Cajuns were beaten back out of the swamp in short order with heavy losses.

Next in line was Colonel Isaac Trimble's brigade, which Ewell pressed into the fight under a major because Trimble was allegedly too drunk to fight. The Butternuts were slammed by a storm of whizzing Minié balls fired by Yankees who were invisible except for muzzle flashes and gun smoke. The fire was too hot to penetrate but the Johnnies were too proud to retreat, so they stood there and slugged it out in a stand-up gun battle.[19]

While he waited for Jackson and the balance of the army to arrive, Ewell rode along his line until his horse was shot out from under him. When finally in place, the rest of Jackson's force began to pour in a steady stream of blistering fire. The victory laurels went to the Butternuts in the center and on the opposite side of the line however, when they crashed through the Yankee defenses with a screaming bayonet charge. Nightfall saved the Federals and allowed them to withdraw and regroup.[20]

With the collapse of the Union line at Gaines' Mill, Jackson's army, due mostly to the luck of positioning, became mostly spectators to the balance of the Seven Days' Campaign. When it became clear that McClellan was neutered and had hunkered down at Harrison's Landing, Confederate attention shifted to Major General John Pope and his Army of Virginia that was lurking in the northern quarter of the Old Dominion State. Within weeks Jackson, and with him Ewell, were marching toward the northwest to meet their next challenge.

---

[19]Sears, *To the Gates...*, pp. 227-230.
[20]Ibid., pp. 230-242.

After sparring with Pope in the triangle between the Rapidan and Rappahannock Rivers, Jackson led his half of the Confederate army in a daring sortie around the unprotected Union right flank and into the Federal rear. Pope's efforts to trap and beat Jackson in detail before Lee could arrive with the balance of the Southern army led to the Second Battle of Manassas and another confrontation between Milroy's Independent Brigade and Ewell's boys.

On August 28, Pope's Federals were struggling to locate Jackson's army, which seemed to have vanished. Eventually, the two armies collided in what has become known as the battle of Groveton. The conflict was relatively minor compared to what was coming, but would prove to be monumental for Richard S. Ewell and his future. While kneeling to peer under a pine tree in preparation for launching an assault against the Union right flank, a Minié ball sliced under the branches and struck Ewell on his left knee. The lead ounce did to the Virginian what often occurred to other victims—the bone was splintered, necessitating the removal of the leg a few hours after Ewell was carried from the field in agony.[21]

Ewell's division remained, and the next day it held the right center of the Confederate line behind the railroad embankment. Isaac Trimble's brigade of Ewell's division, composed of the 15th Alabama, 12th and 21st North Carolina, 21st Georgia, and the 1st North Carolina Battalion, found its right flank resting on the edge of "the dump." It was almost certainly Trimble's brigade that flailed Milroy's ill-fated penetration of the Confederate line, drove the Hoosier's Bluecoats back in disarray and pummeled them throughout the afternoon. To complete their domination of Milroy's brigade, Ewell's division participated in the counter-attack that bulldozed the Federal left, including Milroy's boys,

---

[21]Hennessy, p. 182.

deep into the Union rear.[22] Once their beloved Old Bald Head was able to recover from his wound, his division, and a host of their comrades, would resume the effort to collect the fabled $1,000 bounty on the head of Robert H. Milroy.

That recovery took longer than normal due to a couple of nasty falls that reopened the wound, but on June 1, 1863, four days after marrying Lizinka Brown, one of ante-bellum America's richest women, Ewell took formal command of the Confederate Second Corps.[23] The next day Ewell received a briefing on Lee's invasion plans and marching orders for his corps that numbered somewhat in excess of 20,000 hardhanded veterans.[24] Included in the plan were instructions to evacuate Fredericksburg and to proceed surreptitiously to Culpeper Court House, so as not to alert Hooker's lookouts along the banks of the Rappahannock River.

Major General Robert E. Rodes pulled his division of Ewell's corps out of the trenches on June 4, and late that night Major General Jubal A. Early's division followed. "Sure enough, at 10 o'clock tonight we cooked up three days rations, and at 12 o'clock we took up what little effects we had and started on a forced march...we marched all night."[25] Close behind trailed the

---

[22]Hennessy, pp. 262-269.

[23]Pfanz, *Richard S. Ewell...*, p. 279. The marriage was the first for Ewell, who everyone had believed was a confirmed bachelor, thus eliminating one of his perceived peculiarities.

[24]Ibid., p. 280. Neither Lee nor Ewell provided an exact count of the Second Corps at the start of the campaign. Professor Coddington placed the total number in Lee's army at about 75,000 of all arms. Allowing for artillery and cavalry would leave Ewell's corps, one of three, with at least 20,000 rifles. This number is supported by a head-count performed by Major General Robert Rodes, who commanded one of Ewell's three divisions, and who placed the size of his command on June 3, 1863 at 9,098. Coddington, p. 249; O.R. 1-27-2-564, Rodes. Further, Lee reported his Second Corps' killed and wounded during Gettysburg at 3,977 and its total casualties at 5,937, both of which are consistent with an aggregate force going into the battle in excess of 20,000. O.R. 1-27-2-332, 242.

[25]Reed, p. 34. Private Thomas Benton Reed was a member of the 9th Louisiana Infantry in Early's division.

last of Ewell's divisions, under the command of another of Milroy's former adversaries, Major General Edward Allegheny Johnson.[26] The day's tramp, which carried the dusty Butternuts through Spotsylvania Court House, was finally halted for the day when a Federal barrage across the Rappahannock caused Lee to halt the procession in case it was preparatory to another Yankee incursion.[27] When Lee was satisfied on June 6, that the Union effort was nothing more than a reconnaissance by artillery, Ewell's men resumed their march on the Plank Road that ran from Chancellorsville toward the Orange Court House.[28]

At dawn on June 7, the Johnnies hoisted their packs, shouldered rifles, and strode toward the Raccoon Ford across the Rapidan River. Along the way, Early's men spotted Old Bald Head. "The troops soon recognized Gen. Ewell & began to cheer him as had been their habit with Gen. Jackson, thus transferring to him the ardor they felt for their old commander. He took off his cap & rode rapidly along the line."[29] The next day's march to the vicinity of Culpeper Court House brought more of the same to the Butternuts—plenty of dust to eat while trying to march without dwelling on aching shoulders and raw and oozing blisters.[30]

Although he was totally oblivious to the movement of much of Lee's army, Fighting Joe Hooker fretted about what might be going on beyond the forest on the opposite side of the Rappahannock. While the Rebels plodded or limped along the road, Hooker decided that it could be suicidal to concede the entire initiative to Robert E. Lee. He, therefore, ordered the Yankee cavalry commander Major General Alfred Pleasonton to take his troopers and 3,000 of the best-marching Yankee riflemen in the army, cross the

[26]Coddington, p. 51.
[27]Ibid., p. 51; Reed, p. 34.
[28]Reed, p. 34.
[29]Jed. Hotchkiss as quoted in Pfanz, *Richard S. Ewell...*, p. 280.
[30]Reed, pp. 34-35; O.R. 1-27-2-439, Ewell.

river near Rappahannock Station, and smash whatever Confederate concentration they encountered.[31]   As Ewell's men accumulated around Culpeper, Pleasonton gathered his forces and then, in the predawn twilight of June 9, his troopers splashed across the river at two points and galloped south toward Brandy Station.   In a nearly day-long battle, the Federal horsemen came close enough to beating J.E.B. Stuart at his own game that Rodes' and Early's divisions were both pulled back toward the sound of fighting in case they were needed.[32]

Fortunately for Lee's invasion plans, Ewell's infantry was not required to rescue Stuart's cavalry, leaving the presence of the foot soldiers undetected. Despite what could have been a signal that Hooker had learned of his movements, the next day Lee, in a gutsy move, ordered Ewell to resume the march of his corps. The Second Corps, which traveled in two columns, passed by Gaines' Cross Roads and Flint Hill on their way to the banks of the Hazel River, where the command was permitted to bivouac for the night.[33]   June 11 offered a short but strenuous march through Sperryville and partway up the Blue Ridge.[34]

Starting at dawn on the morning of June 12, and ending late that night, Ewell's 61 infantry regiments and 20 batteries of artillery passed through Chester's Gap, descended the western flank of the Blue Ridge, and sloshed across the Shenandoah River at Front Royal.[35]   Ewell accompanied the procession in a carriage in order to spare his slowly healing stump the unnecessary strain of riding horseback.   Although it may have looked like the Southern leader was on a Sunday promenade, Ewell was actually employing his carriage as a mobile command post.   Near Front Royal, General Rodes was invited to clamber aboard, and as the

[31]Coddington, p. 54.
[32]Reed, p. 35; Pfanz, *Richard S. Ewell...*, p. 281.
[33]Ibid., p. 35; O.R. 1-27-2-440, Ewell.
[34]O.R. 1-27-2-459, Early; Reed, p. 35.
[35]Coddington, pp. 590-592; O.R. 1-27-2-440, 459, 546, Ewell, Early, Rodes.

two jostled along, Ewell explained to the commander of his lead division where Rodes and his men were expected to go and what they were expected to accomplish.[36] While the two Confederate generals discussed his fate, Robert Milroy remained unaware that he would very shortly be called upon to put some substance behind the boasts that he had been making for the last several days.

Long before Ewell's Second Corps waded across the Shenandoah River, Major General Henry W. "Old Brains" Halleck, general in chief of the Union armies, concluded that Winchester was a precarious place to maintain a garrison. The town was strategically important but virtually impossible to defend, which explains why it eventually became the scene of three major battles, numerous skirmishes, and changed hands over 70 times. Although shielded on the west by a long series of low hills known locally as Apple Pie Ridge, the other three sides of the town lay exposed to a flat plain heading off into the surrounding country-side. The town was vulnerable to rapid approach and easy investment because of its location at the convergence of at least seven major roads, two of which, the Valley Turnpike and the Front Royal Turnpike, were the major means of travel to and from the upper Shenandoah Valley. Without even a significant river to act as a bastion, Winchester was an outpost that demanded an emotionally and intellectually secure commanding officer with a clear understanding of the possible—one who could judge when to hold or when to fold. It was not the place for a commander whose personality contained a witch's brew of enormous self-confidence,

---

[36]Reed, p. 35; Pfanz, *Richard S. Ewell...*, p. 282.

reckless physical courage, abolitionist fervor, and a dash of paranoia.

Almost from the inception of its deployment, Old Brains began to fret about the garrison in Winchester, and perhaps about Milroy as well. Conveying those fears to the wealthy and politically well-connected Major General Robert C. Schenck who, from Baltimore, was the commander of the Eighth Corps, and the military district in which Winchester was located, was a somewhat delicate task. Perhaps because he was an accomplished bureaucratic warrior who understood the value of treading softly with political generals, and of never making a commitment until it was necessary, Halleck sent the following telegrams to Schenck which were couched as advice rather than explicit orders.

"January 5, 1863 - No attempt should be made to hold Winchester against a large force of the enemy, but use it simply as an outpost, as advised in our conversation a day or two ago. Isolated posts and columns are too liable to be cut off."

"April 30, 1863 - If you want more troops in the west, and at Harper's Ferry, why do you leave so large a force at Winchester? As I have often repeated to you verbally and in writing, that is no place to fight a battle. It is merely an outpost, which should not be exposed to an attack in force."[37]

Rather than jumping to satisfy the wishes of the second most powerful man in the chain of command, Schenck balked at the advice. Charged with protecting the vital B & O Railroad, Schenck believed that the best way to carry out his assignment was to keep a strong force in Winchester—a conclusion that was based primarily on geography. The portion of the B & O that ran through the lower Shenandoah Valley on the south side of the Potomac formed a rough semicircle with the town of Winchester at the open end. Schenck reasoned that a garrison at Winchester could act more or less like a lid and could provide much stronger

---

[37]O.R. 1-27-2-158, 159.

Henry W. Halleck   Robert C. Schenck
(Author's Collection)   (Author's Collection)

protection against marauding Rebels than could the same number
of troops spread out along the circumference. Emboldened by his
status, and perhaps as leery of West Pointer Halleck as was fellow
volunteer Milroy, Schenck decided to follow his own instincts until
unambiguously ordered to do otherwise.[38]

By early May, Halleck became so concerned about the
exposed division in Winchester that he actually ordered Schenck
to pull Milroy back. "May 8 - Major General Schenck, You will
maintain only a small force at Winchester, as an outpost, and
employ the remainder of Milroy's troops for the protection of the
railroad and operations against the enemy in Western Virginia."[39]
Instead of obeying, Schenck dithered, apparently taking the order
as only more of the same fatherly advice that could be ignored in
favor of his own plans. Rather than demanding compliance,

---

[38]O.R. 1-27-2-187.
[39]Ibid., 1-27-2-159.

Halleck deferred enforcement of his order, perhaps because he was satisfied that he was finally covered no matter what the eventual fate of Milroy's division might be.[40]

During the first 12 days of June, the Federal chain of command may have been oblivious to the details of Lee's movement toward the Shenandoah Valley but all, and especially Milroy, shared a pervasive sense of anxiety about what was occurring below the Rappahannock. The Hoosier's concern was based upon more than just intuition. Throughout the month of May, Milroy had received a number of disturbing intelligence reports from the chief of his special scouts, Colonel J. Warren Keifer.[41] Keifer claimed that his scouts, posing as Rebels, had obtained a steady stream of rumors from residents of the central Valley that Lee was headed north. "So uniform were their reports as to the proposed attacks that I gave credence to them, and advised Milroy that unless he was soon to be largely reinforced it would be well to retire from his exposed position. He refused to believe that any thing more than a cavalry raid into the Valley or against him would be made, and he felt strong enough to defeat it. He argued that Lee would not dare to detach any part of his infantry force from the front of the Army of the Potomac."[42]

Keifer's warnings became more urgent as May turned into June. "...I learned as early as the 1st of June, through correspondence secretly brought within our lines from an officer of Lee's army to which I gained access, that Lee contemplated a grand movement North, and that his army would reach Winchester on

---

[40]Coddington, p. 87. If Halleck had wanted to enforce his orders to get Milroy out of Winchester, he could, at any time, have sent a telegram like the one he eventually sent to Schenck on June 14, 1863. "If you have not executed my orders to concentrate your forces at Harper's Ferry, you will do so immediately.... Unless there is a more prompt obedience of orders, there must be a change in the commanders. See to this immediately." O.R. 1-27-2-181.

[41]Keifer's scouts were distinguishable from regular cavalry scouts because they generally patrolled enemy territory dressed as Confederates. Keifer, vol. 2, p. 4.

[42]Ibid.

June 10, 1863. The Secessionists of Winchester generally believed we would be attacked on that day. I gave this information to Milroy, but he still persisted in believing the whole story was gotten up to cause him to disgracefully abandon the Valley."[43]

Whether or not Milroy actually received Keifer's alleged intelligence and advice, the Hoosier began to act like a commander who expected trouble of some sort.[44] On June 2, the 18th Connecticut was ordered to sleep with loaded muskets in anticipation of an attack although "...the men were incredulous as to the near approach of the enemy." The next afternoon a false alarm generated four or five cavalry patrols into the countryside as well as a large reconnaissance-in-force that sent approximately 170 troopers and 500 riflemen from the same 18th Connecticut pounding up the Pike to Newtown.[45]

The loquacious Mrs. Lee gleefully recorded in her diary on June 5 that "The Yankees are in a panic; the horses are kept to the guns, no officers are permitted to come to town except on urgent

---

[43]Keifer, vol. 2, p. 4. Keifer neglected to provide the name of his informant, any details concerning how he came to make the contact, or why the Confederate officer would have betrayed his cause. Apparently aware that his claims included in a postwar memoir might generate skepticism, Keifer added a footnote that read, in part, "In letters, dated in May, 1863 to Col. Wm. S. Furay (then a correspondent...of the Cincinnati Gazette...), I detailed the general plan of Lee's advance northward, and gave the date when the movement would commence."

[44]There are no definitive reasons to question Keifer's veracity except, perhaps, that he was a lawyer, served four terms in Congress, and showed a penchant for dramatic after-action reports. Keifer, vol. 2, p. 257. On the other hand, Milroy didn't mention the information in his letters home to his wife or directly in any discovered dispatches to headquarters. He may have made one oblique reference in a telegraph sent on June 8, where he wrote that he had information that Lee had mounted a division of infantry to supplement J.E.B. Stuart's cavalry and that more than 24,000 Rebels were probably headed his way for "...a mighty raid...." O.R. 1-27-3-36.

[45]Walker, pp. 100-101. On June 3, Milroy received a dispatch from Schenck that read, "The general commanding directs you to act with caution, keep him advised, and fall back, when forced, in the direction of Harper's Ferry or Martinsburg, as your better judgment may dictate." O.R. 1-27-3-4.

business; the sutlers are ready to go at any moment...."[46] The next day, perhaps in an attempt to alleviate some of that anxiety, elements of the 87th Pennsylvania and the 18th Connecticut were sent on a tramp to Front Royal which uncovered nothing of significance.[47] That night the men of the 12th West Virginia were ordered to sleep on their arms. Their discomfort served no purpose other than denying the Mountaineers the rest that would have made reinforcing the pickets on the Strasburg Road the night of June 7 more bearable.[48] Then, on June 9, four companies of the 12th West Virginia, under the command of the regiment's colonel, were sent out in the dark to support a section of artillery that was posted each night in anticipation of an attack.[49]

The division's Buckeyes did not escape repercussions from Milroy's angst. In a letter posted on the same day that the Mountaineers were dispatched to support some of their gunners, Private Jefferson O. McMillen of the 122nd Ohio advised the folks at home, "We have been doubling the picket nearly every night for a week or two expecting to be attacked by a heavy force but we have never seen any of them yet."[50] That sentiment was echoed by the historian for the 116th Ohio, who wrote, "For two or three days prior to the 12th of June, the whole army was on the qui vive. We were in line of battle ready for orders, or on the move from one point to another, day and night."[51]

Despite having fortifications that were already imposing, on June 11 many of the Bluecoats were assigned to fatigue duty "...chopping down trees. We chopped every tree and bush to have them out of the way so the enemy cannot come in on us without us seeing them. It looks like great destruction here where timber

---

[46]Lee diary, 6/5/1863.
[47]Walker, p. 102.
[48]Hewitt, p. 39.
[49]Ibid., pp. 39-40.
[50]McMillen letter, 6/9/1863.
[51]Wildes, p. 54.

is so scarce but we do not stop for anything where it is in our road."[52] Milroy also sent 114 wagons loaded with quarter-master's stores back to safety at Harpers Ferry while his men toiled on the defensive perimeter.[53] Finally, on the morning of June 12, the Union sick were sent to the rear.[54]

It is not surprising that with all the tension in Winchester, that the debate over whether the garrison should stay or leave was revived. On June 8, Halleck again raised the issue with Schenck. "The indications are that the enemy is massing about 12,000 cavalry and artillery in Culpeper County for a raid. Deserters say the men have been given to understand that it is to be a long and desperate one. I can only repeat the recommendation, so often made to you, to mass your troops more in convenient places for rapid and concerted operations, holding railroad bridges only with small detachments, in block-houses, and exposing no large force in advanced positions, where they are liable to be cut off. We probably shall not know the direction or intention of this raid till it is actually in motion. Hence the necessity of keeping your forces well in hand for a sudden movement."[55]

The following morning, after a telegraphic consultation with his chief of staff, Lieutenant Colonel Donn Piatt, Schenck responded to Halleck's carping with a telegraph seemingly intended to get Old Brains off his back by requesting that the latter take direct responsibility for the advice that he was dispensing. "Does your knowledge of rebel movements enable you to suggest the better points on the railroad to concentrate? I have at Point of Rocks and Frederick 3,400 men; at Harper's Ferry, 6,300; at Winchester, 6,900; at Martinsburg, 3,000; at Romney, 2,300; at

---

[52]Hartley letter, 6/12/1863.

[53]Coddington, p. 89.

[54]Ibid., p. 89; Hartley letter, 6/12/1863.

[55]O.R. 1-27-2-159. Halleck's use of the word "recommendation" in this dispatch seems to validate Schenck's decision to disregard his superior's May 8 telegraph as merely additional advice.

New Creek 2,400. Troops at Winchester can fall back now to Harper's Ferry, in face of enemy, [or] to Martinsburg. Force at Romney can fall back to Green Spring."[56]

To complicate the situation, Schenck also sent Piatt to personally inspect the situation in Winchester and to report his findings. Piatt did so on June 11. "Just in from inspection of fortifications and troops. All looks fine. Can whip anything the rebels can fetch here."[57]   That same day, Brigadier General Daniel Tyler, commander of the brigade at Martinsburg, tossed in his two cents, "Left Winchester at 2 p.m. of this p.m. Milroy deserves credit for his fortifications; it will take all of Lee's cavalry and light artillery to whip him out."[58]   Finally, Milroy weighed in with, "I have the place well fortified, and am well prepared to hold it, as General Tyler and Colonel Piatt will inform you, and I can and would hold it, if permitted to do so, against any force the rebels can afford to bring against me, and I exceedingly regret the prospect of having to give it up, and it will be cruel to abandon the loyal people that are in this county to the rebel fiends again."[59]

Perhaps without knowledge of the traffic between his subordinates, Halleck tried to put the matter to rest with a telegram that seems to have been intended as a direct order to Schenck but which was drafted, perhaps slyly, in terms that were still subject to being interpreted as more fatherly advice. "Harper's Ferry is the important place. Winchester is of no importance other than as a lookout. The Winchester troops, excepting enough to serve as an outpost, should be withdrawn to Harper's Ferry. The troops at Martinsburg should be ready to fall back to Harper's Ferry. No

---

[56]O.R. 1-27-2-159-160.
[57]Ibid., 1-27-2-161.
[58]Ibid., 1-27-2-161.
[59]Ibid., 1-27-2-161.

large amount of supplies should be left in any exposed position."[60]

Schenck, faced with a dilemma over what Halleck meant by the word "should," (i.e., ought or shall), seems to have concluded that he retained discretion but that he had better include some eyewash in the next dispatch to Piatt in case his commander's patience was nearing exhaustion. Accordingly, Schenck's chief of staff was directed to "...take steps for preparing to carry out carefully and judiciously these instructions [Halleck's order of June 11] of the General-in-chief. Be ready but wait for further orders."[61] Piatt reacted to the missive like a soldier rather than a bureaucrat. Milroy was supplied with a copy of Halleck's telegraph with instructions, added by Piatt, to prevent the Hoosier from playing the same game as his superiors, "It must be considered an order, and obeyed accordingly. Take immediate steps. You understand this."[62]

Predictably, Milroy ignored the aide and resumed the debate directly with Schenck. "Have just received an order from Colonel Piatt to immediately take steps to move my command to Harper's Ferry, leaving only a sufficient force for a lookout. I have sufficient force to hold the place safely, but if any portion is withdrawn the balance will be captured in forty-eight hours. All should go or none. Please designate what portion of my forces must be left here for the enemy."[63]

Then, on the chance that his benefactor was seriously considering pulling the Second Division back to Harpers Ferry, Milroy also sent a separate letter to Schenck that was a combination plea and brief. "Having received some orders looking to the evacuation of this place and falling back upon Harper's Ferry, I hope you will pardon me for making a few suggestions.... First.

---

[60]O.R. 1-27-2-162-163.

[61]Ibid., 1-27-2-124.

[62]Ibid., 1-27-2-125.

[63]Ibid., 1-27-2-162.

This place is the key to the Baltimore and Ohio Railroad. Let this point be abandoned, and our forces withdrawn to Harper's Ferry, and no force that it would be practicable for our Government to place at Harper's Ferry, and at points along the...Railroad west of that place, would or could secure it against raids from the enemy occupying this place [Winchester] as a base.... Secondly. The fortifications on the hill near this place are now so perfect, and all approaches to them so well protected by outworks, that I can hold them against five times our number [i.e., 35,000 to 45,000 Rebels]. Thirdly. The Union men and women of this and adjoining counties have been so often disappointed and abandoned to the demons of treason, that they had become very timid and doubtful, but our six months' occupation here has begun to give them confidence in, and many of them have come out and taken a decided stand for, the Union, and in both town and country the Union sentiment has recently been rapidly improving.... Fourthly. There is a large amount of wheat in this and the surrounding counties of the last two years' crops, still unthreshed, which the rebs would get, if we abandoned the country to them. I am, therefore, decidedly of [the] opinion that every dictate of interest, policy, humanity, patriotism, and bravery requires that we should not yield a foot of this country up to the traitors again."[64] Milroy obviously wanted to stay in command at Winchester very, very badly.

Whether because of a bond formed with Milroy during months of campaigning, because he had more faith in the judgment of a fellow volunteer, or because he wanted to keep his prickly subordinate as far from Baltimore as possible, Schenck succumbed to Milroy's persuasion and issued another order to the Hoosier that modified the preceding one.[65] "Lieutenant-Colonel Piatt has, I

---

[64]O.R. 1-27-2-177-178, Milroy.

[65]Milroy did not mention any particular relationship with Schenck in any of his letters, but given the fact that the Hoosier was never critical of Schenck, a marked contrast to the way he savaged other commanding officers in his letters, it may be

learn by copy of dispatch sent me, ...misunderstood me, and somewhat exceeded his instructions. You will make all the required preparations for withdrawing, but hold your position in the meantime. Be ready for movement, but wait for further orders. I doubt the propriety of calling in McReynolds' brigade at once. If you should fall back to Harper's Ferry, he will be in part on the way and covering your flank; but use your discretion as to any orders to him. Below I give you a copy of a telegram of the General-in-Chief. Nothing heard since. Give me constant information."[66]

With hindsight, it is hard to understand Schenck's continued resistance to the obvious wishes of his commanding officer, and easy to judge his insistence on maintaining the garrison in Winchester as at least imprudent. The real-time context in which the players were operating made the situation much more ambiguous, however. Schenck's plan to guard the railroad was sound, since the force at Winchester must have been far more effective at deterring raids than the same number of men strung out along the railroad would have been. Perhaps as significant to the commanders in the field, the administration placed a great deal of pressure on its generals to be aggressive, and sacked the beloved McClellan only months before because of his lack of that trait. Halleck, who Schenck undoubtedly believed would survive any outcome, had left himself enough wiggle room to shift the blame to Schenck in the event of either a disastrous defeat or an embarrassingly needless retreat.[67] Weighing all the confidence exuded by his officers in

---

inferred that the two shared mutual respect if not friendship. As for the logic of Milroy's argument, a cavalry force left in Winchester would certainly have been less vulnerable to capture than any of the numerous large patrols of cavalry and infantry which Milroy had repeatedly sent deep into contested territory throughout the winter and spring.

[66]O.R. 1-27-2-162.

[67]If Schenck believed that the president would side with Halleck regardless of the eventual outcome, he was probably correct. In July 1863, Lincoln supposedly confided the following to one of his personal secretaries, John Hay: "...Halleck

the field against the dreaded perception of timidity that would settle on him if he issued an order to prematurely or unnecessarily withdraw, Schenck made his best attempt to appear to comply while deferring a commitment at least until an actual enemy appeared on the horizon.

Unlike his superiors who were struggling to insulate themselves from the consequences of a bad decision, Milroy was spoiling for a fight and totally focused on the certainty that if he could manage to manipulate a stay in Winchester, he could finally demonstrate that he was superior to the despised West Pointers.[68] Holding an order which enabled that predisposition, Milroy boldly girded himself for whatever challenge the Confederates could offer his garrison of approximately 7,000 effectives out of a total of 9,000 men.

Milroy's command, designated as the Second Division, Eighth Corps, remained divided into three brigades. The First Brigade, under Brigadier General Washington L. Elliott, consisted of the 110th, 116th, 122nd, 123rd Ohio Infantry regiments, the 12th and 13th Pennsylvania Cavalry regiments, and Battery L of the 5th United States Artillery. Colonel William G. Ely's Second Brigade was comprised of the 87th Pennsylvania, 12th West

---

thinks Schenck never had a military idea & never will learn one. Thinks Schenck is somewhat to blame for the Winchester business. President says, however you may doubt or disagree from Halleck[,] he is very apt to be right in the end." By early 1864, Lincoln's opinion of Halleck had apparently changed dramatically. According to Hay, the president complained, "'[w]hen it was proposed to station Halleck here in general command, he insisted, to use his own language[,] on the appt. of a General-in-Chief who shd. be held responsible for results. We appointed him & all went well enough until after Pope's defeat [in August 1862] when he broke down—nerve and pluck all gone—and has ever since evaded all possible responsibility—little more since that than a first-rate clerk.'" Hay diary, 7/16/1863, 4/28/1864.

[68]This interpretation of Milroy's mind-set is based upon the general tone of his previous letters, the pugnacious stance taken in his early June dispatches, and the fact that he must have known that if he didn't want to fight, he could easily tip the scale in favor of withdrawal by sending an apprehensive-sounding telegram.

Virginia, 18th Connecticut, 5th Maryland, Company K of the 1st West Virginia Cavalry, Companies D and E of the 3rd West Virginia Cavalry, and Battery D of the 1st West Virginia Artillery. The 6th Maryland, 67th Pennsylvania, 1st New York Cavalry, and the Baltimore Artillery Battalion formed Colonel Andrew T. McReynolds' Third Brigade.[69]

It is somewhat difficult to compare the punch of the Hoosier's 10-infantry regiment division to the more common 12 to 15 regiment-sized divisions that populated the Army of the Potomac at that time. Milroy's regiments were relatively fresh and thus nearly fully manned with the desired complement of men. On the other hand, most of his riflemen had not yet been involved in serious combat. In partial compensation for fewer regiments and limited experience, the Hoosier's division boasted the attributes and the striking power of a small army, thanks to its three cavalry regiments and three artillery batteries.

Milroy's real source of confidence (or overconfidence) rested on his defensive works. Despite the fact that his assertion that he could hold Winchester "...against any force the Rebels can afford to bring against me..." was pure propaganda, he was legitimately bolstered by the strength of his position. Even though Winchester itself was vulnerable, the garrison was protected by heavy earthen fortifications and interlocking rifle pits that stretched along the northwestern side of the town atop the commanding heights of Apple Pie Ridge. The northern end of the emplacements, about a mile and a half to two miles out of town, was anchored by a closed dirt fort appropriately named the Star Fort due to its numerous pointed bastions. Three-quarters of a mile southeast of the Star Fort loomed the largest Federal emplacement, known as the Main or Flag Fort. A line of rifle pits ran from there along the ridge to Bowers Hill, located about a half mile southwest of town, completing the main defensive line. In

---

[69]O.R. 1-27-2-41, 43, Milroy.

addition, four small partially completed earthen redoubts, the largest of which was known as the West Fort, were positioned about a half mile west of the Main Fort and about the same distance east of Little North Mountain.[70]

Those Yankee fortifications could be studded with Milroy's 18 field guns and two 24-pounder howitzers. Even more impressive were the pillars of Milroy's defenses, four 20-pounder Parrott guns manned by the 14th [First] Massachusetts Heavy Artillery, that had just arrived on June 11 after a 22-mile march from Martinsburg.[71] The iron brutes which the Bay Staters served, could throw 17- to 20-pound case shot, shells, or solid shot with accuracy as far as 6,200 yards (about three and a half miles). Thanks to the height of Apple Pie Ridge, the Federals were able to project their might in a complete circle, including over top of Winchester and at least a mile beyond its southeastern outskirts.[72]

The bravado contained in Milroy's dispatches to Schenck appears to have been partly a reflection of genuine confidence in

---

[70]O.R. Atlas, Plate 39, #4. That map, drawn by Milroy's chief engineer, Captain W. Angelo Powell, included a table that provided that: the Star Fort was designed for an eight-gun battery and 1,500 men; the Main Fort could shelter 14 guns and 2,000 men; while the West Fort was planned for three guns and 2,000 men. Three of the four redoubts west of the Main Fort could not be manned due to a lack of manpower and ordnance. There was also an unmanned emplacement north of the Star Fort and another a few hundred yards south of the Main Fort. The latter redoubt was probably occupied on an intermittent basis during the engagement at Winchester as circumstances dictated.

[71]Ibid., 1-27-2-72, Hanson.

[72]Coddington, p. 89; Thomas pp. 33-36, end. A solid shot was just a conical lump of iron while a shell was hollowed out and filled with explosives so as to generate shrapnel. For those situations where a shell would not be lethal enough, the cannoneers had case shot, which was a shell with small iron balls imbedded within the explosive to add to the carnage. Some shells and case shot were designed to have a fuse inserted so that they could burst near the enemy while others had percussion devices that allowed detonation on contact. For close work all the cannons could fire canister, which consisted of a flimsy tin can filled most often with one inch diameter iron or lead balls that spread out like shotgun pellets when fired.

the strength of his position, as well as a healthy dose of spin intended to wangle more time as an independent commander in Winchester. Although perhaps apocryphal, the following anecdote concerning the beginning of Milroy's day on Friday, June 12, related 47 years after the fact by A. J. Hertzog, who had served as a trooper in the 14th Pennsylvania Cavalry, may provide an insight into the mind-set of the Union commander. The young cavalryman allegedly reported to Milroy that he had just returned from delivering some dispatches on the other side of the Blue Ridge. Then Hertzog and Milroy supposedly had a brief but possibly telling exchange:

"He [Milroy] asked me if I saw many Johnnies [on the way back from Leesburg]."

"I said: 'General, I saw about 15,000 or 20,000 and counted 16 batteries.'"

"He said: 'My boy, you are excited....' As we stepped out on the veranda the chief of the Jessie Scouts ran up the steps and saluted. 'General,' he said, 'there are about 25,000 rebels coming down from toward Leesburg.' He [Milroy] replied, 'I don't care a ____ how many there are. We will give them a warm reception.'"[73]

---

[73]Hertzog, *National Tribune*, 3/31/1910. Hertzog did not explain how he came to be carrying dispatches to Winchester by way of Leesburg. Further, the anecdote certainly deserves some healthy skepticism because Leesburg was 35 miles from where Ewell was then located. The tale may contain a nugget of fact that became distorted by the passage of time and a desire for a little personal aggrandizement, however. On June 8, 1862, Major Melvin Brewer of the 1st Michigan Cavalry sent a report from Milroy's headquarters in Winchester, concerning a scout he had just conducted through the Loudoun Valley to Front Royal. In that report Brewer wrote, "...General Ewell, with a corps, was encamped 1 mile this side Culpeper [55 miles from Winchester]. Stuart, with a large force of cavalry, is between Culpeper and Front Royal." How Brewer obtained this intelligence despite his patrol having gone no closer than 20 miles from Culpeper was not disclosed. O.R. 1-27-2-785. Perhaps the exchange that Hertzog attributed to himself and the Jessie Scout was really an artistically embellished conversation he overheard between Milroy and Brewer.

Like wishes, one should always be careful about what one boasts.

5

"LET THE REBELS COME"

Major General Schenck:
    The Twelfth Pennsylvania Cavalry had a slight skirmish with a rebel cavalry force, about 500, 12 miles from here, on road to Front Royal, this afternoon...."
                                                            —Robert H. Milroy[1]

Whether he had actually taken to heart the warnings allegedly provided by three different sources, or was merely responding to a nagging sixth sense, Milroy accelerated the normal pace of his surveillance during the morning of June 12 by repeatedly dispatching strong patrols deep into the Valley. Around midday, two such reconnaissances-in-force left the security of the fortifications at Winchester and headed south. One, under Colonel John W. Schall, with 400 men of the 87th Pennsylvania, 200 troopers from the 13th Pennsylvania Cavalry, and one section of Battery L, 5th United States Artillery, marched south toward Strasburg on the Valley Turnpike.[2] Lieutenant Colonel Joseph L. Moss, leading about 400 troopers from the 12th Pennsylvania Cavalry, cantered southeast on the Front Royal Road with the other.[3] Milroy's explanation for sending the Hussars in the direction of a purported

---

[1]O.R. 1-27-2-163.
[2]Prowell, p. 65.
[3]O.R. 1-27-2-43, Milroy.

131

force of 20,000 Rebels without the same screen-busting allocation of infantry and artillery allowed to Colonel Schall was that "...I did not expect an advance on that road, and did not dream that any forces would approach me except what were in the Shenandoah Valley."[4]

After traveling about nine miles up the Valley Turnpike, Schall's cavalry advance bumped into Confederate videttes. Colonel Harry Gilmor, commander of the picket force, was at that same moment lying on his sick bed in Middletown. The sound of gunfire on the picket line, which might have been a warning that the Yankees were attempting to breach the screen shielding Ewell's advance into the Valley, was strong enough medicine to yank Gilmor out of bed and propel him, after hastily donning a "spang-new" uniform festooned with gold braid, out onto the field. The partisan leader quickly rallied his troopers, and after a brief skirmish, led them in pursuit of the suddenly redirected Blue-coats.[5]

Gilmor was not the only officer to respond quickly and decisively to the sounds of a tussle in the offing. Colonel Schall "...immediately halted his command and posted it for action in the following manner: five companies of infantry were sent ahead, about two hundred yards, to the brow of a hill to the right of, and facing the pike, in a position screened from the view of the rebel cavalry as it would advance; the section of artillery was planted in a position to the left of the pike, with guns ranged to sweep the brow of the hill over which the enemy would come, with an enfilading fire, the remaining three companies of infantry were posted in support of the artillery; the cavalry, with the exception

---

[4]O.R. 1-27-2-92, Milroy.

[5]Achinclose, pp. 52-54. There is disagreement over who was in command of the first Confederate pickets encountered by the 13th Pennsylvania Cavalry. See Nye, pp. 75-77.

of the advance guard, was massed on the pike, a little distance in rear of the point opposite to which the artillery was posted...."[6]

Colonel Gilmor grew progressively more uneasy about the uncontested progress of his horsemen. When he approached the far side of the hill behind which the Federals were massing, he and a few scouts crept forward to see if the Yankees were actually retreating. Apparently unable to spy directly upon the Union dispositions, but nonetheless more convinced than ever that an ambush was in the works, Gilmor decided to lead his riders back toward Middletown. Soon after Gilmor's men got themselves redirected southward, they received an unwelcome jolt when a dust cloud was spotted on the southern horizon that could have been a warning that instead of having cleverly avoided an ambush, they had been surrounded.

The suspense was relieved in a few minutes when about 70 reinforcements, assembled from Company E of the 1st Maryland Cavalry Battalion (C.S.A.) and a company of the 14th Virginia Cavalry that was temporarily detached from Brigadier General Albert G. Jenkins' cavalry brigade, all under the command of Captain William Raisin, galloped close enough to allow identification.[7] Raisin yanked his horse to a stop and received a quick report which included Gilmor's suspicions about the Federals' too-timid behavior. After a brief discussion it was agreed that the partisan leader, with eight skirmishers, should return and ascertain the actual intentions of the Yankees before the main body advanced.

As Gilmore and his scouts approached Newtown, they encountered a line of blue-coated troopers who brandished sabers and taunted the Johnnies to charge if they dared. That last bit of uncharacteristic boldness erased any lingering doubts that Gilmor harbored about an ambush waiting over the brow of the next hill,

---

[6]Prowell, p. 65.
[7]Ibid., p. 66.

so he waived his pistol over his head to warn Raisin off. Almost simultaneously, several Rebelettes crowded up to a gable window on the end of their house that overlooked the Federal ambush, and began to scream and wave their handkerchiefs in a frantic attempt at a warning.[8] Unfortunately, Raisin mistook Gilmor's warning as a signal to charge, shouted the order, and in a few moments the entire Butternut force was racing over the top of the hill despite the lacey warning which the Butternuts either failed to observe or misinterpreted as further encouragement.[9]

The Federals were ready and waiting, with the gunners poised at their pieces and the infantry lying prone in a field of sweet-smelling clover.[10] "This disposition of our force had hardly been made when the advance guard of [our] cavalry made its appearance on the hill, coming in on the run, closely pursued by the enemy, who were howling like demons. After the head of the rebel column had crossed the hill, our forces opened fire, raking them with artillery and pouring a destructive broadside fire of musketry into them from the right of the pike, creating great confusion in their ranks, when our cavalry made a charge and sent them whirling in the direction of Strasburg, and picked up a number of prisoners...there were no casualties on our side."[11]

Four Confederates paid the ultimate price for the misunderstanding including a "...Mr. FitzPatrick...[who] led the charge with drawn sabre...[until a] ball went in near his left ear and came out his right ear...."[12] In addition, from 30 to as many as 50 Confederates, depending on the source, were wounded, captured,

---

[8]Prowell, p. 66; Kate Sperry, as quoted in Grunder, p. 25.

[9]Ackinclose, pp. 52-54.

[10]Kesses letter, 1895.

[11]Prowell, pp. 65-66.

[12]Kate Sperry, as quoted in Grunder, p. 26. In a dispatch, Milroy provided a short summary of the ambush of Raisin's men near Middletown that included a recitation that "...[e]ight of the rebels were killed, a number wounded, and 37, including a captain and 2 lieutenants, taken prisoners."

or both. Captain Raisin received such a severe saber wound to the head that he was presumed dead and abandoned, but he survived, was exchanged, and served out the balance of the war.[13] The Yankees may have gotten the better of the engagement but the Rebels accomplished their mission. Satisfied with the punishment they had administered and the negative results from another hour's scouting, Schall's Yankees trudged back toward Winchester without having penetrated Ewell's screen on the Valley Turnpike.

Meanwhile, the detachment from the 12th Pennsylvania Cavalry under the command of Lieutenant Colonel Moss trotted up the Valley on the Front Royal Road. At Cedarville, 10 miles southeast of Winchester and three miles short of the town of Front Royal, Moss' men "...found a large rebel force, consisting of cavalry, infantry, and artillery. After skirmishing with them awhile and ascertaining their strength, the regiment fell back to Winchester [with] two men wounded...." Moss reported the contact to Milroy at 3:00 p.m.[14]

It is likely that the Hussars collided with Brigadier General Junius Daniel's brigade that had crossed the Shenandoah River at noon in advance of Major General Robert E. Rodes' division. Daniel reported that he followed the road toward Berryville, which branched off from the Front Royal Road just south of Cedarville, and also that "[n]ear Millwood, my advance guard came in contact with a small party of the enemy's cavalry, which retired before them...."[15] Further confirmation of the fact that the 12th Pennsylvania Cavalry actually made contact with the main

---

[13]Prowell, p. 66; Ackinclose, p. 54; *Confederate Veteran*, 24, p. 466. Raisin died in 1916. Presumably because failure is an orphan, responsibility for the ill-fated charge was denied by both Gilmor's and Raisin's men. The historian for the Maryland Line maintained that the entire operation was under Raisin's control until Gilmor, in his impressive uniform, showed up and led the charge. See Goldsborough, *The Maryland Line in the Confederate Army*, Baltimore, Kelly, Piet, 1869 and Nye, pp. 75-77.

[14]O.R. 1-27-2-69, Titus; O.R. 1-27-2-42, Milroy.

[15]Ibid., 1-27-2-565, Daniel.

Confederate force is provided by an after-battle report quoted from the *Richmond Dispatch* which confirmed that soon after leaving Front Royal, advanced elements of Ewell's corps skirmished with a contingent from Milroy's garrison.[16]

In his after-action report, Milroy expressed dissatisfaction with Moss' recapitulation of the skirmish near Cedarville. "It did not appear, however, that he [Moss] had placed himself in a position to ascertain the number or character of the force which he had encountered, or exercised the usual and necessary efforts to obtain that essential information. Officers of his command and reliable scouts [all un-named] who were present gave contradictory reports. This report was discredited by myself and by General Elliott, my second in command. There was nothing in the report which indicated the presence of General Lee's army. It was supposed [by Milroy] that the force on the Front Royal road could not be other than the enemy which we had faced during the occupancy of Winchester, or that the anticipated cavalry raid of General Stuart was in progress, against either or both of which combined I could have held my position. I deemed it impossible that Lee's army, with its immense artillery and baggage trains could have escaped from the Army of the Potomac, and crossed the Blue Ridge...."[17]

---

[16] *Philadelphia Inquirer*, 6/24/1863.

[17] O.R. 1-27-2-134, Milroy. To that point Milroy had not received any intelligence from Washington that would have warned him that anything other than a possible cavalry raid was in the offing. It was not until 7:00 p.m. on June 12 that General Pleasonton, chief of cavalry for the Army of the Potomac, sent the following dispatch which was the first specific warning of Lee's advance into the Valley: "A colored boy captured on the 9th states that Ewell's corps passed through Culpeper on Monday last, on their way to the Valley, and that part of Longstreet's has gone also. A second negro just across the river confirms the statement. I send a reconnaissance to find out the truth." O.R. 1-27-2-184-185. Curiously, despite numerous earlier suggestions and two orders based solely upon general apprehensions, Halleck did not respond to Pleasonton's dispatch with a preemptory order to Schenck.

Milroy's assistant adjutant general, Major John O. Cravens, was apparently present when Moss made his report. Either as a result of different recollections, or less urgent motivation, Cravens provided a version of the 12th's encounter with the enemy near Cedarville in his later court of inquiry testimony that differed markedly from Milroy's. According to the staff officer, Lieutenant Colonel Moss reported to Milroy that the "'...enemy was in some considerable force with infantry and artillery: that they had a full battery of artillery, and that twelve shots were fired at him from their artillery.' A number of his subordinate officers and the scouts who were with him [all un-named] represented that there was not any artillery at all, and but about *1,500 infantry.*"[18]

Rather than inform Schenck of the substance of Moss' report, Cravens' version of that report, or even a recitation of the reasons why he discredited the Pennsylvanian's assertions, Milroy offered what may be judged to be a deliberate deception intended to forestall an order to pull back. "The Twelfth Pennsylvania Cavalry had a slight skirmish with *a rebel cavalry force, about 500*, 12 miles from here, on road to Front Royal, this afternoon.... The enemy are probably approaching in some force. I am entirely ready for them. I can hold this place. Please state specifically whether I am to abandon it or not."[19]

Supporting an interpretation that the Hoosier was deliberately spinning the facts so as to avoid an order to withdraw, he apparently failed to place Lieutenant Colonel Moss under arrest, which would have been the expected fate of an officer who was believed to have shirked his duty and knowingly provided false information to his commanding officer.[20] Even more damning,

---

[18] O.R. 1-27-2-134, emphasis supplied.

[19] Ibid., 1-27-2-163, emphasis supplied. In his after-action report the Hoosier praised Schall's effort at the same time he discredited Moss'.

[20] On June 24, 1863, Lieutenant Colonel Moss tendered his resignation from the service. Two reasons were cited: a sick wife who was unable to care for the Moss' six small children, and the reduction in the size of the 12th Pennsylvania Cavalry

the never-before-timid Milroy failed to send the 12th Pennsylvania Cavalry and a section of artillery back up the Front Royal Road with mandatory orders, given to an officer whom he trusted, to smash through any Rebel screen they encountered and either confirm or debunk Moss' report. Under cross-examination during the subsequent court of inquiry, Milroy offered, as a dubious excuse for his failure to launch another probe, "[d]arkness came on, and there could nothing more be done."[21]

The asserted justification for failing to take further action seems to have been consciously disingenuous and definitely out of character for the Hoosier, given that Moss made his report at 3 p.m. If the Union commander had acted promptly, there would have been ample time to summon artillery and for a mounted force to race back up the road and gather the crucial intelligence before total darkness fell around 8:30 p.m. Although the troopers would probably have had to return in the darkness, the potential gravity of the situation should clearly have warranted the risk.[22] One

---

to a point that no longer warranted a lieutenant colonel. Milroy endorsed the request with the note "...the best good of the service requires that this resignation of Lt. Colonel Moss be promptly accepted." Moss Military Records, National Archives. There are three possible reasons for the resignation and Milroy's prompt endorsement. The first is that Moss really needed to resign. The second is that Milroy encouraged Moss to resign so that he would not be available as a hostile witness in a court-martial or court of inquiry. Finally, Milroy might have offered Moss the opportunity to resign honorably rather than face court-martial. The latter possibility is discounted because of the Hoosier's earlier treatment of General Cluseret and because although Milroy was not above using spin to further his aims, there is no indication that he was ruthless or unethical enough to use charges to falsely turn a fellow officer into a scapegoat.

[21]O.R. 1-27-2-92, Milroy.

[22]Under compelling circumstances, horsemen could cover at least five miles per hour for moderate distances. Since the initial encounter was approximately 10 miles from Winchester (and as far as Milroy knew the Confederates might have been approaching him at two miles per hour) it could have been anticipated that a horse-borne force that left Winchester at 4 p.m. would have reached the enemy between 6 and 7 p.m., allowing ample time before dark to punch through even a determined screen. In the alternative, running up against a screen that was too strong to be

may legitimately conclude either that Milroy didn't want to know information that might eventually cost him his independent command, or that he was so confident of the infallibility of his own assumptions that he didn't feel the need to be troubled by the facts.

Further incriminating information is found in the fact that although it may have been too dark to send Moss' regiment back to Front Royal, it wasn't too dark to send them up the Valley Turnpike to reinforce the 13th Pennsylvania Cavalry. On the way, the 12th "...met them [the 13th] returning with some prisoners. Both regiments returned to camp. At about 7 p.m. the regiment [the 12th], by order from General Milroy, left camp on scout for Strasburg, or to go as far as Middletown. We proceeded to Middletown and beyond. Saw no rebels, and returned to camp at 2 a.m."[23] Not only does Milroy's order to send the 12th to Strasburg at 7 p.m. impeach his earlier assertion about the limiting effects of darkness, but it also indicates that he may have deliberately diverted all of his cavalry away from the Front Royal Road when prudence would have dictated at least a heavy cavalry picket somewhere between Winchester and Cedarville.

Although he seems not to have wanted to know the true composition of the enemy that he faced, Milroy did take immediate steps to warn Colonel McReynolds in Berryville that trouble might also be headed in his direction. Along with the warning, the Hoosier ordered the commander of his Third Brigade to "...keep a strong party of observation in the direction of Millwood..." and also to "...place his command in readiness to move at a moment's warning...," which would consist of four blasts from the big guns in Winchester. Finally, McReynolds was given discretion to fall

---

breached by a full cavalry regiment, supported by artillery, would alone have provided significant intelligence.

[23]O.R. 1-27-2-69, Titus. Strasburg is about 12 miles from Winchester, and Middletown about eight.

back on the rest of the division by any practical route in the event he was attacked by superior forces.[24]

    McReynolds wasted little time in dispatching contingents of the 1st New York Cavalry on patrols deep into the countryside. It wasn't long thereafter that one of them, under the command of Captain Friedrich Hendrich, collided with the Rebels near White Post, a village which was four miles north of Cedarville, three miles south of Millwood, and nine miles south of Berryville. Within moments the New Yorkers found themselves embroiled in a "...lively skirmish..." with the Confederate vanguard comprised of "...two regiments of infantry and a small party of cavalry...." Hendrich dutifully reported the skirmish and soon thereafter received orders to remain in contact with the enemy but to fall back slowly toward Berryville. Carrying out those orders cost two New Yorkers their lives.[25]

    Exactly when McReynolds chose to report Hendrich's encounter to Milroy remains a mystery, since both were silent on the point. It is likely, given the fairly urgent nature of the Hoosier's dispatch to Berryville, that it came into Winchester sometime later in the evening of June 12. That Milroy actually received the information at some point, and that he may have deliberately delayed forwarding the news to headquarters, is evidenced by a telegram he sent to Schenck through Piatt at 11 a.m. on June 13. "A small detachment of First New York encountered *a body of rebel cavalry* at White Post, supposed to be the advance of force met by Twelfth Pennsylvania on Front Royal road.... Am perfectly certain of my ability to hold this place."[26] Piatt appended his own laconic postscript to Milroy's message: "Have received the following dispatches from General Milroy.

---

[24]O.R. 1-27-2-43, Milroy.
[25]Stevenson, p. 183; Beach, p. 230; O.R. 1-27-2-108, McReynolds.
[26]O.R. 1-27-2-164, emphasis supplied.

Am sorry that you interfered with me."[27] He would become even sorrier.

The Hoosier allegedly ended Friday night with a final act of denial. Colonel Keifer of the 110th Ohio, who was also in charge of the division's undercover scouts, reported that on the night of the June 12 his disguised troopers were unable to advance more than four or five miles south of town because of Confederate pickets. Convinced that the Rebel cavalry pickets would only have been so obstinate if backed by large numbers of foot soldiers, Keifer claimed that he requested an audience with Milroy to discuss the new development and to reiterate the Ohioan's previously offered opinion that the garrison ought to retreat. According to Keifer, "Milroy persisted in the notion that only cavalry were before him, and he was anxious to fight them and especially averse to retreating under circumstances that might subject him to the charge of cowardice. He also sincerely desired to hold the Valley and protect the Union residents.... During my acquaintance with Milroy he had evinced confidence in and friendship for me; now he manifested much annoyance over my persistence in urging him to order a retreat at once, and finally he dismissed me rather summarily."[28]

Saturday, June 13, came early for both the Federal garrison in Winchester and Ewell's corps bivouacked between the Blue Ridge Mountains and Cedarville. Before daybreak, a small party of Rebel cavalry took a swipe at the Yankee picket line four miles southeast of Winchester, but they were beaten off by determined volleys of musketry.[29] Lacking the adrenalin rush from a sudden

---

[27] O.R. 1-27-2-163.

[28] Keifer, vol. 2, pp. 6-7. In addition to the other reasons, Milroy also supposedly rejected Keifer's advice because the Ohioan's sources had previously predicted that an attack on Winchester would commence on June 10. Keifer's source might have been correct had it not been for the delay caused by the battle at Brandy Station on June 9, 1863.

[29] Walker, p. 105.

attack, it required blaring bugles and swearing sergeants to roust the men of the 12th and 13th Pennsylvania Cavalry from their bedrolls that morning because the former had just returned from their scout to Middletown a few hours earlier and the latter were mustered in the pitch darkness of 3 a.m.[30] With bleary eyes and leaden muscles the Keystone troopers boiled their coffee, gulped down a few hard tack crackers, tended and saddled their horses, and then fell into formation for action.

At about 7 a.m., the 12th Pennsylvania Cavalry trotted toward the Union Mills (also known as Milltown or Barton's Mill), that were located along the banks of Abraham's Creek about a half mile south of Winchester. From there, Moss' regiment and Keifer's 110th Ohio were detailed to conduct a scout out the Cedar Creek Road toward the southwest. The combined column marched four or five miles before reaching the most distant outpost on the Union perimeter. Once into no-man's-land the Pennsylvanians and the Buckeyes "...proceeded on the Strasburg road [Valley Turnpike] about three miles farther. Remained an hour or so; then fell back to the force which had collected and was in line of battle near the mill. We [the 12th Pennsylvania Cavalry] were placed on the extreme right of the line."[31]

In true army fashion, Colonel Michael Kerwin's 13th Pennsylvania Cavalry, after having been dragged out of bed well before dawn, was forced to wait five and a half hours in camp (probably to allow time for the 12th to move out first), until they were permitted to follow their sister regiment up the Pike. Instead of the original plan, after a trot of a mile and a half, Kerwin's troopers were ordered to peel off to the left of the Pike and to form an extended skirmish line facing south, perpendicular to the Front Royal Road.[32]

---

[30]O.R. 1-27-2-70, Titus & Kerwin.

[31]Ibid., 1-27-2-69, Titus; O.R. 1-27-2-57, Elliott. The Valley Turnpike was sometimes referred to as the Strasburg Road.

[32]Ibid., 1-27-2-70, Kerwin.

As the Federal troopers were feeding and saddling their horses around 4 a.m., the Butternuts were, pursuant to Ewell's master plan, beginning to file onto the roads toward Winchester and Berryville.[33] Major General Rodes, with the lead division and Jenkins' 1,600 horsemen, drew the assignment to proceed northward and seize Berryville. Major General Edward Johnson, whose division was next in line, was directed to continue towards Winchester on the Front Royal Road. Finally, Major General Jubal A. Early received orders to approach Winchester from the southwest, which he set out to accomplish by following the Front Royal Road to Nineveh, then west to Newtown and from there down the Valley Turnpike.[34]

Not surprisingly, the first serious Union contact with the approaching Rebels that morning occurred on the Front Royal Road, where a Federal cavalry patrol recoiled from a collision with the Confederate vanguard at approximately 8 a.m. Milroy accepted the challenge and rushed the 87th Pennsylvania, 18th Connecticut, 5th Maryland, 13th Pennsylvania Cavalry, and one section of Randolph's Battery L, 5th United States Artillery, all under the command of Colonel Ely, toward the point of contact.[35] About a mile south of Winchester the 18th Connecticut, whose prior experience was comprised of "...reconnaissance and

---

[33]O.R. 1-27-2-499, 523, Johnson, Newton.

[34]Early, pp. 240-243; Coddington, p. 90. No explanation was offered as to why the shorter route was assigned to Johnson, whose division was second in line while Early, at the end of the column, was given the longest march. Perhaps to have sent Johnson toward Nineveh would have required his men to double-back.

[35]O.R. 1-27-2-44, Milroy. In his report written two weeks after the fact, Milroy stated that Ely's cavalry regiment was the 12th Pennsylvania, but it is this writer's assessment that he either confused the 13th Pennsylvania for the 12th, or that only a detachment of the 12th was involved. As will be seen later, Major Titus reported the 12th in action on the Valley Turnpike throughout the day, a fact that was confirmed by Colonel Keifer of the 110th Ohio. It is presumed that the participants had a better knowledge of their activities than did the general in overall command.

picket...," shook out companies A, B, H, F, and I into a skirmish line on the right side of the Front Royal Road in order to probe some suspicious-looking woodlands in their front.[36]

Earlier in the week some of the Connecticut Yankees had echoed the confidence of their commander by boldly proclaiming, "...let the rebels come..." and "...we'll give them all they want..."[37] Perhaps the rookies were braced for their first potential glimpse of "the elephant" by echoes of those jaunty words, as well as the two-gun section of regular army artillery under Lieutenant Edmund D. Spooner that was arrayed on a hill behind them.[38] At about 10 a.m. the neophytes' skirmish line entered the northern end of a long farm field that was entirely boxed in by a loose stone farm fence. After all of the rookies had clambered over the wall, they began to cautiously approach the deeply shaded fence and tree line 400 yards to their south. Even though the Yankees had not yet experienced the horror that could suddenly explode from the shade of a peaceful-looking forest, not all of the sweat that stung their eyes and rolled down their chests into pools atop their waist belts was due to woolen uniforms and the already sweltering mid-June sun. Undoubtedly as they pressed forward, a few of the farm boys on the line absentmindedly noted the type of plants being tramped down or puzzled over the lack of bird songs in the treetops. The rest peered into the shadows as if sufficient concentration would suddenly illuminate any gray-coated marksmen kneeling in the semidarkness.

Before they had gone a quarter of the way across, the bucolic tranquility was suddenly rent by the loud, sharp, staccato cadence of a ragged volley of rifle fire unleashed from behind the

---

[36]Walker, p. 106; O.R. 1-27-2-75-76, Peale.

[37]Ibid., p. 106.

[38]"Seeing the elephant" was an expression used during the earlier part of the war to reference experiencing combat for the first time. The source of the phrase is unknown but it may refer to the experience of the Roman legionnaires when they encountered Hannibal's war elephants for the first time.

southern wall. For a moment the buzz of Minié balls passing over their heads, uncertainty of what was expected of them, and the paralyzing effects of emotions that simultaneously screamed run, shoot, or dive to the ground, froze the rookies in their tracks. Before the Butternuts could reload and adjust their sights, though, a quick-witted Federal officer realized that the mission to develop the possible presence of the enemy had been cheaply accomplished and led his charges back to their own wall at a jog. Whether any of the Yankees returned the fire was forgotten in the excitement.[39]

Unfazed by what to them was a familiar occurrence, the two spit-and-polish regular army gun crews prepared to let fly as soon as the rookie riflemen got out of the way. When he obtained a clear field of fire, "...Lieut. Spooner, in command of the battery [section], gave the order: 'Number one, fire, and be sure of your aim. Number two, fire,' and the shells went whizzing and screaming into the woods...causing great commotion among the concealed rebels."[40] For the next half hour the Federal gunners flogged the trees in hopes of either dispersing the Confederates or failing that, revealing the number or intentions of their adversaries.

While the Yankee cannoneers toiled, both sides made tactical adjustments. On the northern end of the field the 87th Pennsylvania filled in behind the stone wall alongside of their comrades from Connecticut.[41] On the southern side, Confederate Lieutenant William T. Lambie surreptitiously led his six-gun battery of brass 12-pounder Napoleons through the woods and into position behind their portion of the wall.[42] Just about the time that the Connecticut boys' first opportunity to observe artillery in combat had evolved from awe into tedium, the Rebel-occupied tree

---

[39]Walker, p. 106.
[40]Ibid.
[41]O.R. 1-27-2-78, Ruhl; Prowell, p. 71.
[42]Ibid., 1-27-2-500, 540, Johnson, Latimer. A 12-pounder Napoleon was a brass field cannon with a smooth bore.

line erupted with jets of flame, six nearly simultaneous gut-thumping concussions, and billows of white roiling smoke. Within the blink of an eye, barely visible swarms of "...terrible...grape and canister..." splattered against the Yankees' wall or buzzed and hissed over their startled, sweat-soaked heads.[43]

It wasn't long thereafter that the shrieking death emanating from the southern woods convinced the Federal gunners that numbers and position favored the enemy. After firing a few rounds for honor's sake, Spooner and his regulars decamped for safer ground, and Ely's infantrymen wasted no time in following their more experienced brethren toward the rear.[44] Although intimidating, the Confederate barrage claimed only three casualties when, during the retreat, a lucky shot exploded a powder-filled limber and killed three Union gunners. For their part, the Johnnies lost two killed and one wounded to the brief Federal counter-battery fire.[45]

Ely's brigade soon reestablished itself a short distance outside of town near the intersection of the Front Royal Road and Valley Turnpike. Behind them, Lieutenant Wallace F. Randolph positioned his entire six-gun Battery L in an orchard on the top of another small hillock.[46] The Southern gunners, covered by Colonel J. Q. A. Nadenbousch's 2nd Virginia skirmish line, limbered up, followed the Federal retreat, and within a relatively short time resumed the noisy, but generally harmless, artillery argument.

While the blue and gray gunners generated huge clouds of smoke and expended chests full of expensive ammunition, Confederate General Johnson began to feed his division into battle formation as his troops gradually marched down the Front Royal

---

[43]O.R. 1-27-2-78, Ruhl.
[44]Walker, pp. 106-107.
[45]O.R. 1-27-2-73, 500, 540, Spooner, Johnson, Latimer.
[46]Ibid., 1-27-2-44, 73.

Road.[47] The Stonewall brigade under Brigadier General James A. Walker and Brigadier General George H. Steuart's brigade peeled off the road to the right into a sheltering ravine, while Johnson's other two brigades under Brigadier General John M. Jones and Colonel J. M. Williams occupied a stand of trees on the left.[48] Apparently pursuant to orders from Ewell not to attack until Old Jubal's division was in position on his left, Johnson allowed his gunners to do the fighting while he held his men back and remained in battle line out of Federal view.

The artillery duel was eventually ended not by a bloody Union infantry assault, but through the intervention of the heavy artillerists from Massachusetts who manned the big guns in Milroy's Main Fort.[49] According to 1st Lieutenant J. B. Hanson, commander of a section of the Heavies, "A part of the time the enemy was in sight of the fort, distant about 5,000 yards, and some 70 shells were fired at them from the fort...."[50] "The third shot struck and broke one of the brass cannon in two pieces. At this the remaining [Rebel] guns limbered up and fled to a more secure place."[51]

The Bay Staters almost made a greater contribution to Federal fortunes. One of their 70 rounds blew a gaping hole out of another stone wall behind which the skirmish line of the 2nd Virginia was pausing for a blow. Several of the flying rocks barely missed General Ewell, who was observing Johnson's progress from a much-too-forward position. After some prompting from staff officers about Ewell's safety, and a suggestion offered by a cheeky 2nd Virginia private about theirs, Old Bald Head sent the Virginians forward into a protected hollow where they hunkered down in relative safety, while he rode off to check on the

---

[47]Prowell, p. 71; O.R. 1-27-2-515, 520, Walker, Nadenbousch.
[48]O.R. 1-27-2-500, Johnson.
[49]Walker, p. 107.
[50]O.R. 1-27-2-72, Hanson.
[51]Powell, *National Tribune*, 5/16/1889.

progress of Early's division.[52]   For the balance of the day,
Johnson's Southerners gave the Federal 20-pounder Parrotts plenty
of leeway and the situation on Milroy's southeastern front, but for
an occasional skirmish with some pesky Butternut cavalry, lapsed
into a tense standoff.[53]

At the same time that Colonel Ely's brigade was commencing its sortie up the Front Royal Road, Brigadier General Elliott
was ordered to deploy his First Brigade along the Valley Turnpike
and to "...feel the enemy...." Elliott reported that he "Formed
line of battle, Thirteenth Pennsylvania Cavalry on my left flank,
with vedettes to the front; One Hundred Twenty Third Ohio on the
left and One Hundred Tenth Ohio on the right of the Strasburg
road [Valley Turnpike], with section of [Captain John] Carlin's
battery [Battery D, 1st W. Virginia Artillery] in the rear of the
One Hundred and Tenth Ohio. The Twelfth West Virginia Volunteer Infantry, Colonel Klunk, of the Second Brigade, reported to
me, and was assigned a position on the right of the One Hundred
and Tenth Ohio."[54]

At first, the Federals didn't "feel" enough of the Southern
lines to even get slapped. Colonel Ely's withdrawal on the Front
Royal Road exposed Elliott's left flank, requiring a redeployment
back to a stronger defensive position which was in closer proximity to the right flank of the Second Brigade. Elliott chose a line
behind the headwaters of Abraham's Creek at Union Mills because
it had a "...boggy stream, at its base, and the steep ascent to the
hill [Bower's] on the other side."[55]

---

[52]Pfanz, *Richard S. Ewell...*, p. 283.

[53]O.R. 1-27-2-44.

[54]Ibid., 1-27-2-57, Elliott. The historian for the 12th West Virginia recorded
that his regiment marched out to join Elliott at 11 a.m., and while in transit they
heard the commencement of the artillery duel on the Front Royal Road. Hewitt,
p. 40.

[55]Ibid., 1-27-2-57, Elliott; Early, p. 241.

Milroy, who was struggling to maintain a share of the initiative rather than allow himself to become a sitting duck, ordered Elliott to send a reconnaissance-in-force back up the Valley Turnpike toward Kernstown. Elliott retained the 123rd Ohio, the 12th West Virginia, the 13th Pennsylvania Cavalry and possibly a portion of the 116th Ohio in support, and sent the 110th Ohio and the 12th Pennsylvania Cavalry in search of the enemy.[56] "At 2 p.m. I [Colonel J. Warren Keifer, 110th Ohio] received an order to take my regiment, the Twelfth Pennsylvania Volunteer Cavalry, commanded by Lieutenant-Colonel Moss, and a section of Carlin's battery [two 3-inch rifled cannons], commanded by Lieutenant Theaker, and make a reconnaissance. I moved at once up the Strasburg road [Valley Turnpike], forming my infantry upon the right and center, artillery in the center and cavalry upon the left.... After proceeding about one mile, the infantry and cavalry skirmishers became closely engaged with the enemy's advance. The enemy were driven back to the woods on the left. I immediately withdrew the cavalry skirmishers, who were beginning to suffer severely from the enemy's sharpshooters, and placed my artillery in position, and shelled the woods, where the enemy were concealed in large force. After a few moments' brisk firing, the enemy [the 2nd Maryland Infantry Battalion (C.S.A.) and Griffin's Baltimore horse artillery battery] fell back to the woods on the left of Kernstown. I advanced with my entire force under a heavy infantry fire to within a quarter of a mile of the town, and opened upon the enemy with canister, producing a telling effect. At the same time the infantry upon my right became closely engaged. After a few moments' brisk firing, the enemy fell back to the woods on the left of Kernstown."[57]

---

[56]O.R. 1-27-2-57, 69, Elliott, Titus; Wildes, p. 54; Keyes, p. 44.

[57]Ibid., 1-27-2-60, Keifer; Nye, p. 82. In that initial skirmish the 12th Pennsylvania Cavalry suffered the only specifically reported casualties, one man killed and two wounded. O.R. 1-27-2-69, Titus.

When he heard sounds indicative of a serious firefight, Elliott rushed the riflemen of the 123rd Ohio and the 12th West Virginia, and possibly three companies of the 116th Ohio, forward to support their embattled comrades.[58]   Lieutenant Colonel Thomas F. Wildes, historian for the 116th Ohio, based upon what may have either been personal observations or an account cobbled together from the recollections of other Ohioans, wrote a vivid description of what could have only been the end of the skirmish described by Keifer.[59] "Soon after passing our picket lines, we [the 116th Ohio] met the enemy's skirmishers, which we drove back beyond Kernstown.... We met a strong line a short distance beyond Kernstown. The 116th was quickly thrown around to a position from which it enfiladed the line, and pushing our advantage, pressed them under a hot fire, until they broke, when we charged and drove them from the field in a rout."[60]

The Federals had only a few moments to bask in their achievement and to catch their collective breath. "It was soon seen, however, from a point of high ground which we reached in the pursuit, that we had met but a small portion of the force actually in our front. The roads for miles up the valley indicated the approach and near presence of a large force."[61] That force

---

[58]The sources were unclear whether the entire brigade moved out together, with Keifer's and Moss' men out front and the rest in support, or whether Keifer's contingent went first and the others came up when the fighting started. Interpretation is made more difficult by Colonel Keifer's emphasis on his own achievements.

[59]Some skepticism of Wildes' account is justified since he dated the described action as occurring on the previous day (although it clearly didn't happen on June 12), no other source placed any portion of the 116th Ohio with Keifer, and his own colonel mentioned that Wildes was sent to West Fort during the afternoon in command of three companies. The quotations were included because although embellishment and exaggeration were common in regimental histories, fraudulently reporting involvement in identifiable battles was not. Further, it is possible that either Milroy or Elliott latched onto Wildes' detachment and, without their colonel's knowledge, sent them from where they were not needed to where they were.

[60]Wildes, p. 54.

[61]Ibid.

was the rest of Jubal Early's division, which had been tramping toward Winchester all morning intent on mayhem. Lee's Bad Old Man, as the Confederates' top general somewhat affectionately nicknamed Early, was not about to allow a few winded Federal regiments to impede his progress.

Elliott reacted as soon as a breathless messenger brought news of the discovery of the approaching Confederate column. Rather than pull his brigade all the way back to Abraham's Creek, the Union general elected to assume a defensive posture across the Pike just north of Kernstown. Perhaps he chose the location as a charm since it was the same field on which Stonewall Jackson received one of his few defeats the previous year. In any case, around 3 p.m. the Yankee riflemen established a line of battle with their right flank doubly anchored by Theaker's artillery atop Pritchard's Hill and by the Mountaineers of the 12th West Virginia, who took up a position to the gunner's right rear on a slight ridge that offered the shelter of both a stone wall and a stand of trees.[62] Undoubtedly ignorant of what was coming their way, most of the privates in the thin blue line probably used the pause to gulp some lukewarm water from their canteens and to absent-mindedly rearrange equipments or double check their supply of cartridges and caps.

When the Confederate general and the bulk of his division arrived at Kernstown, Early recalled that "...the only force in sight...was a cavalry force, but I was informed that a strong infantry picket occupied the town, and the supposition was that a stronger force was in the neighborhood. Just beyond Kernstown and Pritchard's Hill and a ridge extending from it to our left, which was covered with trees...was a position on which a considerable body of troops might be posted out of our view, and I soon discovered a battery of artillery on Pritchard's Hill which

---

[62]O.R. 1-27-2-80, Klunk; Early, p. 242.

opened on us. I then reconnoitred the ground carefully.... "63

Confident that he enjoyed a substantial numerical superiority that would trump his adversary's geographic advantage, Early began to deploy his troops in order to sweep the Federals out of his path. "I moved Hay's brigade to the left, through a skirt of woods and a meadow, to a small road in from Bartonsville towards the Cedar Creek pike, and then along that to a suitable position for advancing against the artillery on Pritchard's Hill; and ordered it to advance and get possession of the hill...."64 Brigadier General Harry T. Hays led his command about a half mile to the east of the Middle Road (approximately a quarter mile west of the Valley Turnpike) and then deployed the 9th Louisiana under Colonel L. A. Stafford as his skirmish line. Hays was able to push his line over the top of Pritchard's Hill with little if any bloodshed because Theaker had withdrawn his artillery only moments before, and the Federal sharpshooters who were left behind pulled back rather than attempt to seriously contest the Confederate advance.65

After Hays spread his line further to the left the Butternuts encountered more determined resistance from the 12th West Virginia.66 Upon receiving news of the threat to his flank, Early "...immediately moved [Brigadier General John B.] Gordon's brigade over the same route Hays' brigade had taken, and ordered him to advance and clear the ridge on Hays' left...."67 As soon as Gordon and his Georgia brigade arrived on the scene around 4 p.m., he "...deployed a line of skirmishers, [that incorporated six companies of Hays' skirmishers] and moved forward to the attack,

63Early, p. 241. Jubal Early hated the Union from at least the time the war started until he drew his final breath. He consistently omitted from his memoirs any reference to events which might have reflected favorably upon the Union army, and his failure to mention the initial action around Kernstown was consistent with that pattern.
64Ibid., pp. 241-242.
65O.R. 1-27-2-460, 466, 477, Early, Hays.
66Ibid., 1-27-2-80, 460, 476, Klunk, Early, Hays.
67Early, pp. 241-242.

Kernstown Skirmish

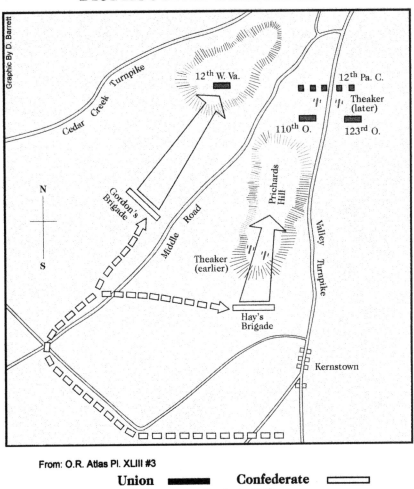

Graphic By D. Barrett

12th W. Va.

12th Pa. C.

Theaker
(later)

110th O.

123rd O.

Cedar Creek Turnpike

Gordon's
Brigade

Middle Road

Prichards
Hill

Theaker
(earlier)

Valley Turnpike

Hay's
Brigade

Kernstown

N

S

From: O.R. Atlas Pl. XLIII #3

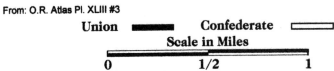

Union   Confederate

Scale in Miles

0   1/2   1

holding two regiments (the Thirteenth and Thirty-first Georgia) in reserve." After pushing ahead several hundred yards, it became obvious that neither Gordon's skirmish line nor his original battle line were going to be strong enough to pry the Mountaineers away from behind their wall and off the ridge. In order to achieve the necessary heft, Gordon fed his reserves into the line with the 31st Georgia on his right and the 13th Georgia on the left.[68]

The 12th West Virginia was another one of Milroy's green regiments that, despite never having faced hostile fire, was placed in a critical position because of Elliott's urgent need to patch together a defensive line.[69] The Mountaineers probably sensed they were about to receive their fiery baptism when an order raced down the line to drop and pile their knapsacks. Like the Connecticut boys earlier in the day, they soon thereafter heard "...those peculiar sounds, the whistling of the minnie-balls.... So unaccustomed were they to the whistling sounds, that they began to question among themselves as to what they were, some saying that they were the sounds of flying bullets: others that they were not. An officer hearing the talk said: 'Boys those are bullets as sure as you live.' This assurance together with the increasing frequency of the sounds, settled the matter in their minds...."[70] Despite the novelty of their circumstances, the West Virginians quickly began to bite, pour, ram, and fire like veterans, and at least for a time, the Mountaineers fought the gray avalanche to a standstill.[71]

With a line that was two regiments longer, General Gordon was able to angle his brigade so as to flank the West Virginians.

---

[68]O.R. 1-27-2-491, Gordon.

[69]Ibid., 1-27-2-80, Klunk.

[70]Hewitt, pp. 40-41.

[71]In order to fire a rifled musket the soldier had to: extract a paper cartridge from his cartridge box; tear its end off with his teeth; pour the powder down the barrel; insert the bullet in the barrel; remove his ramrod from under the gun barrel; shove the bullet down to the powder with his ramrod; replace his ramrod; cock his rifle; extract a cap from his cap box; and place the cap on the nipple under the hammer. A dexterous rifleman could fire a maximum of three shots per minute.

When properly aligned, the Georgians began to drive with increasing momentum towards the Pike. As the Rebels approached, the Mountaineers both intensified their fire and attempted to respond to the impending threat to their right flank. Company A under Lieutenant Burley sprinted over to the vulnerable flank and upon arrival his men quickly let loose with a smattering of rifle fire from an improvised skirmish line. They were too few, and too late, to halt Gordon's advance.

When the futility of their situation became obvious, Colonel John B. Klunk ordered his Mountaineers to abandon the sheltering wall and woods and to fall back. Due to lack of experience and the nearly overwhelming, stress-induced, disorientation that many officers experienced during their first exposure to the responsibilities of command amidst death and whizzing bullets, Klunk fouled up the retreat. "We filed off the field by the left flank, and in doing so the right had to march the length of the regiment before gaining a step to the rear. It was while thus marching to the point of filing left to the rear, Lieut. Bradley, of Company I, was shot dead. We left our knapsacks in the woods, where we had unslung them. They, of course, fell into the hands of the Johnnys, who, no doubt, examined them with a good deal of interest."[72]

The Confederates poured over the wall that had only minutes before been a Union bastion. After carefully stepping over or around nearly a dozen dead or wounded Bluecoats, who littered the ground behind it, the Georgians pursued Klunk's regiment toward the Turnpike—a maneuver that drew them

---

[72]Hewitt, p. 41; Powell, pp. 8-9; O.R. 1-27-2-80, Klunk. Colonel Klunk, perhaps anticipating some censure, recorded that "...we retreated in perfect order...." Both Klunk and Milroy reported that the 12th West Virginia held their position for approximately two hours. Given the timing of subsequent events and the fact that Keifer did not report remaining disengaged for over an hour while the Mountaineers fought alone, the stated time period must have encompassed the entire time from the West Virginians' advance until their withdrawal, rather than just the amount of time they contested Gordon's main assault. Historian Hewitt estimated that his regiment maintained a steady fire for about an hour. Hewitt, p. 41.

obliquely across the front of Hays' brigade. When Gordon's boys finally cleared his front, Hays' brigade took a position on Gordon's left flank and together they shoved their combined weight against the Union line.[73]

Despite the pressure from several times their numbers, the Federals "...withdrew...in perfect order, keeping...skirmishers well to the front, [while] embracing every opportunity the ground offered to halt, and, with artillery, [to] pour a heavy fire into the enemy's ranks."[74] For over an hour the adversaries remained locked in a rolling gunfight as the thin blue line volleyed, loaded, fell back, volleyed, and fell back, all the while bracing for the sight of retaliatory billows of gun smoke and the whine of Minié balls that marked another countervolley from their pursuers. During most of the retrograde movement, Union casualties were minimized thanks to the terrain and the cover of trees and bushes. In one bloody incident, though, a fusillade ripped into the midst of the 123rd Ohio, downing a number of the Buckeyes as they rushed to cross an exposed stretch of the Valley Turnpike.[75] The fighting retreat continued until the Union forces had been pushed back to the front of the defensive perimeter from which their sortie had commenced at the beginning of the afternoon.[76]

---

[73]Early, p. 242. The fighting claimed one West Virginia officer and six enlisted men killed and 16 wounded. General Gordon acknowledged losing 75 men. Although the text implies the losses were inflicted by the Mountaineers, it is probable that the tally covered his brigade's losses for the entire day. O.R. 1-27-2-80, 491, Klunk, Gordon.

[74]O.R. 1-27-2-60, Keifer. The sharpshooters of the 110th Ohio were particularly effective because they were armed with Henry repeating rifles. O.R. 1-27-2-63, Keifer. One resident of Winchester purportedly saw 40 to 60 wounded Rebels being cared for in Kernstown the day after the fight. Grunder, p. 30.

[75]Keyes, p. 46.

[76]At about this time Milroy sent the following telegraph: "Considerable skirmishing with artillery all forenoon.... It is reported that Stuart is crossing the run at Berry's or Snicker's Ferry. I fear the attack is only a feint to cover the great raid." O.R. 1-27-2-164, Milroy.

While Elliott's men struggled to avoid being engulfed by the flood of gray washing down the Valley at them from the south, Ewell's forces poked and probed at other portions of the Federal perimeter in hopes of finding an isolated post that they could "gobble up." Like Johnson and Early, General Rodes roused his division, which had bivouacked for the night a short distance south of Millwood, and sent them marching toward Berryville while the morning mists still clung to the lowlands. Before long, Rodes became aware of the first of a string of perceived failures by his mounted arm under the command of Brigadier General Albert G. Jenkins. As his riflemen tramped through Millwood, they were discovered by a detachment of the 1st New York Cavalry, an outcome Rodes believed could have been avoided had Jenkins' troopers occupied Millwood the night before as he had ordered.[77]

A few hours later, Rodes left his toiling column and rode ahead to personally investigate the defenses around Berryville in anticipation of having to assault the Union garrison that was known to be holed up there. Upon arrival, the Rebel general found Jenkins' horsemen stalled south of town thanks to what Rodes believed was a halfhearted effort to penetrate the Yankees' outer works. Assuming that the Federals were preparing to flee, Rodes, "...determined to surround them, if possible, and ordered General Jenkins to march to the left of the town, to cut off the retreat of the enemy toward Winchester. The infantry, save one brigade, without being halted, were ordered to move to the right and left of the place, to unite in its rear." When it became apparent that at least some of the Bluecoats had already taken flight, Rodes ordered

---

[77]O.R. 1-27-2-547, Rodes.

his Alabama brigade under the command of Colonel Edward A. O'Neal to storm the Union fortifications.[78]

The Alabamian's hustled into line of battle, braced themselves for a lethal dose of bullets and canister, gave the Rebel yell, and rushed the enemy emplacements. Instead of fire and death however, "When we got to their breastworks the birds had flown. They did not take their nests with them. Their camp, with all their cooking utensils, quartermaster and commissary stores, were all left in our hands. They were evidently cooking a meal, for plenty of pots full of eatables were still on the fire when we got into their camp. We ate up all we could, and filled our haversacks...."[79]

Rodes pronounced that he was "...mortified to learn that the enemy...had left his cavalry and artillery to keep our cavalry in check, and had some time before retreated with his infantry toward Charlestown, without being discovered [by Jenkins]."[80] What was one side's embarrassment was often another side's successful operation, and such was the case at Berryville. Sometime close to 9 a.m. four simultaneous blasts from the big guns in Winchester, and the intelligence gleaned by his troopers at Millwood, compelled Colonel Andrew T. McReynolds to make immediate preparations to evacuate his Third Brigade from Berryville in favor of Winchester.[81]

First, McReynolds assembled his train of wagons with his acting quartermaster, Lieutenant William H. Boyd, Jr., designated as its commander. When collected, the train rumbled down the

---

[78]O.R. 1-27-2-547, Rodes.
[79]Ibid., 1-27-2-591, O'Neal; Leon, p. 31.
[80]Ibid., 1-27-2-547, Rodes.
[81]Stevenson, p. 184; O.R. 1-27-2-108, 109, McReynolds. One may legitimately ponder why a threat that was grave enough to justify a recall order to McReynold's brigade early Saturday morning was not similarly serious enough to prompt Milroy either to withdraw his whole division, or at least to wire a more concerned dispatch to headquarters.

road toward Bunker Hill under the protection of a company of infantry and Company H of the 1st New York Cavalry under Lieutenant Franklin G. Martindale.[82] Then he sent most of the balance of his command down the road that led to Harpers Ferry because the Berryville Pike that led directly to Winchester was already becoming clogged with Butternuts.

Finally, "I [McReynolds] remained behind with four companies of the Sixth Maryland Infantry, a section of Alexander's battery, and 150 of the First New York Cavalry. I placed the infantry across the road, and threw out the cavalry as skirmishers. We shelled the enemy vigorously, in order to give my advance column more time, and I detained their advance three-quarters of an hour, perhaps more."[83] When Rodes' Alabamians finally began to advance on the Union works, McReynolds sent his infantry scurrying north at the double quick. After a few parting cannon and carbine shots, the remaining Bluecoats were permitted to pull out as well, leaving the Johnnies with a fresh meal but no captives. When it appeared that his column was well separated from the Confederates, McReynolds galloped ahead to catch up with the larger contingent of the 1st New York Cavalry that was leading his parade, and left responsibility for the rear guard to the 150 troopers who had stayed with him in Berryville.[84]

Vexed that the mouse had evaded the pounce, Rodes directed Jenkins, by what was probably a curt and pointed order, to intercept the fleeing Bluecoats before they got to Winchester. Not being sure exactly which route the Yankees had chosen however, either Jenkins or Rodes split the Rebel cavalry into portions, with one taking the more direct route toward Winchester while the other, a battalion under Major J. W. Sweeney, pursued northward down the Charlestown Road. After the Butternut troopers were on their way, Rodes regrouped his division and

---

[82]Stevenson, p. 184; Beach, p. 231.
[83]O.R. 1-27-2-109, McReynolds.
[84]Ibid.

commenced the long tramp that he hoped would end with the capture of Martinsburg pursuant to Ewell's master plan.[85]

Near Brucetown, about two miles shy of the Opequon Creek, Major Sweeney's 350 Rebel troopers and their heavily lathered horses caught up with the hindmost troopers from New York under the command of one of the 1st's best officers, Captain William H. Boyd. Boyd's horsemen tried their best to delay the Butternuts long enough to allow a messenger to warn the main column and to make enough noise so that their comrades would know trouble was coming in case the messenger was intercepted. McReynolds received both warnings and immediately commenced preparations to beat back the Southern pursuers. A staff officer was dispatched with orders that the four companies of the 6th Maryland and the Baltimore Battery, who were at the end of the column as a result of having been with McReynolds in Berryville, should immediately deploy on the western side of the Opequon Creek. McReynolds also sent the balance of the 1st New York Cavalry rushing back toward the clatter of small arms fire.[86]

The Marylanders soon heard the pounding hooves and cracking pistol and carbine shots indicative of a mounted skirmish hurtling in their direction. Then, out of the distance "...the enemy were...approaching, uttering frightful yells, and driving Boyd's rear guard before them. Captain Alexander had posted his guns in a commanding position in the road, and as the enemy appeared in view, he burst shell after shell among them, which threw them into considerable confusion, killing and wounding quite a number of them."[87]

As Alexander's gunners began to slam shells into the Rebel formation, Major Adams arrived with about 200 troopers and ordered that "...the fences [be] thrown down along the right flank of my command [to facilitate a cavalry charge], and formed the

---

[85]O.R. 1-27-2-548, Rodes.
[86]Ibid., 1-27-2-109, 83, McReynolds, Adams.
[87]Stevenson, p. 185.

squadrons in a field on my right.... When the rebels approached within easy carbine distance, I opened upon them, emptying many of their saddles, and, for the moment, confused and checked their charge upon us." Seeking to capitalize on the momentary confusion in the Confederate ranks, Adams ordered a charge across the river. However, to his extreme disappointment (or good fortune) he discovered, before colliding with the enemy, that a significant portion of his regiment remained standing and gawking on the other side of the creek. Adams reined his horse to a short stop, wheeled, and led his followers, and then the others, back behind a ridge on the western side of the creek to regroup.[88]

Enticed by the apparent retreat of the New Yorkers, Sweeney sent his howling and splashing horsemen headlong across the Opequon. "As the...[Confederate] column appeared around the bend in the road, I [Adams] again ordered the charge, which was promptly obeyed."[89] "...[O]ur regiment [the 1st New York]...burst upon them with the sabre, cutting and thrusting right and left. Not a shot was fired by our boys; but their flashing steel could be plainly seen from the hill, where the colonel commanding [McReynolds] and his staff stood with the infantry in line of battle, and the shouts of the combatants could be distinctly heard as each party strove desperately to drive the other back."[90] In the midst of the mayhem, "...One stalwart [New York] German meeting an antagonist face to face, brought down his sabre with such

---

[88]O.R. 1-27-2-83, Adams. Adams asserted that the actions of Captain Lambert J. Simons, who commanded the reluctant squadron, and Lieutenant Frank Passegger whose Company L also failed to charge, were criminal. Anti-Adams historian Beach wrote that the 1st New York hesitated to follow Adams because the "...officers and men had very little confidence in him...his effusive and pompous manner and his much talking did not indicate judgment and discretion. He was more apt to think of gaining some credit for himself than of gaining success with the least loss among his men. Beach, p. 233.

[89]Ibid., 1-27-2-83, Adams.

[90]Stevenson, p. 185.

tremendous force that he cleaved his foeman from the neck almost to his sabre belt, muttering, as he withdrew his weapon, 'Gott fur damn!'"[91]

After he watched the contending horsemen pull back to their respective sides of the creek, Captain Alexander concluded that his artillery was superfluous and began to limber up and pull away from the riverbank, leaving only one gun to guard the crossing. Encouraged by the sudden disappearance of most of the Federal battery, the plucky Rebels, who had managed to regroup on the east bank, launched another assault across the ford. In midstream several of the leading Johnnies and their horses were shredded by a blast of canister. Undaunted by the gore that splattered onto their faces, the survivors closed ranks and charged ahead, churning crimson-tinted water into pink froth. As they began to splash ashore on the Federal side, another swarm of canister scythed through their ranks.

In short order the several hundred riflemen of the 6th Maryland, who had been patiently waiting along the bank, slammed a volley into the accelerating Rebel horsemen. "This staggered the enemy, but some of them succeed[ed] in reaching the rearmost gun; and a regular melee ensued between the rebel horsemen and our gunner[s], in which several of the enemy were killed. This did not last long, as a second volley from the infantry sent the enemy flying to the rear, hotly pursued by our regiment [the 1st New York Cavalry], which drove them clear out of sight and hearing, capturing a number of prisoners."[92] With "...thirty men killed, including two captains...fifty wounded and captured,

---

[91]Beach, pp. 234-235. The 1st New York Cavalry had a large contingent of ethnic and immigrant Germans, a fact that led to dissension and a riot during the first months of the regiment's existence.

[92]Stevenson, p. 186.

including a colonel and a major...," and the fight thoroughly beaten out of them, the Southerners abandoned their pursuit.[93]

Curiously, the defense of the ford, which should have justified some hearty chest thumping by the Empire State troopers, became instead a vehicle for the anti-Adams faction in the regiment to vent its displeasure over his performance, and perhaps to express bitterness over his success. The New Yorkers had hardly wiped and resheathed their sabers when Timothy Quinn, a junior major, "...evincing unmistakable signs of jealousy and envy, remarked that it was the opinion of most of the officers that I [Major Adams], had sacrificed my men by risking a battle at that place; that they were dissatisfied, and wanted him to take command, and that I should have fallen back upon the main column and upon batteries for protection, &c. I told him that I would permit no such remarks in presence of the officers and men; that it was well calculated to excite mutiny with officers and men."[94] Much to Adams' chagrin, within a short time one of the rebellious officers returned with orders, ostensibly from brigade commander McReynolds, to place Adams under arrest. Late that night, word finally reached Winchester that one of his division's officers had been arrested for *attacking* the enemy. An undoubtedly incensed Milroy fired off a personal order, probably to the accompaniment of an oath or two, countermanding the arrest and freeing Adams.[95]

-----

[93]Stevenson, p. 186. Adams' official tally was more conservative, claiming that his men killed 20 Confederates and wounded twice that number while suffering only two killed and 10 wounded. Major Sweeney was badly wounded while fighting at the head of his troopers. O.R. 1-27-2-83, 548, Adams & Rodes.

[94]O.R. 1-27-2-84, Adams.

[95]Ibid.

McReynolds' warriors made the rest of the journey to Winchester unmolested, but trouble, and approximately 1,200 gray-coated cavalry, stalked the Third Brigade's wagon train, which had departed Berryville first and followed a different route in hopes that it could escape to the north.[96] Traveling with as much speed as the swearing teamsters could wring from their exhausted animals, the train lurched and jolted toward a ford over the Opequon just to the east of Bunker Hill. At the ford, all was peaceful until the train arrived, followed shortly thereafter by Jenkins' Confederate cavalry. The wagons were hustled across the creek and on to Carlisle, Pennsylvania, in good order.[97] The four Union rifle companies which remained to guard the ford, G and H from the 87th Pennsylvania and two from the 116th Ohio, about 300 men in all, were not so fortunate.[98]

The commander of the detachment, Major W. T. Morris of the 116th Ohio, quickly drew his men into a line of battle with skirmishers in front, in order to meet the impending Rebel onslaught. In response, a contingent of Rebel horsemen dis-mounted and advanced in their own skirmish line, precipitating a 20-minute duel between sharpshooters.[99] Dissatisfied with the rate of progress, Jenkins ordered the balance of his command to assail the Union line on horseback. The blue-coated foot soldiers stood their ground against at least one mounted charge but in the process paid a fearful price, losing nearly half their contingent in killed, wounded, or captured.[100] When the weight of the

---

[96]The Confederate force was the bulk of the cavalry brigade that had originally been sent on the more direct route toward Winchester, but which somehow managed to pass McReynolds' column and pick up the trail of his wagon train. Nye, p. 87.

[97]At least according to one of the historians for the 1st New York Cavalry, the train guard was forced to fend off Jenkins' cavalry near the ford. In the process a carriage with the wife, son, and daughter of Captain William H. Boyd, overturned and all three were captured by the Confederates.

[98]Prowell, p. 67.

[99]Ibid., p. 68.

[100]Wildes, pp. 55-56.

Confederates' numerical advantage could no longer be resisted, Morris ordered his riflemen to fall back to the sheltering cluster of three brick churches on the edge of Bunker Hill.[101] Backing and fighting, the harried Federals traded fire as "...the enemy made an effort to cut them off from it, but they fought their way into it [one of the churches] bravely, and using loop-holes which they had previously made for their rifles, soon drove the enemy beyond their reach."[102]

The trailing Yankee company was led by Ohio Lieutenant A. B. Frame, who had just received command moments earlier after his captain was shot down. "Under the most galling fire, he [Frame] covered the retreat to the church, keeping his men in hand as well and as coolly as on a parade ground. More than half of his company were made prisoners, by being cut off from the church, and from reaching him from the skirmish line."[103]

"About this time John Lemon, a citizen of Bunker Hill, was sent to them by a Confederate officer with a flag of truce, asking them to surrender."[104] With the curt response "'[w]e are not doing that kind of business...,'" the offer was declined, and the small brick church instantly became double-wreathed with the gun smoke and muzzle flashes from both attackers and defenders.[105] The chapel quickly filled with a choking haze of acrid and sulfurous smoke as well as the deafening roar from dozens of rifles being fired from every window and loophole. It is doubtful that the tearing and squinting Federals were able to hit much, but because they probably spent little time exposed to view, the defenders suffered no additional casualties while barricaded in their sanctuary. Much to their frustration, the surrounding Confederate troopers had the numbers to push the Federals into the church but

---

[101]Prowell, pp. 68-69.
[102]Wildes, pp. 55-56.
[103]Ibid.
[104]Prowell, pp. 68-69.
[105]O.R. 1-27-2-67, Washburn.

lacked the artillery to blast them back out. As a result, the two sides traded bullets, and probably insults, until late in the evening, when darkness, lack of ammunition, and fatigue ended the hostilities. Around 2 a.m. the next morning, after it became apparent that the Butternuts had departed, the Union survivors crept off to Winchester, where they bedded down for the night near the Star Fort.[106]

Like the narrow escapes of the Third Brigade and the detachment at Bunker Hill, it was a close question whether Elliott's troops on the southwestern flank would be able to reach the shelter of Abraham's Creek before being cut off and destroyed. The last bastion between the onrushing Confederates and the shelter of the creek was a three-sided stone farm fence that over-looked the Turnpike. Blue-coated riflemen were crammed into the impromptu fort, but at 5 p.m. the Rebels flanked and then over-ran it.[107] When that last road-block was engulfed by a torrent of gray and butternut, the Yankees fell back to within about 600 yards of the haven beckoning from behind Abraham's Creek and the adjacent millrace. Right behind them, two gray battle lines, inflamed with the scent of victory and straining to deny them that sanctuary, descended upon the Federal right flank.[108]

"[A] large body of rebel infantry [came] in view of the four guns I [Captain John Carlin, Battery D, First West Virginia Artillery (U.S.A.)] had on the range of hills [Bowers Hill]. The

---

[106]Prowell, pp. 68-69; O.R. 1-27-2-67, Washburn. Company H of the 87th Pennsylvania was reported to have lost 20 members during the action. Crowl Letter, 6/16/1863.

[107]O.R. 1-27-2-45, Milroy.

[108]Ibid., 1-27-2-44, 45, Milroy.

enemy was in a dense wood adjacent, and marched forward through an open field some three-quarters of a mile distant. I withheld the fire of my guns until they were within about 800 yards, when I opened on them with the four pieces. That column succeeded in getting some of the men to the stone wall adjacent. Immediately another column was formed in the same dense woods adjacent, and marched in the same direction. Having the range of the ground, I opened fire upon them at 1,200 yards distance. The fire was so destructive, and kept up with such energy, that they were prevented from gaining a position."[109]

The same action was described in more florid terms by David Powell of the 12th West Virginia. "The enemy [Rebels] in their haste and wild pursuit filled the pike with masses of men and right in front of them behind a hedge fence in the old cemetery, ...lay Captain Carland's [Carlin's] battery, stoutly shotted with grape and canister. Like crouching bulldogs they were waiting their chance to hurl death and destruction upon the too exultant enemy. The word 'fire' was given and crushing and crushing and crushing went grape and canister through masses of men. The cry of 'Oh, Lord!, Oh Lord!, Oh, Lord!' came loud and plaintive, full one-fourth of a mile away."[110]

General Elliott seized the opportunity offered by the stunned and bloodied Gray ranks to launch the 123rd Ohio and at

[109]O.R. 1-27-2-105, 106, Carlin. Both Milroy and his aide-de-camp recorded in their after-action reports that Carlin's battery was stationed on what was referred to as "Milltown Heights," probably the southernmost portion of Bower's Hill. O.R. 1-27-2-44, 45, 54, 58, Milroy, Palmer, Elliott.

[110]Powell, Memoirs, p. 8. At least one participant indirectly indicated that this phase of the action occurred as Gordon's troops were attempting to storm the bridge at the Union Mills over which the Union artillery had just made its escape. Keifer, vol. 2, pp. 8-9. The distances provided by Captain Carlin in his testimony quoted above at the court of inquiry raise a question about whether the Rebel advance was broken with canister or shells.

least two companies of the 12th West Virginia in a sudden counter-attack.[111]   The Buckeyes smashed into Gordon's line and knocked the Georgians back on their heels, while the Mountaineers overran, and briefly held, the farm fence fort that had just been captured by the Confederates a short time earlier.[112]   The counterattack blunted the Southern onslaught long enough to allow most of the Union brigade time to cross the creek.[113]

The Federal defensive perimeter was further consolidated when a contingent from the 87th Pennsylvania was dispatched by Milroy, who had apparently assumed personal command of the action, to drive some Rebel snipers out of one of the mills. In short order the soldiers from York County, Pennsylvania, assaulted the position and sent the Johnnies fleeing in wild confusion.[114] When the men of the 123rd Ohio and the 12th West Virginia finally splashed across the creek and rejoined their comrades, the Federals presented a solid line of battle snugly positioned behind daunting natural defenses.

Two grizzled old veterans from Early's division described what was probably either an attempt by the Yankee cavalry to assist the counterattack or an effort to distract the enemy so that the Northern infantrymen would not be caught while in the

---

[111]Elliott reported the counterattack was carried out by the 123rd Ohio but Milroy attributed the assault to both the 123rd and the 110th Ohio. Colonel Keifer, commander of the 110th, who was not shy about claiming credit for his unit, did not mention participation in the action, so it is assumed that only the 123rd, and a few of the mountaineers, participated. O.R. 1-27-2-45, 57, 60.

[112]O.R. 1-27-2-45, Milroy.

[113]The 123rd Ohio's historian reported that his regiment lost 76 men killed or wounded on June 13, while Captain W. H. Bruder put their casualties at 50. Keyes, p. 46; Bruder, Memoirs, p. 2.

[114]Prowell, p. 71.

Elliott's Counterattack
June 13, 1863

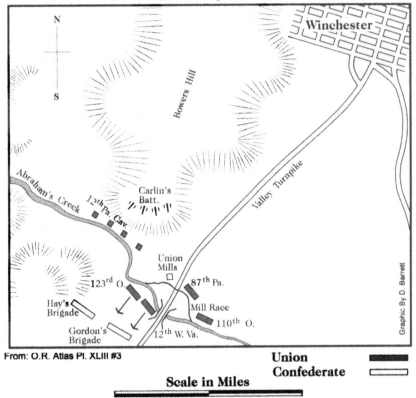

Winchester

Bowers Hill

Abraham's Creek

Carlin's Batt.

12th Pa. Cav.

Valley Turnpike

Union Mills

123rd O.

87th Pa.

Hay's Brigade

Mill Race

110th O.

Gordon's Brigade

12th W. Va.

N

S

Graphic By D. Barrett

From: O.R. Atlas Pl. XLIII #3

Union
Confederate

Scale in Miles

0   1/3   2/3

vulnerable process of wading across the creek.[115] "...[W]hile we [Early's division] lay here in the open field under the bursting shells from the fort, we saw one of the most splendid spectacles I have ever seen. The sally port toward us was open and out of it rode squadron after squadron of well-mounted cavalry, with their shining swords drawn and other equipment reflecting the bright sunshine. They formed so as to occupy the entire width of the pike...."[116]

"After waiting some time we [the 9th Louisiana Infantry of Hays' brigade] heard their horses. Then the Captain came to each of us and said: 'Now, boys, don't shoot until you hear the report of my pistol; then each man be sure he strips a saddle.' The Pike road did not come square across this rock fence, but came in an angle, so that when they came in sight of us on the right, they were not in front of those on the left; that was why the Captain gave us the orders he did. Well, it took the Yankees some time to get ready to come, but after awhile here they come—clatter! clatter! down the pike road."[117] "The rattle of their steel scabbards, the clanking of their spurs, and the noise of the iron shoes of their horses as they struck the hard surface of the pike were awe-inspiring, but doomed to result in an ignominious failure...."[118] "I [Private Thomas B. Reed] was on the extreme right and the Captain was on the left, and I began to think that he was going to let them go by altogether; but finally, I heard his pistol. Then such a roar of muskets, the like of which you never did hear, and then such a stampede of cavalry. We did strip

---

[115]Neither the Hussars' Lieutenant Colonel Moss in his official report, nor any of the numerous postwar sources from the 13th Pennsylvania Cavalry mentioned this clash, and the 1st New York Cavalry was still fighting its way back to Winchester. Therefore, it appears that troopers from West Virginia performed the mission.

[116]Brachwell, p. 331.

[117]Reed, p. 35.

[118]Brachwell, p. 331.

several saddles...but a few of them returned the fire with good effect, for they wounded Captain Montgomery S. Harrison and M. McGowin."[119]

The rout of the Union cavalry probably rekindled Old Jubal's fighting spirit. But despite his hostile inclinations, Early's efforts to quickly regroup his exhausted and disorganized troops for another push were thwarted by the continuous pounding being administered to his battle line from the Federal artillery that maintained a steady drumbeat from Bower's Hill and the Main Fort. The frustrated Confederate commander ultimately managed little more than to press his skirmish line up against the Union perimeter, and to pace his line to the accompaniment of the staccato popping from dueling marksmen and the shriek from incoming Federal ballistics.[120]

As the last of the sharpshooting dwindled out in the twilight, a Confederate prisoner, who had been captured by the 12th West Virginia when it briefly reclaimed the makeshift stone-walled fort beside the Pike, was brought before Milroy for interrogation.[121] Whatever else the Johnny may have divulged, he allowed that he was a member of Hays' Louisiana brigade of Ewell's division, and threw in the lie that some of Major General James Longstreet's corps were in the vicinity as well. Incredibly, despite having spent the entire day watching his forces being beaten back virtually into the streets of Winchester, Milroy maintained in his after-action report that "...This was the first intimation that I received that Lee's army had quietly retired before the lines of the Army of the Potomac, and performed a five

---

[119]Reed, pp. 35-36. If the troopers were Mountaineers, their losses were slight. The combined total casualties for all West Virginia cavalry at Winchester was only two wounded. O.R. 1-27-2-53.

[120]O.R. 1-27-2-45, Milroy.

[121]Ibid.

or six days' march. The Blue Ridge screened the operations of Lee's army from me."[122]

At 9 p.m. the Union commander attempted to send another telegraph which showed that he may have obtained additional information but that either he had still not gotten the message or that his pride prevented him accepting and divulging the reality of his situation. "Have been skirmishing; occasionally pretty severe.... We captured some prisoners of a Louisiana brigade, who say they belong to Ewell's...corps, and that this corps is all in front [of] us; also Jenkins and Imboden. McReynolds will soon be here...[but] he is closely pursued and hard pressed by a heavy body of cavalry. I can hold this place for five days if you can relieve me in that time. They will surround me, but can't take my fortifications."[123]

Apparently still in denial, Milroy began to redeploy his forces in an attempt to put some substance behind his boasting. Various Federal regiments, and even companies, were shifted from place to place as Milroy sought figuratively to rearrange the chairs on the deck of the *Titanic*. Convinced that the Confederates would not subject their own civilians to the perils of a house-to-house fight through the town, Milroy maintained only a scratch force, comprised mostly of men from the 18th Connecticut, in the rifle

---

[122]O.R. 1-27-2-45, Milroy.

[123]Ibid., 1-27-2-182. Several days after Winchester had fallen the *Richmond Dispatch* reported that at this point in the action Ewell offered Milroy the opportunity to surrender. Supposedly, "The officer commanding [Milroy] replied that he would abide the issue of battle, and if attacked would burn the town. Gen. Ewell answered, if any house was burned, other than those fired by the bombardment, the black flag would be hoisted and no quarter given." *Philadelphia Inquirer*, 6/24/1863. Corporal John Service of the 18th Connecticut included among his recollections that Milroy provided the following written retort to demands for his surrender, "Go to ____. Come and take us." Service failed to include how he gained the information. Service Memoirs. Mrs. Lee, a pro-Southern resident of Winchester, reported in her diary that "...Milroy says if our [Confederate] Infantry enter town he will shell it." Lee diary, 6/14/1863.

pits on the east side of Winchester.[124]   McReynold's brigade, which rejoined the division at approximately 9:30 p.m., was posted near the Star Fort, while Elliott's men were withdrawn from the banks of Abraham's Creek almost into the southern suburbs of the town.[125]

The redeployment, and some terrible weather, made it a long night for the men in blue.   The 12th Pennsylvania Cavalry "...was ordered back near to Winchester; there remained in line with the Thirteenth [Pennsylvania Cavalry] during a heavy thunder-storm until about 12 o'clock, when we were ordered to camp, which was located on the Martinsburg road about one mile from town, and to remove everything out of camp, excepting tents, to the west side of the fortification, and for the regiment to locate on the Pughtown road, about one mile west of the main fortification."[126]   On the other side of town the Connecticut boys stood all night in trenches filled with several inches of mud with "...water streaming down their backs to their feet...."[127]

Perhaps there was something about squatting or standing in a puddle under a rubberized blanket in a torrent of rain, after spending the day retreating from an overwhelming number of men with guns, that imparted a grasp of reality unavailable to generals in their tents.   Although Milroy still was not willing to accept the peril of his division's situation, the men in the ranks certainly did.[128]   The thunderstorm, which drenched both sides equally,

---

[124]Walker, p. 108.   Mrs. Hugh Lee, the diarist who lived in Winchester throughout the war, repeatedly maintained that Milroy had threatened to shell the town if it was occupied by Rebels, and these threats were undoubtedly known to General Ewell. Lee diary, 6/13, 14/1863.

[125]O.R. 1-27-2-46, Milroy.

[126]Ibid., 1-2-7-2-70, Titus.

[127]Walker, p. 108.

[128]Although Milroy would maintain as part of his defense that he was compelled to remain at Winchester pursuant to his last order to hold until told to withdraw, he certainly understood that the military practice of the time, where communications were slow and unreliable, allowed a field commander discretion to disregard out-

dampened only the confidence of the Yankees as they waited for morning and the opening of "business."[129]

   For the Federals forced to spend the night out on the picket line, the wait was even worse. "I [Captain W. H. Bruder, 123rd Ohio] was ordered by the officer of the day to hold the picket line [on the southern line of defense] during the night and the regt.s. all returned to the fort leaving me with sixty men in possession of the picket line with a heavy body of Rebels in the front of us.... During the night it stormed and rained very hard and became very dark which made our situation still more terrible. There we stood during the night at our posts of duty as soldiers only know how to stand, the rain falling in torrents which wet our clothes through in fifteen minutes, not leaving a spot under the apple tree for those that were not on the sentinel post to sit down, but they had to remain standing the whole night. About 12 o'clock in the night while I was visiting the sentinels I discovered some of the enemy within three rods [forty eight feet] of our sentinel posts, there being only a small stream of water intervening between us.... You may imagine my feelings—anything but pleasant for I expected to be surrounded during the night and have my men and myself gobbled up as soon as it became light."[130] Captain Bruder and his pickets may have been physically alone but emotionally, they had about 9,000 blue-coated companions.

---

dated orders that had become obsolete due to changing circumstances. He must also have known that under the circumstances (especially given Halleck's views) that it would have been extremely unlikely that he would receive any censure if he pulled his division out of Winchester on the night of the June 13, given the days developments. Further, Milroy had never shown himself to be blindly obedient to orders with which he did not agree.

[129]Keyes, p. 44.

[130]Bruder, Memoirs, pp. 1-4.

6

WEST FORT

Major General Schenck:
   Force at Bunker Hill arrived this morning at 6 o'clock. I was sharply engaged with the enemy on last evening; prospect of a general engagement, but will hold this place in spite of fate.

—Robert H. Milroy[1]

The first rays of sunlight that crested the Blue Ridge on Sunday, June 14, 1863, illuminated both Blue and Butternut forces making preparations to have at each other as soon as there was enough light to aim a musket. In the palest light of dawn, Milroy dispatched troopers to scout the Berryville and Martinsburg Roads to the east and northeast. Both details were quickly beaten back by Confederate sharpshooters. On the southwestern side of Winchester, Old Jubal began his day with a predawn survey of his line, which stretched from the west of Bower's Hill to just over the Valley Turnpike and was manned by Brigadier General William Smith's three regiment brigade of Virginians on the left,

---

[1]O.R. 1-27-2-166. The dispatch was allegedly sent by courier at 10 p.m. on Saturday, June 13, but the date and time provided in the *Official Records* must have been incorrect since the message referred to the arrival of the Bunker Hill survivors at 6 a.m. on June 14.

Hays' Louisiana Tigers in the center, and Gordon's Georgians on the right.[2]

When it became light enough to reveal that the Yankees had contracted their line and virtually abandoned Bower's Hill, Early ordered Hays and Gordon to send one regiment apiece to occupy it.[3] In order to avoid the sharp tongue and salty language of the Bad Old Man, the 9th Louisiana under Colonel D. H. Penn and an unidentified Georgia regiment hustled to form a battle line and then advanced up the side of the hill until they encountered a Union skirmish line strung out through the woods. The blue-coated skirmishers, who managed only a smattering of rifle fire, intended more to cover their retreat than slow the Confederate advance, fell back until the Butternuts decided that possession of the majority of the hill was sufficient.[4]

It was probably Captain Bruder's soggy and bedraggled riflemen from the 123rd Ohio who halfheartedly opposed the Butternut advance up and over Bower's Hill. "As soon as it became daylight we discovered a number of the enemy in a piece of woods about 80 or 90 rods [1,300 to 1,400 feet] to our front. We immediately commenced firing on them & they without waiting for any further ceremony returned the compliment. We continued skirmishing until 10 a.m. when the enemy made an advance on the left of our line in order to flank the pickets to the left of our position. I immediately sent orders for them to fall back. We took a position about 40 rods to the rear of picket line when the rebels made a rush across an open meadow intervening between us with about four times our number. We gave them one volley & still continued to fall back until we reached our camp which we found deserted, our Regt. having packed up everything

---

[2]Hoke's brigade, Early's fourth, spent the night guarding the trains in Kernstown. O.R. 1-27-2-461, Early.

[3]O.R. 1-27-2-461, Early.

[4]Ibid., 1-27-2-477, Hays.

in the wagons the night previous except the tents & moved them over to the forts...."[5]

Most likely in response to the Confederate advance up Bower's Hill, the 12th West Virginia was dispatched to occupy a long stone fence that was located between the Valley Turnpike and the Romney Road, about a mile southwest of town and just beyond the western slope of Bower's Hill.[6] After cautiously settling in behind the wall, the Mountaineers were treated to the spectacle of some Union cannoneers abusing the left flank of Early's division. "In front of this battery off to the southwest the Johnnys were behind a stone wall. Our artillery did some very accurate shooting, knocking several holes in the wall behind which the Johnnys were, causing them, when the wall was struck, to scatter in a lively manner, and thus affording for the time being, at least, great sport for our boys, though they were quite worn out from want of sleep, having had little or none the night before." The sport turned deadly though, when a sniper shot and mortally wounded Lieutenant Ben Gough of Company F from a distance of 900 yards, as he lay stretched out on the ground trying to make up for the sleep that he lost the previous night. When it became apparent that the Confederates had a firm grasp on the high ground on their left flank, the bulk of the West Virginia regiment pulled back closer to the forts, leaving their stone fence in the possession of a very nervous skirmish line.[7]

The available sources do not provide conclusive evidence concerning whether or not Early's division eventually managed to capture all of Bower's Hill. Jedediah Hotchkiss, the credible map maker for the Army of Northern Virginia, indicated on the map

---

[5]Bruder memoirs, pp. 4-6.

[6]Hewitt, p. 42.

[7]O.R. 1-27-2-80, Klunk. Klunk also reported that Gough expired that night at the Taylor Hotel. Historian Hewitt recalled Gough's passing differently, writing that the unfortunate lieutenant died when he was struck by some return artillery fire as he lay sound asleep. Hewitt, p. 43.

that he drew to accompany Ewell's after-action report that the Confederates occupied only the southern half of the hill.[8] Milroy described the location of some of Elliott's troops as "...about a quarter of a mile south of the Romney road...," which placed them somewhere on the hill. Union Colonel William H. Ball of the 122nd Ohio claimed that his Companies A, D, and E under Lieutenant Colonel Granger occupied the "crest" of the hill until noon and that Companies I, K, and B retained the position thereafter.[9] Finally, Early vaguely asserted that his men "...had advanced to Bower's Hill...," which supports the reasonable interpretation, based upon Early's consistent refusal to write anything positive about his adversaries, that the Federals managed to hold on to at least a portion of the hill.[10] Whatever the exact location of the contending lines, blue and gray sharpshooters arrayed somewhere north of the hill's crest continued to pop away at each other until late in the afternoon.

The sporadic rifle fire that punctuated the woods and fields on Bower's Hill quickly spread to the south and east sides of town. The 18th Connecticut, under the temporary command of Major Henry Peale, was rushed from its bivouac outside the Star Fort and ordered to guard the removal of some unprotected quartermaster's stores—an assignment that required that they repulse several small Rebel sorties that pushed into the outskirts of town.[11] About the same time that the Connecticut boys finally managed to establish control over the streets in their sector, some of the Georgians in Gordon's brigade, who were strung out behind a wall of their own about 200 yards south of Winchester near the Turnpike, began to trade potshots with Yankee pickets.

Emboldened by newly arrived reinforcements from the Maryland Line, and itching to be the first Confederates to liberate

---

[8]O.R. *Atlas*, plate 43, #3.
[9]Ibid., 1-27-2-67, 68, Ball.
[10]Ibid., 1-27-2-45, Milroy; Early, p. 243.
[11]Ibid., 1-27-2-76, Peale.

a portion of Winchester, some of Gordon's men launched an impromptu miniassault that quickly carried them onto Loudoun Street. As the Butternuts sprinted from house to house on their way toward the center of town, they encountered a small gang of adolescent boys. The youngsters, whose heads were filled with dreams of glory and whose relatives were probably toting rifles in the Stonewall Brigade, began to tag along and offer warnings about the location of Union snipers, and suggestions about shortcuts and hidden passageways that could be used to ferret them out.[12]

Despite the help from the boys, and encouragements shouted through open windows by impassioned Rebelettes such as "Go to it gray coats, kill the nasty rascals...," the unsupported incursion proved to be short-lived.[13] As soon as word of the attack reached Milroy, he rushed the 87th Pennsylvania to the scene with orders to repulse the invaders. When the Pennsylvanians collided with the Johnnies, a nasty door-to-door tussle quickly erupted. Although trained to fight in a line with a comrade on either shoulder, the Federals rapidly adapted to street fighting, which required sprinting, hopefully some distance ahead of whizzing bullets, for a building corner or fence row from where a newly exposed enemy rifleman could be gunned down before he could retreat to a better protected position of his own.

Probably the unexpected appearance of one such quick-triggered Yankee rifleman from around a street corner tragically aborted the family reunion of a Johnnie who momentarily forgot the unwritten rules of the engagement. "...[W]hile they were fighting considerable in the streets a Rebel left the ranks and ran into the house to see his wife. She met him at the door and while

---

[12]Residents of both Winchester and Frederick County, Virginia, also had a substantial presence in the 13th and 33rd Virginia Infantry regiments and the 1st, 11th, 12th, 18th, 23rd, and 39th Virginia Cavalry regiments as well as a smattering in dozens of other Confederate regiments. Delauter, pp. 53, 120-130.

[13]As quoted in Delauter, p. 53.

her arms were around him he was shot down by a Pennsylvanian. She had not much satisfaction in meeting him...."[14]

The Confederates were swept out of town in short order but mopping up almost cost several of the Pennsylvanians their lives. "...Charles E. Zimmerman, B. F. Frick, Lewis Frey and Alfred Jamison, of Company A, were ordered to search a house on one of the main streets, for a sharpshooter supposed to be in it. They entered the basement and passed up to the landing of the second stairs, when a volley from the enemy, a distance away, came in the windows. One of the balls grazed the left temple of Zimmerman, making a scar several inches in length, and cut off two-thirds of his hat rim. Another ball pierced the arm of Jamison, causing a painful flesh wound."[15]

Another York Countian in the 87th Pennsylvania, Johnson H. Skelley, probably dodged a few Rebel bullets sent his way as his regiment was shoving the Butternuts out of Winchester, but he would not be so fortunate the next morning.[16] The poor Bluecoat suffered until he finally expired from his wound on July 12. It was the poignant circumstances that surrounded his death, rather than the agony he endured, that made his passing noteworthy. Skelley (or Shelley) was engaged to Mary Virginia (Jennie) Wade, a 20-year-old woman who resided in Gettysburg. Perhaps it was

---

[14]Hartley letter, 6/26/1863. This anecdote may have been apocryphal since the attackers were from Georgia and Maryland and the reporter was a member of the 123rd Ohio rather than the 87th Pennsylvania. However, given the proximity of Winchester to Maryland, the unfortunate Johnny may have either been a resident of Winchester who for some reason found it expedient to join one of the Confederate Maryland regiments, or perhaps his wife moved from Maryland to a more congenial location in Winchester after her husband chose to fight for the Confederacy.

[15]Prowell, p. 86.

[16]Ibid., pp. 84-85. The roster which Prowell provided with his regimental history listed the soldier's last name as Shelly. In the Bates roster for the 87th Pennsylvania, Skelley was listed as having been mortally wounded on June 15 at Carter's Woods.

thoughts of her absent lover, whose picture she kept nestled in her apron pocket, that compelled the courageous and compassionate girl to stand over her oven baking fresh bread for other Union soldiers while the battle of Gettysburg raged outside her house on July 3. As she toiled in the summer heat, a stray bullet passed through the front door and struck her in the back, killing her within minutes.[17] The only consolation in the tragedy was that neither lover ever learned of the other's fate.[18]

At approximately 9 a.m., after at least the heights of Bower's Hill had been seized by the Confederates, and while brief firefights were flaring and subsiding on the southern and eastern fringes of Winchester, "General Ewell came up...and together we [Early and Ewell] proceeded to reconnoitre from that point [Bower's Hill], from which we had a very distinct view of the works about Winchester."[19] The two generals soon discovered an unexpected impediment to an assault on the Union fortifications. In addition to the anticipated line of emplacements and rifle pits that ran from Bower's Hill northward along Apple Pie Ridge to the Star Fort, Ewell and Early observed that a small hill west of the main line, about halfway between Apple Pie Ridge and Little North Mountain, had also been fortified and occupied by Yankee infantry and artillery.[20]

---

[17]Wade was the only civilian killed during the battle of Gettysburg. Pfanz, *Gettysburg: Culp's Hill...*, pp. 329, 358.

[18]According to the historian for the 87th Pennsylvania, the Gettysburg G.A.R. Post was named after Skelley even though he was not at the battle fought there. Prowell, pp. 84-85.

[19]Early, p. 243; O.R. 1-27-2-440, Ewell.

[20]Little North Mountain was approximately three-quarters of a mile from that forward redoubt and about one and one-half miles from the Main and Star Forts. There is some disagreement whether Early incorrectly identified his intended staging area as Little North Mountain. The map drawn by Milroy's engineer after the battle (it shows troop movements but the underlying topography may have been drawn during the occupation) shows Early's destination to have been an unnamed ridge between Little North Mountain and the West Fort. This designation is supported in at least one text. See O.R. *Atlas*, plate 39, #4, and Nye, p. 98. On

Shortly after the Confederate brass discovered the little emplacement (hereafter referred to as the West Fort) that blocked the approach to the Main and Star Forts, Union general Elliott came to the conclusion that if the fort was to be held, more rifles would be required. Orders were immediately issued to Colonel Keifer dispatching his 110th Ohio to join the company from the 116th Ohio under Captain Frederick H. Arckenoe, and Battery L, 5th United States Artillery commanded by Lieutenant Wallace F. Randolph, who already manned it. Keifer was not pleased with his new assignment. "...[T]he earthwork [was] of slight strength about three-fourths of a mile from the main fort, ...[and was] fully commanded by Round Mountain [Little North Mountain] to the west."[21]

Another of Milroy's artillery officers recognized the hazards inherent in the position and confirmed Keifer's assessment: "The position was not a very good one. Only a portion of the timber in front of the work was cut away, and the enemy could come very near without being seen. The timber in some places was only 50 yards off...[t]he work had been commenced a few days before, and was incomplete." Not only was the little redoubt vulnerable to surprise attack, but getting reinforcements in, or getting everyone out, would be difficult "...on account of the hill, which was very steep, and, to get out on the Pughtown road, we would have to pass through a little lane, and ravines were in the way...."[22]

Probably for the same reason that Colonel Keifer was leery about defending the place, Major General Ewell concluded that it

---

the other hand, Jedediah Hotchkiss, the Confederates' pre-eminent cartographer and a Valley resident, labeled Early's destination as Little North Mountain, which this writer accepts as dispositive. O.R. *Atlas*, plate 43, #3. In either case, the intended Confederate staging area should not be confused with North Mountain which was more than six miles to the west of Winchester.

[21]O.R. 1-27-2-58, Elliott; O.R. 1-27-2-60, Keifer.
[22]Ibid., 1-27-2-146, Spooner.

was essential "...to take that hill, which was the key to the position, by assault, and having discovered a ridge back of it [referred to variously as Little North Mountain, Flint Ridge, or Round Mountain] from which it might be attacked, I [Early] was ordered to leave a brigade and some artillery, where I then was [Bower's Hill] to amuse the enemy in front, while I moved the rest of my command around by the left to the point from which I could make the assault, taking care to conduct my movement with secrecy so that the enemy would not discover it."[23]

Sometime after giving Early orders to prepare to storm the West Fort, Ewell sent directions to General Johnson to make the necessary dispositions, so that his division could generate a diversion that would both mask Early's movements and freeze as many Bluecoats as possible on the opposite side of town.[24] "For this purpose, the Stonewall Brigade...was moved across the Millwood pike to a range of hills east of and fronting the town and between the Millwood and Berryville pikes. Steuart's brigade was posted in rear and within supporting distance of Walker. The Fifth Virginia Regiment, Lieut. Col. H. J. Williams commanding, was thrown forward as skirmishers, encountering the enemy on the crest of the hills...driving them to the edge of the town, from which position, sheltered by houses and fences, they kept up a brisk and continual fire upon our line, which occupied the stone fence at the western base of the hills and within easy musket-range."[25]

---

[23]Early, pp. 243-244.
[24]O.R. 1-27-2-440, Ewell.
[25]Ibid., 1-27-2-500, Johnson.

That innocuous sounding "...brisk fire..." between the 5th Virginia and the 18th Connecticut actually developed into a nerve-wracking, and often deadly, contest between keen-eyed snipers who dueled with each other while occasionally harvesting a careless soldier who raised his head too high or moved too slowly.[26] The baking sun, the all-too-frequent thumping sound of another bullet tearing through flesh, and the incessant screams and groans of wounded and dying comrades made Peale's Blue-coats irritable and aggressive. Around 4 p.m., when the sun was hottest and nerves were twisted nearly to the breaking point, the Yankees began to focus their growing rage on "...a large brick house within rifle distance, immediately in front of company H, which had been taken possession of by the rebel sharp-shooters, who greatly annoyed the Eighteenth by delivering their fire whenever a head showed itself above the rifle-pits. The order was given to Companies F and H to dislodge them. A twenty-four pound brass howitzer was procured from the fort and turned upon the building. The gun was served by Capt. McDonald, of the commissary department. After the firing of several shots, some of which penetrated it, and at a signal, which was a shell from a thirty-two pounder from the fort, Capt. Bowen, with the companies under his command, sprang out of the pits, and amid the crashing of shot and shell charged the house. The work was short and bloody. Several of the enemy were killed and wounded and thirteen prisoners were captured."[27]

Major James W. Newton of the 5th Virginia reported that he pulled his men back "...in order to keep the enemy from shelling the house," a statement that wrapped a kernel of truth in a thick husk of spin. After the house was secured, Yankee sharp-shooters occupied its upper windows on the side facing the

---

[26]O.R. 1-27-2-76, 523, Peale, Newton.
[27]Walker, pp. 109-110; O.R. 1-27-2-76, 500, 516, 524, Peale, Johnson, Walker, Newton.

Southerners, from where they had a clear shot down their adversaries' line. Within moments, small dust geysers from errant Minié balls began to creep progressively closer to their intended victims as the Federals gradually acquired the correct range. Coerced by the danger, the Butternuts at the center of the Virginians' line fell back from their exposed salient. As the Johnnies sprinted up the ridge to safer ground, the 5th Virginia's Lieutenant Colonel Williams took a bullet in the foot.[28]

The assault on the brick house was the last offensive action by either Connecticut or Virginia, but the sniper battle continued for another hour or two until the Yankees were recalled to reinforce the Union fortifications. In all, the 18th Connecticut lost 15 men killed or wounded despite their determined effort to keep under cover. Surprisingly, the Bluecoats, who were not known for their marksmanship, managed to pick off 19 skirmishers from the 5th Virginia, of whom three were killed and 16 were wounded.[29]

Thanks to a semicircle of gun smoke and rifle clatter, Milroy had a fairly good idea of the location of his adversaries to the east, southeast and southwest, but not to his west. Although the Federal line of fortifications sitting atop Apple Pie Ridge made that approach to the city the most secure, the Union commander nevertheless decided that a scout to Pughtown, on the far side of North Mountain, would be a worthwhile undertaking. The job was handed to the 12th Pennsylvania Cavalry. At about 9:30 a.m., two companies of Pennsylvania horsemen trotted west on the

---

[28]O.R. 1-27-2-524, Newton.

[29]Ibid., 1-27-2-516, Walker. Perhaps the unusual similarity in the body count was due to the Federals having better shelter or because the Rebels, who were firing down hill, would have had a tendency to fire high.

Pughtown Road with orders to check the road's namesake, move south, and then return by the Romney Road—a scout of about 12 to 15 miles that should have taken three or four hours.[30]

Major Darius Titus, author of the 12th Pennsylvania's after-action report on his regiment's involvement at Winchester, neglected to supply the name of the officer who led the scout. Milroy and two other witnesses during the postmortem court of inquiry maintained that the scout was under the command of a "Captain Morgan." It is possible that Titus failed to include the man's name because Morgan's little patrol would only assume importance later, when Milroy highlighted the incident as part of a defense intended to try to save his career. Possibly, though, the name was excluded in protest over how Titus believed that Morgan came to be a member of his regiment.

Morgan's suspicious introduction to the Hussars was recounted in charges Titus would later press against Colonel Lewis B. Pierce, the commander of the 12th Pennsylvania Cavalry whose frequent absences from his regiment included the fight at Winchester. In those charges, Titus alleged that in 1862, Pierce "...received [as] compensation for rank promotion & commission one brown stallion of [from?] Capt. C. B. Morgan a citizen who was appointed by Col. L. B. Pierce to the rank of Capt. and placed in command of Co. E...."[31] Regardless of how he attained the position of a captain in the Union army, Charles B. Morgan would soon assume the role of a scapegoat for General Milroy.[32]

About an hour and a half after the mysterious Captain Morgan and his patrol departed from the Hussars' campground in

---

[30]O.R. 1-27-2-70, Titus; O.R. 1-27-2-152, Powell.

[31]Pierce Military Records, National Archives.

[32]Although his first name and middle initial are never mentioned in the text, the index to the *Official Records* for the pages where he was mentioned refers to him as Charles B. Morgan, as do his military records. Morgan Military Records, National Archives.

front of the Main Fort, Jubal Early surreptitiously pulled Hays' and Smith's brigades and some artillery back about two miles from the previous night's battle line, and along with Hoke's command that had been summoned from Kernstown, began to feed his division onto the Cedar Creek Turnpike by regiment.[33] After a mile's tramp on that road's relatively good surface, the Butternut strike force turned north. They then struggled for about two and a half miles "...through fields and the woods, which latter was here sufficiently open to admit

Jubal A. Early

(Author's Collection)

of the passage of the artillery...." After crossing the Romney Road, Early left the 54th North Carolina Regiment of Hoke's brigade to guard his rear while the rest of his strike force began the final leg of their journey.[34]

It is likely that the Rebels crossed the Romney Road at the Lupton house between the hours of 2 and 3 p.m., and from there hiked "...along a small obscure road to the rear of the position [the north end of Little North Mountain] from which I [Early] wished to assault the enemy's works.... I reached this position about four o'clock p.m., and as the day was exceedingly hot, and

---

[33]Hays reported that he got his order to move at 11 a.m., the colonel of the 31st Virginia, noted that his regiment moved out around midday, and Thomas Reed, one of Hays' men recorded that his regiment fell in between 10 and 11 a.m.. O.R. 1-27-2-461, 477, 489, Early, Hays, Hoffman; Reed, p. 36.

[34]Grunder, p. 36; Early, p. 244.

the men had marched a circuit of eight or ten miles.... I massed them in the woods in the rear of the position and gave them time to rest."[35] Immediately after their arrival on the hidden, western side of Little North Mountain, the Johnnies formed a battle line, stacked their arms, dropped to the ground in place, wolfed down whatever greasy morsels could be scavenged from the dark recesses of their haversacks, and washed the meal down with warm, stale canteen water.[36] Then, as they relaxed in the shade and daubed sweat from lean, hard, and weathered faces, imaginations undoubtedly explored the possibilities of what might be waiting on the other side of that peaceful, wooded ridge.

While his foot soldiers enjoyed some much needed rest, Early began to deploy the 20 cannons that had been allotted to him to crack open the West Fort. Eight guns under Captain James M. Carrington were moved to a point north of the West Fort while Captain Willard Dance's remaining 12 pieces were placed in an orchard somewhat to the south of it, creating what was hoped would soon become a deadly converging fire. When at their designated positions, the gunners unlimbered their pieces and then tried to claim a few minutes' rest of their own, knowing that they would soon have to shoulder their guns up the backside of the ridge into firing position.[37]

Early was justifiably proud of his covert march and stealthy disposition. "My route had been a very circuitous one, in order to check the enemy's vigilance, and I was conducted over it by a very intelligent and patriotic citizen, ...Mr. [James C.] Baker...and

---

[35]Early, pp. 245-246. Early did not supply the time that he crossed the Romney Road. This writer's estimate is based upon: the time that Early's division began their movement, the usual rate of an infantry march which was about two miles per hour, the fact that the distance from the Romney Road to the final destination was about two miles, and that the rate of travel was probably somewhat slower due to the poor quality of the road behind Little North Mountain.

[36]Reed, p. 36.

[37]Grunder, pp. 38-39.

Early's March

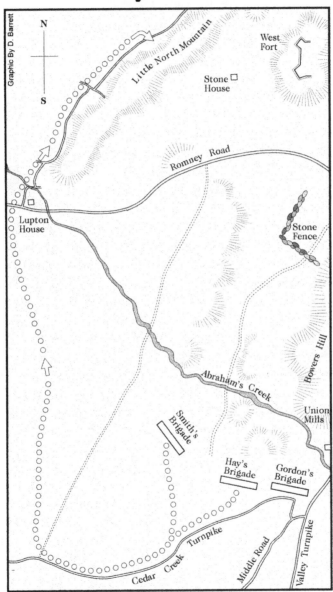

N
S

Little North Mountain

West Fort

Stone House

Romney Road

Lupton House

Stone Fence

Bowers Hill

Abraham's Creek

Union Mills

Smith's Brigade

Hay's Brigade

Gordon's Brigade

Cedar Creek Turnpike

Middle Road

Valley Turnpike

Graphic By D. Barrett

From: O.R. Atlas Pl. XLIII #3

Scale in Miles

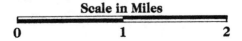

0   1   2

it was mainly owing to the intelligent and skillful manner in which he guided me that I was able to get there without attracting the slightest attention from the enemy."[38]   Although competently managed, Early received significant assistance.   The previous night's rainstorm prevented development of a dust cloud that would have heralded his movement from miles away.   Benign geography hid the last stages of the march from Federal view and Milroy inexplicably failed to post videttes along the crest of Little North Mountain, from where the Confederate advance would certainly have been discovered.   The key factor, however, was another one of those odd coincidences that often appeared to favor the Confederacy.   Captain Morgan's cavalry patrol passed by the Lupton house on the Romney Road around noon, preceding the approaching vanguard of the Rebel column by a few hours, or perhaps even less.

As Morgan's detachment rode back through the Union picket line, one observer reported that he did not see any flankers riding out on the sides of the column as it ambled along the road.[39]   It is possible that Morgan was sloppy or inexperienced enough to have patrolled in such a reckless fashion, but it is equally likely that he pulled his flankers in when the Yankee troopers came in sight of friendly pickets and before Captain Powell noticed their approach.   Due to the timing and the geometry, however, it is unlikely that Early's column would have been discovered even if flankers had been deployed.   In any event, the patrol returned to the Main Fort at approximately 1:30 p.m.

---

[38]Early, pp. 244-245.

[39]O.R. 1-27-2-152, Powell. Flankers were troops who marched or rode parallel to, but at some distance to the sides of, a moving column in order to prevent a surprise attack, or to extend the scope of observation. Milroy wrote in his after-action report that Major Adams and Lieutenant Spooner informed him that the Hussars never ventured beyond sight of the Union pickets, but both denied any personal knowledge about Captain Morgan's patrol when questioned on the issue at the subsequent court of inquiry. O.R. 1-27-2-96, 43, 147, Milroy, Adams, Spooner.

and soon thereafter Captain Morgan reported to Milroy that he had not observed any Grey-backs.[40]

Later, in his exculpatory after-action report, Milroy wrote that "...the report of Captain Morgan relieved me from all apprehension of an immediate attack in that direction, and induced me to turn my attention to the approaches in other directions."[41] One must wonder what the Union commander would have done had his attention remained focused toward the west. The only real options that he had were either to stand pat, send reinforcements to the West Fort, or abandon the small crescent-shaped dirt emplacement. Given that he had chosen to construct and man it in the first place, it is doubtful that Milroy would have abandoned the vulnerable little redoubt even if the approach of the enemy had been detected. Had he learned of the advancing danger, Milroy's feisty personality might very well have led him to send additional riflemen to supplement the Buckeyes who had been deployed there earlier in the morning, rather than to allow the position to serve merely as a trip-wire. If he would have been so inclined, subsequent events probably made the Hoosier secretly grateful for his ignorance, even while he decried Morgan's implied dereliction of duty.

Secure in the assumption that his western flank remained unchallenged, Milroy turned his attention to the Confederates who, since midmorning, had been using their skirmish line on the high ground of Bower's Hill to harass Elliott's brigade. But before the

---

[40]Milroy and Captain Z. Baird reported that the patrol returned around 2 p.m. while Titus thought between 1 and 2 p.m. O.R. 1-27-2-46, 70, 140, 152, Milroy, Baird, Titus, Powell.

[41]O.R. 1-27-2-46, Milroy.

Hoosier could commence an attack on Bower's Hill, it became necessary to repulse another Butternut diversionary sortie into the southern streets of Winchester. The 122nd Ohio drew the assignment to expel the pesky Rebels. At about 1 p.m. Companies F and H of the 122nd became "sharply" engaged on the southern fringe of town with an approaching Confederate skirmish line as well as with some secessionist bushwhackers who shot at the backs of the Ohioans from parlor and bedroom windows.[42] Undoubtedly because they never had any intention of trying to hold any territory, the Southerners were quickly evicted.

Then, about the same time that Early's men were forming ranks behind Little North Mountain, the 122nd Ohio and the 12th West Virginia, with the 123rd Ohio in reserve, began to make final preparations to reclaim Bower's Hill. Sometime between 4 and 5 p.m. the Mountaineers, who held the right end of the line, moved up to the stone wall that they had all briefly occupied earlier in the morning and which their skirmish line held throughout the afternoon. After the 122nd Ohio took its position on the Mountaineers left flank, the West Virginians clambered over their wall and began to press toward the Rebel's defensive line that consisted of rifle pits anchored by another stone farm fence.

Simultaneously, the 122nd Ohio advanced to within 60 feet of the Confederate line that was manned, according to the estimate of the Buckeyes' Colonel William H. Ball, by a battalion of Butternut riflemen. The exposed Ohioans and the emplaced Rebels traded virtually point-blank rifle fire long enough for the Federals to unleash three volleys. Finally convinced by one death and eight woundings that he was bound to lose the duel, Ball led his men back beyond effective range.[43] When Colonel Klunk saw the Buckeyes stop and then withdraw, he halted his Mountaineers for a moment and then, after withstanding some additional scalding

---

[42]O.R. 1-27-2-68, Ball.
[43]Ibid., 1-27-2-67, 68, 80, Ball, Klunk.

gunfire, allowed his regiment to resume the position behind the stone wall over which they had boldly leaped only a few minutes before.[44]

As the adversaries on the southwestern front resumed their bitter little firefight from behind opposing stone fences, General Early gave the signal directing his 20 artillery crews, who had been permitted barely enough time to stretch out on the ground and get comfortable, to manhandle their pieces into firing position on the crest of the ridge.[45] After a massive struggle to heave their guns uphill through bushes and over rocks and gullies, Jones' cannoneers were disgusted to find that a stone fence impeded their line of fire. Keeping below the wall in order to avoid detection, the Johnnies hurriedly removed enough stones to create embrasures for their muzzles. When Jones' cannons were finally rolled up to the wall, 20 Confederate gun crews sighted in on their target and began to stuff vent holes with friction primers.[46]

Neither the commander of the Union garrison nor the commander of the contingent that manned the West Fort had any idea of the threat that was lurking behind the hills to their west. Colonel Keifer of the 110th Ohio felt so secure that at approximately 3 p.m. he rode back to the Main Fort, left his horse with an orderly for feeding, and requested a conference with Milroy. The Ohioan found the Hoosier "...in high spirits. He complimented me on the strong fight I put up the previous day, and declared his belief that the enemy were only trying to scare him out of the Valley. He referred to the quiet of the day as evidence that they

---

[44]O.R. 1-27-2-80, Klunk.
[45]Early, p. 247.
[46]Grunder, p. 40.

had no purpose to assail him in his works. He said the cavalry had just reported no enemy in my front on any of the roads."[47]

The men of the 110th and 116th Ohio who lounged behind the dirt walls of the West Fort were as oblivious to the presence of the enemy as were their commanders, a situation verified by Confederate Captain William J. Seymour, assistant adjutant to Brigadier General Harry T. Hays. The Southern staff officer recorded that "...we discovered several men lying on the ground under the shade of a tree that stood just outside of the [West] fort, the sentinel lazily paced the rounds and everything betokened a total ignorance of our proximity...."[48]

That drowsy tranquility abruptly ended when nearly simultaneous concussions from the massed Rebel artillery suddenly thundered and echoed across the valley, causing thousands of blue-capped heads to snap toward the west. In the next instant, those Buckeyes who were not already napping on the ground, frantically dove for cover from the exploding shells which showered their fort with red hot shrapnel, and from the screaming iron shot that alternately punched into their earthen rampart, flashed overhead, or gouged sheets of dirt and rock out of the hilltop.[49]

"So taken by surprise were the Yankees that they made no response for several minutes...," except, perhaps, to further compress themselves into the sheltering earth.[50] Colonel Keifer responded as quickly as he could to the sounds of the barrage that was pounding his boys in the West Fort. Rather than wasting the time to locate, retrieve, and resaddle his own mount, the Buckeye

---

[47]Keifer believed that the censure of the 12th Pennsylvania Cavalry and Captain Morgan for not discovering Early was "unjust" because when the report was given it was true. He added, "There was, however, a lack of vigilance on the part of somebody; possibly General Milroy was not altogether blameless." Keifer, vol. 2, pp. 11-12.

[48]Seymour diary, 6/14/1863.

[49]Ibid.

[50]Ibid.

colonel commandeered a team horse from a handy supply wagon and galloped bareback across the shell-rent valley. Because of the terrain, Keifer was forced to dismount at the base of the hill upon which the West Fort was constructed, "...and then, hastening on foot through a storm of shot and exploding shell, I was [within about five minutes of leaving the Main Fort] soon in it."[51]

After the initial shock to the West Fort's garrison had subsided, and while Keifer frantically raced to rejoin his command, the courageous regulars of Battery L formed around their pieces despite the blizzard of flying iron whizzing around their heads. Ignoring the progressive slaughter of 50 battery horses, caissons and limbers being blown up or knocked to pieces in their midst, and the gradual reduction of the battery from six operable pieces to two, the Union gunners continued to respond as best they could with a determined, but understandably wild, counterbattery fire.[52]

General Early had ordered Hays, whose Cajun brigade was assigned to make the charge, to wait for a signal to attack in hopes of knocking out all the Federal artillery in the West Fort before the ground assault began. Instead, after the barrage had lasted about a half hour, Hays launched his Louisiana Tigers forward on his own authority out of reasonable concern that the solid shot that had begun to crash through the trees overhead meant that the presence of his brigade had been discovered.[53] Upon hearing the command to advance, the 6th, 7th, and 9th Louisiana regiments in the first line and the 5th and 8th Louisiana in support emerged from the woods. "[O]ur boys had to cross several open fields, jump fences, etc. but so hot was the fire of our artillery, that the Yankee infantry had to keep as close behind their breastworks that they did not observe us...." On the way, Butternut as well as Blue suffered from the artillery fire that scorched the valley between Little North

---

[51]Keifer, vol. 2, p. 11.
[52]O.R. 1-27-2-61, Keifer.
[53]Reed, p. 36; Jones, p. 232.

Mountain and West Fort. "I [Thomas Reed of the 9th Louisiana] looked and saw a man raising our flag. A shell had burst near and a piece of it had struck our flag-bearer, James Stewart, on the head and killed him instantly."[54]

On the perilous trek across the valley, the Tigers marched past a lonely farmhouse where two women, Lizzie and Alma Yonley, stood on their porch transfixed by the spectacle of "...banners flying and our own and the enemy's shells screaming over...." It was a sight that Lizzie would later recall as "...the grandest sight my eyes ever beheld."[55] The opportunity to bask in the admiring gaze of the two females allowed the Louisiana boys a few moments' respite from thoughts about what would happen when the Federals finally lifted their heads above their earthworks long enough to unleash a torrent of leaden death. After Lizzie and Alma receded from view, a few more tense minutes of marching brought the Tigers to an abatis of felled trees that the Yankees had erected 150 yards in front of their emplacement.[56] Without the slightest hesitation, Hays' men waded into the barrier made of "...trees fallen or dragged, with the tops of them outward...and the small ends of the limbs were cut sharp."[57]

As the Butternuts clawed their way through the tangle, "...our artillery ceased firing and the Yankee infantry opened a brisk fire upon us...."[58] When finally clear of the abatis, Johnnies screaming the Rebel yell and wielding bayonet-tipped rifles poured around, over, and into the little fort. For a few moments Captain Arckenoe of the 116th Ohio attempted to stem the flood with his revolver by blasting each Confederate face that appeared

---

[54]Reed, p. 37. It is not clear whether the shell came from Milroy's main fortifications, the West Fort, or from a Rebel shell that detonated early.

[55]As quoted in Jones, p. 232.

[56]Seymour diary, 6/14/1863.

[57]Reed, p. 37.

[58]Seymour diary, 6/14/1863.

Assault on West Fort

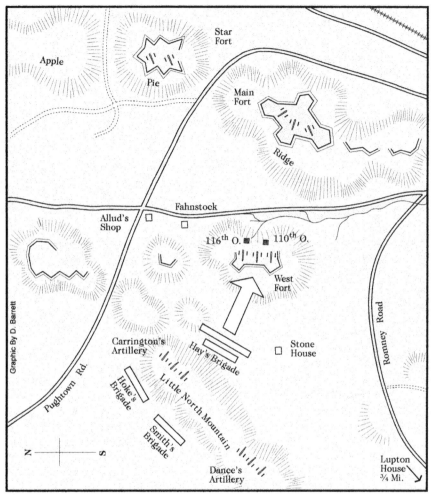

Apple

Star
Fort

Pie

Main
Fort

Ridge

Fahnstock

Allud's
Shop

116th O.   110th O.

West
Fort

Graphic By D. Barrett

Carrington's
Artillery

Hay's Brigade

Stone
House

Romney Road

Pughtown Rd.

Hoke's
Brigade

Little North Mountain

Smith's
Brigade

Dance's
Artillery

Lupton
House
¾ Mi.

N — S

From: O.R. Atlas Pl. XLIII #3

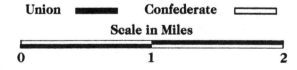

Union   Confederate

Scale in Miles

0   1   2

on the top of the wall in front of him. Before he could reload, his valiant stand was terminated by a Minié ball in the brain.[59]

At another point in the melee, three quick-witted Yankees snatched a regimental flag from the grasp of a Cajun who was trying to clamber over the parapet. Armed only with his sword, Confederate Adjutant John Orr of the 6th Louisiana attempted to rescue his regimental colors from its captors. His quest was aborted by a bayonet in the gut.[60]

The defenders' recollections of the storming of the fort were somewhat different, but the outcome remained the same. "About 6 p.m. the enemy came up behind a ridge with at least five regiments of infantry...in deep columns of attack. The advance regiment carried the United States Colors. The infantry and artillery opened fire upon him with fearful effect, mowing down his advance regiment almost to a man. My [Keifer's] sharp-shooters shot down the officers on horseback. We checked the enemy's column for a few moments only, and with terrible loss he effected an entrance into the works near the center of my regiment, my men fighting him until he outnumbered us inside the works. The trenches and breastworks were of such a character as to afford no obstruction to the entrance of the enemy."[61] Regardless of whose version was the more accurate, General Hays conceded that the brief but ferocious Federal resistance claimed two officers and 10 men killed as well as eight officers and 59 men wounded.[62]

Once inside the Federal redoubt, the Confederates shot down the surviving artillery horses before the Yankee gunners could limber up and save any of their ordnance.[63] With their artillery in the hard hands of the Rebels, the surviving defenders

---

[59]Wildes, p. 57.
[60]Seymour diary, 6/14/1863. Orr eventually recovered from his wound.
[61]O.R. 1-27-2-61, Keifer.
[62]Ibid., 1-27-2-478, Hays.
[63]Seymour diary, 6/14/1863; O.R. 1-27-2-477, 478, Hays.

broke and ran for the shelter of the Union fortifications on Apple Pie Ridge.[64] Unfortunately, some of the Ohioans weren't quick enough to escape Southern revenge. Corporal John Service of the 18th Connecticut, who apparently had just arrived at the Main Fort from the east side of town, claimed to have seen some of the "...Confederates club the brains out of our men after they surrendered, the only act of barbarity...[he] ever witnessed."[65] Other Cajuns tried to shoot the refugees before they could reach the Main Fort. One Tiger recalled, "Then you ought to have seen those fellows run, and as they ran down the hill we poured it into them, but they soon scampered away and we were in possession of the breastworks."[66]

The carnage among the Bluecoats could have been worse, but the hungriest of the conquerors never got to the firing line. As soon as it became apparent that the Federals were on the run, a goodly number of Rebels began to ransack abandoned Union haversacks. While the demoralized Buckeyes sprinted for shelter, the scavengers consumed what was readily edible and stuffed their own haversacks with what was not.[67]

While many of their comrades looted or gawked, other Tigers, who were still engorged with battle rage or blood lust, spun Battery L's two remaining operable guns in the direction of the rapidly retreating Ohioans in hopes of stopping a few, and speeding the rest, with a few loads of canister. Knowing full well what they would have done had the situation been reversed,

---

[64]By a quirk of fate, at dusk on November 7, 1863, the Louisiana Brigade was overrun and mostly captured by the Third Brigade, First Division, Sixth Corps while defending its own earthen emplacements at Rappahannock Station. After the Confederate works were taken, it was discovered that three of the cannons seized by the Federals belonged to Randolph's Union battery which the Cajuns had captured five months earlier in the West Fort. Maier, pp. 111-120; Early, pp. 307-313; Keifer, vol. 2, p. 55.

[65]Service papers.

[66]Reed, p. 37.

[67]Jones, pp. 233-234.

Keifer's men sprinted to get out of canister range before the Butternuts could reverse, load, aim, and fire the captured pieces. So determined was their flight that the routed Buckeyes raced right through the lines of the balance of the 116th Ohio and the 87th Pennsylvania, who were marching in line of battle to reinforce the West Fort at the moment that it fell. The Confederates rammed powder and canister down the throats of their newly captured weapons, while the advancing Yankees braced themselves to receive the deadly blasts. Undoubtedly to the Bluecoats' unanimous relief, just before the two regiments came under canister fire an adjutant, who Colonel Washburn had dispatched to confirm Milroy's earlier order to advance, rushed back to the line and delivered an order calling them back to the fort.[68]

The thunder and lightning unleashed by Early's cannoneers, the sight of Rebels storming the West Fort on their right flank, and Milroy's recognition that he might soon need all of his rifles to save his main fortifications, promptly ended whatever was left of the rather tepid attempt by the Federals to reclaim Bower's Hill. "We [the 122nd Ohio] marched up to make the charge when we halted and laid flat on the ground and sent for another Regt. to help us while the battery played on them to try to rout them. We got ready to charge when the Rebels opened from two points on our fort. We were ordered back to the fort as quickly as we could go which was the luckiest thing for us that ever happened for when we started back they opened on us and shelled us all the way to the

---

[68]O.R. 1-27-2-64, Washburn. In the fighting, Company C of the 116th Ohio reported that one-third of its number were captured, while the 110th Ohio acknowledged losses of 40 killed, wounded, or captured. Wildes, p. 57; O.R. 1-27-2-61, Keifer.

fort. If we had made the charge we would have been all cut to pieces for they had 3 regiments and some cannon there waiting for us...."[69]

The Yankee withdrawal from Bower's Hill was only somewhat less nerve-wracking than an assault would have been. "When the enemy opened a battery from an eminence on the west of our position and proceeded to shell the fort, ...we...retreated back, the shells flying upon all sides of us...." The gauntlet run, the 12th West Virginia along with the 122nd and 123rd Ohio, "...took a position outside of the [Main] fort in the entrenchments expecting every moment to be attacked by a storming party...."[70]

As the Federals on Bower's Hill began to scurry back to the Main Fort, Early, who was confident that his newly won position was secure, ordered the left portion of his temporarily dormant artillery to be rolled out into the West Fort, so that the reduction of the main Federal defenses could commence.[71] The shells which the Federals tried to ignore on their jog back to the Main Fort were part of the ensuing artillery free-for-all that pitted the Confederate gunners on Little North Mountain and in the West Fort against their counterparts in the Main and Star Forts.[72]

---

[69]Hartley letter, 6/15/1863.

[70]Bruder, Memoirs, p. 7; Keyes, p. 46.

[71]Early, p. 248.

[72]All relevant points were within artillery range of the Union forts. Milroy's 20-pounder Parrotts had a range of 2,100 yards at five degrees elevation, 4,400 yards at 15 degrees, and 6,200 yards at 35 degrees of elevation. The 12-pounder Napoleons could reach just under a mile at five degrees while the 10-pounder Parrotts and the 3-inch Ordnance Rifles could add an additional 200 or 300 yards at the same five degrees and could throw projectiles almost as far as a 20-pounder when fully elevated. Thomas, pp. 28, 33, 39, back cover; Naisawald, p. 28.

Although Early claimed that the West Fort commanded the Union forts on Apple Pie Ridge, the little redoubt was clearly accessible to the Federal artillery. "The guns in the Star Fort greeted them, with shell after shell planted among them with astonishing precision, and each one as it burst in the ranks of the enemy was followed by exulting cheers from the Union troops in the larger forts. A gallant [Confederate] officer on a spirited horse came riding out in front of the works that had been taken. A shell from one of Alexander's guns seemed to strike directly beneath the horse, bursting, and raising a cloud of smoke and dust that enveloped the horse and the rider. Loud and long were the cheers that again broke from the Union men."[73] It is possible that it was that blast that tore the bridle arm off a Rebel captain who rode out to rally his cannoneers.[74]

It appears that because Captain Frederic W. Alexander's gunners of the Baltimore Light Artillery Battery had previously practiced on this field from their position in the Star Fort, they knew the range of their new targets to be between 1,500 and 1,700 yards. That knowledge allowed the Marylanders to inflict fearsome punishment upon their Confederate counterparts. Three times the Rebel gunners were driven behind the hill on which the West Fort was built in order to escape the deadly accurate Union fire that dismounted two of their guns and demolished a limber.[75] One Federal gun crew used chain shot to rip the roof off the Fahnstock house, a lonely farmhouse which was stuck between the West and Star Forts and which probably sheltered a few Butternut sharpshooters. A well-directed shell lobbed by Alexander's men "...struck a caisson, (which consists of three chests of ammunition) and it blew up with a terrific crash...[while another] struck one of their guns, and it was seen to fall over...." Yet another shell was

[73]Beach, p. 238.
[74]Grunder, p. 42.
[75]O.R. 1-27-2-87, Alexander.

sent whistling toward a horse-drawn caisson that appeared out of some trees. The shell burst over top of the team horses, causing "...them to stampede down the hill towards us...[until they] disappeared in a ravine."[76]

That stampede commenced a nightmare for its Rebel gun crew. The terrified horses galloped over a boulder which jolted Major Robert Stiles and three other members of the gun crew off the limber chest and into the dirt. Unfortunately, Stiles came down in front of the cannon rather than along its side, was run over, and received such grievous wounds that he was abandoned on the field as a goner. Another Johnnie was gutted when he was pinned between a stone gatepost and the wildly careening gun.[77]

With each successful shot the enthusiasm of the Union gunners intensified. At one point, "Our little Lieutenant Peter Leary Jr. [of Alexander's Battery] whom the boys did not think much of, up to that time; stripped off his coat, and took a hand in loading and firing a cannon in his shirt sleeves; cheering and hurrahing at every successful shot; and there were many such...." The same irrationality that often overcomes soldiers in the heat of battle almost cost Alexander's historian, Frederick W. Wild, his life and shortly thereafter, a leg. At the commencement of the artillery fight, Wild stuck his head above the parapet to get a better look at the havoc that he and his comrades were inflicting and almost lost it to a sniper's bullet that sizzled past his ear. Later, he noticed "...a fragment of a shell...spinning along the ground, at times standing still like a spinning top; I was going to give it a kick, but something said don't! This innocent looking thing touched against a cannon wheel, glanced off and broke a horses leg. What might it have done to mine, if I had kicked it?"[78]

While the artillery fire stormed back and forth across the valley, Milroy had himself repeatedly hoisted to the top of the

---

[76]O.R. 1-27-2-87, Alexander; Wild, pp. 59-60.

[77]Grunder, p. 42.

[78]Wild, pp. 62-63.

Main Fort's flagpole in a huge basket, where "...with remarkable coolness and bravery, exposed to the greatest danger, [he] took observation of the enemy, concentrating in front of him while solid shot were whizzing by him, and large shells bursting in all directions around him. He then massed all his troops in the two forts, which were near each other, and in the rifle pits in front of them."[79] Each time he was hauled to the top, his men cheered "lustily" (presumably from admiration rather than ill will). Whether his repeated exposure to sniper fire and artillery shells resulted from the same battle rage that infected his gunners, from his rash courage, from an exaggerated sense of duty, or from the hope that his actions would inspire his troops will never be known. Whatever its source, and whatever suspicions may linger about his judgement, no one can question the Hoosier's physical courage.

Incredibly, despite Milroy's exposure to shot, shrapnel, and long-range sniper fire, it was Ewell who got himself hit during the assault on West Fort. While observing Hays' progress from a distant hill and shouting "'Hurrah for the Louisiana boys...[t]there's Early; I hope the old fellow won't be hurt...,'" the Confederate commander was struck square on the chest by a spent Minié ball. Ewell was only bruised but the shot nevertheless proved to be temporarily incapacitating. Old Bald Head's surgeon confiscated the one-legged general's crutches in order to force him to lie down for awhile as well as to try to keep him out of harm's way. Regardless of the doctors good intentions, within minutes Ewell was watching and cheering as he hopped about on his good leg.[80]

The well-directed Union artillery fire failed to disperse the stubborn Southern cannoneers, who defiantly responded with shot,

[79]Prowell, p. 73; Hewitt, p. 43. There is some controversy over how Milroy accomplished his observations. Another version maintained that the Hoosier employed a huge tripod constructed for the purpose. Nye, p. 98.

[80]Pfanz, *Richard S. Ewell*, p. 286.

shell, and allegedly even with railroad iron.[81]   It was only the
setting of the sun, not a lack of courage or energy on the part of
any of the artillerists, that finally halted the contest. Similarly, it
was the lack of visibility, and the inability to discover another
assault in the offing, rather than a loss of nerve, that finally
brought Milroy down from his perch above the Main Fort.

Whether Early actually attempted an additional infantry
assault after twilight had ended the artillery duel remains an open
question. The Southern commander implied in his memoirs that
he did not. "The enemy's force occupying the works, and around
them, was quite large, and deep and rugged ravines interposed
between us and the two occupied works, which rendered an assault
upon them from that direction very difficult...the capture of the
other works by assault would evidently require the co-operation of
the other troops around Winchester."[82]   Although it would have
been consistent with the rest of his recollections if Early had
neglected to mention a failed assault, there were a number of
Union sources who agreed that the involvement of the Confederate
infantry ended with the capture of the West Fort.

Curiously though, at least seven other Union sources
reported that the bloody work resumed after the artillery argument
concluded. "At nightfall...the firing ceased, and the silence was
oppressive—all was quiet. Soon the outstanding pickets began to
fire. In a moment they came rushing into the rifle-pits. There
was plainly to be heard the firing and steady tramp of men. On
they came. The order is 'Be still—hold your fire.' The step is
coming painfully near. At last a sheet of flame bursts from the

---

[81]Black letter, 6/16/1863; Hartley letter, 6/26/1863. About the railroad iron
Wild wrote, "We also received an allotment of railroad iron fired at us, in chunks
of various lengths, which made a terrible roaring noise. This was a wise economy
of the enemy, (every shot we fired cost ten dollars,) and where no accurate shooting
was required and terrifying noise was a factor, the railroad iron answered every
purpose and cost much less." Wild, p. 63.
[82]Early, p. 248.

mouths of more than 30 cannon, double-shotted with grape and canister.... Yet they are still heard advancing. Another shot of grape and canister; the infantry opens fire from the trenches below; another shot from the cannon above, and all is quiet save the moaning of the men out in the dark."[83]

From his position in the West Fort, the Baltimore Battery's historian added: "...as they were coming up, we fired grape and canister into them as fast as the guns could be loaded, and with the thousands of muskets blazing away and the shells flying through the air, were followed by a streak of fire like a sky-rocket, and the flash of the shells from the heavy guns as they burst over the enemy, made a display of pyrotechnics, that was awfully! terribly, grand!"[84]

Sergeant John H. Black of the 12th Pennsylvania Cavalry, who had moved along with his regiment "...along the Pughtown road to the front or south of our fortification...," corroborated the allegations of a final failed Rebel assault when he wrote home to his fiancée the day after the battle. "...[T]hey made a desperate charge [at dark] with 20,000 infantry and came near taking our forts."[85] The obviously exaggerated numbers aside, one may conclude that the Confederates launched at least a limited sortie against the portion of the Union line where the 12th West Virginia, 116th Ohio, 87th Pennsylvania, 1st New York Cavalry, and the 12th Pennsylvania happened to be located.[86]

---

[83]Powell, *National Tribune*, 5/16/1889; Kesses (87th Pa.) letter, 1895; Wildes, p. 57; O.R. 1-27-2-85, Adams; Walker, p. 111; Wild p. 62. All of these accounts, except for Sergeant Black's contemporaneous letter, were written years after the fact, and Powell was often confused about dates and times. It is difficult to conclude, however, that these recollections were all either total fiction or, if true, that the fighting happened at a different time or place.

[84]Wild, p. 62.

[85]O.R. 1-27-2-70, Titus; Black letter, 6/16/1863.

[86]There has been speculation that the last fusillade of the day was triggered by some extremely tense Bluecoats who heard the Rebels maneuvering to occupy a small, abandoned dirt emplacement that was located a short distance to the north of

-----

At the same time that Milroy's division may or may not have been subjected to a final failed assault, the last act in a smaller drama was concluding about 25 miles to the north at Martinsburg, West Virginia. Having driven the Federals out of Bunker Hill in the early hours of Sunday, June 14, Brigadier General Albert G. Jenkins' cavalry brigade, numbering about 1,600 riders, trotted north on the Winchester Turnpike with the intention of adding Martinsburg to their prize list.[87] Around 8 a.m. a contingent of Jenkins' brigade dismounted and drove in the Union videttes who had been stationed on the outskirts of that town. Almost simultaneously, Union Brigadier General Daniel Tyler arrived from Baltimore with orders to relieve Colonel Benjamin F. Smith and take command of the Martinsburg garrison, which consisted of eight companies of the 126th Ohio Infantry, eight companies of the 106th New York Infantry, Maulsby's Independent West Virginia Battery and the 1st Battalion of the Potomac Home Brigade Cavalry.[88]

Tyler was hardly out of the saddle when he learned that Smith was in the process of pushing his entire garrison about a mile south of town into a defensive position behind a stone wall which ran between the Winchester Turnpike and the Charlestown Road.[89] Perhaps for reasons other than courtesy, Tyler chose not to assume command, other than to order the garrison's supply train to flee to Williamsport. Instead of taking over, the brigadier

---

the West Fort.

[87]O.R. 1-27-2-547, Rodes.
[88]Ibid., 1-27-2-16, Tyler.
[89]Ibid., 1-27-2-37, Smith; O.R. 1-27-2-17, Tyler.

informed the colonel that if Smith needed advice he should feel free to ask.[90]

For the next several hours the blue battle line lazily watched their artillerymen lob shells at the Butternut troopers who had the occasional temerity to show themselves on the top of the adjacent ridge to the south. That detached curiosity ended with a jolt when word raced along the line that at 11 a.m. a courier had arrived with a dispatch from Milroy, warning that the Rebels had captured the garrison at Bunker Hill and that 15,000 to 18,000 Rebels were prowling around the vicinity.[91] Despite the news, except for some stomachs that twisted into knots, a few random potshots between contending sharpshooters, and a Federal contraction closer to the town's available escape routes, nothing of significance happened for the next two hours.

Then, at 1 p.m., Jenkins offered the Yankees an opportunity to surrender, coupled with a threat to shell the town in an hour if his generosity was refused.[92] Tyler believed that Martinsburg should be held as long as possible both to prevent the supply train from being intercepted and also to try to keep an escape hatch open should Milroy choose to evacuate Winchester and head north.[93] As a result Smith, with Tyler's blessing, responded to Jenkins' offer with, "Martinsburg will not be surrendered. You may commence shelling as soon as you choose. I will, however, inform the women and children of your threat." Many of the inhabitants heeded the warning and used the lull to skedaddle.[94] Rather than trying to raze the town, Jenkins was ordered by Major General Robert E. Rodes, who had just arrived on the scene ahead of his division of infantry, to send most of his troopers to the left

[90]O.R., 1-27-2-17, Tyler.
[91]Ibid., 1-27-2-17, 33, Tyler.
[92]Ibid., 1-27-2-17, Tyler.
[93]Ibid., 1-27-2-34, Tyler.
[94]Ibid., 1-27-2-38.

to sever one of the possible Federal escape routes.[95] Cowed by
the expectation of masses of the enemy appearing over the horizon
at any moment, Smith limited his response to "...occasionally
shelling the enemy when they appeared within range..." and
watching his skirmish line keep "... up a desultory fire...."[96] As
the Yankees continued to peer into the distance, the number of
sightings of Rebel infantry, who were spreading out along both
flanks after having covered the 25 miles from Berryville to
Martinsburg at quick-time, increased dramatically.

Convinced that his left flank was about to be assailed,
Colonel Smith directed Colonel Edward James, commander of the
106th New York, to shift his regiment to Union Hill on the east
side of town.[97] Still not satisfied, at 6:00 p.m. Smith detached
one section of Maulsby's battery from the two that faced south,
and sent those two gun crews to a position from which he hoped
that a possible assault from the west could be repulsed. Cognizant
of the likely fate of unsupported artillery, Smith also relocated the
left wing of the 106th New York, which quickly filed into position
about 150 yards behind the undoubtedly apprehensive gunners.[98]

All the maneuvering and relative tranquility came to an
abrupt end at sunset when "...the enemy opened upon us a terrific
fire of shot, shell, and grape...," from six or eight pieces of
Rodes' newly arrived artillery.[99] "The first shot passed over
Captain Maulsby's four guns, and plunged into the detached
section, killing and wounding some horses, and producing a bad
effect in the infantry supports, a battalion of the One hundred sixth
New York Volunteers, which fell back in disorder." The reaction

---

[95]O.R. 1-27-2-548, 549, Rodes. Jenkins' ultimatum may have been a bluff
since it is not clear from the records that he had any artillery at Martinsburg, since
he apparently had none at Bunker Hill.

[96]Ibid., 1-27-2-40, James.

[97]Ibid.; Leon, p. 31.

[98]Ibid., 1-27-2-35, Tyler.

[99]Ibid., 1-27-2-40, James.

of the 126th Ohio to the sudden barrage of "...concentrated [artillery] fire...from three different points...." " was not much better, but after a short period of confusion the Buckeyes marched off the field in allegedly "...good order....."[100] In his haste though, Smith apparently left the 106th New York and Maulsby's gunners behind without orders, a warning or even a waive good-bye.

For its part, the balance of the 106th New York "...staggered for a moment under the storm of missiles, rallied again in an instant, and marched steadily from the field, fortunately without the loss of a man."[101] Tyler, who finally assumed command as the foot soldiers were hoofing off the field, personally directed counterbattery fire for about 20 minutes in hopes of buying some additional time for his fleeing infantry. After delaying the Rebels as long as prudence allowed, the Union general ordered his gun crews to limber up and follow the infantry toward safety—but only after each crew had fired a dozen more shots at the approaching enemy.[102]

Most of the Union infantrymen were able to escape the Confederate noose by turning onto the road toward Shepherdstown after the timely discovery that the Johnnies held the northern side of town and the Turnpike that led to Williamsport. As a result, only a small minority of the Union infantrymen fell into Confederate hands. The first captured were the riflemen in Company I of the 126th Ohio, who were taken earlier in the day when their block house on the Opequon Creek was surrounded. The last were a few hundred stragglers who were scooped up in the dark along the Shepherdstown Road by Jenkins' pursuing troopers.[103]

Maulsby's gunners were not so fortunate. Descending darkness and the delay necessitated by firing 12 additional rounds

---

[100]O.R. 1-27-2-38, Smith.
[101]Ibid., 1-27-2-40, James.
[102]Ibid., 1-27-2-35, Tyler.
[103]Ibid., 1-27-2-39, Smith.

and limbering up caused the Union gunners to lose contact with the infantry. In the rush to get to Williamsport, Maulsby failed to discover the Southern roadblock on the Turnpike north of town, was trapped by Jenkins' cavalry, and after a brief and futile fight, he surrendered all five of his surviving guns.[104] The fall of Martinsburg left in question only the fate of Milroy's division at Winchester.

---

[104]O.R. 1-27-2-38, Smith; O.R. 1-27-2-549, Rodes.

7

CARTER'S WOODS

Major-General Schenck:
    Get General Milroy from Winchester to Harper's
Ferry if possible. He will be 'gobbled up' if he remains, if he
is not already past salvation.

—Abraham Lincoln, June 14, 1863[1]

After the last angry echo had passed into the darkness that
divided the contending armies, but before he abandoned his vigil
from above the walls of the Main Fort, the Union commander
must have watched as the valley and slopes below him became
carpeted with guttering campfires and bobbing lanterns carried by
those searching for the wounded. At that moment Major General
Robert H. Milroy must have felt like the loneliest man on earth.
In his heart he surely knew that it was his intransigence that had
delivered his troops into the Confederate vice and that he was
solely accountable for their fate. If he stayed and fought, perhaps
thousands of his men would be killed or injured in a hopeless
gesture. If he surrendered, his men would live but his reputation
would die in their place.

---

[1]O.R. 1-27-2-167, Lincoln. Shortly after sending this order Lincoln interrogated Hooker with "Do you think it is possible that 15,000 of Ewell's men can now
be at Winchester?" O.R. 1-27-1-38.

As the options and their ramifications chased each other around his imagination, he must have reviewed over and over, in an effort to accept the personally unacceptable, the implications of what was probably the last dispatch received from headquarters. That telegraph, sent to Winchester by Schenck to Piatt sometime on June 13, read: "Instruct General Milroy to use great caution, risking nothing unnecessarily, and to be prepared for falling back in good order if over-matched.... In the meantime, go on with your concentration of forces...."[2] Another man might have been overcome with self-recrimination for failing to promptly heed those orders, whose pertinence to his situation should have been compelling. But there is no indication that the Hoosier suffered even a twinge of regret. For days, Milroy had dodged and parried orders to abandon Winchester and even though it is unlikely that he experienced any second thoughts about his earlier decisions, at that moment he surely longed for one more order to withdraw, so that the awful weight of the decision to fight, flee, or surrender could be lifted from his shoulders.

Perversely, the telegraph lines that had been such a nuisance before, but which at that moment might have provided relief from the terrible responsibility, had been severed sometime before 11 p.m. on Saturday evening.[3] Either after McReynolds'

---

[2]O.R. 1-27-2-165, Schenck. Because the telegraph line to Harpers Ferry was cut at some point on June 13, there is some question as to whether this telegraph, which was sent at an unspecified time, was actually received by Milroy. Lieutenant Colonel Piatt, without providing his source, testified that the dispatch "...was communicated by the operator to General Milroy...." even though it was apparently sent while Piatt was in transit from Winchester to Baltimore. Piatt's opinion that Milroy received it was apparently based upon his further testimony that the Hoosier "...sent it after me by express...." O.R. 1-27-2-126-128, 131, Piatt.

[3]Ibid., 1-27-2-175. Exactly when on June 13 the line was broken was the subject of disagreement. The telegraph operator at Harpers Ferry reported that communication ended at 9 p.m.; Milroy claimed it was cut at noon; General Schenck testified that he got a telegraph from Milroy "...later in that day...," but also sent a telegraph to Halleck that indicated a message came in from Winchester as late as 11 p.m.; while General Elliott testified "...the telegraph wires were cut

men arrived at Winchester at 9 p.m. that same night, or early on Sunday morning, June 14, an attempt was made to reopen communications with headquarters. Captain William H. Boyd, of the 1st New York Cavalry, whose wife had been on the Third Brigade's wagon train, volunteered to lead a small band of his men to Martinsburg.   When Boyd reached Martinsburg, presumably before it fell to Rodes' division, he learned of Lincoln's June 14 telegraph quoted at the opening of this chapter. Three of Boyd's men, Sergeants John V. Harvey, George Pitman, and John D. Humphrey volunteered to take the order back to Milroy. "After dark they set out, one a few rods behind another, the last one carrying the message." The mission was successful but the daring troopers and the order from President Lincoln did not arrive until after the Hoosier had already made his decision.[4]

Without the benefit of the directive from his commander in chief, at 9 p.m. on Sunday evening, when further procrastination would have decided the issue by default, Milroy convened a council of war which included all three of his brigade commanders. After reviewing the situation and the options, Milroy decided that their best hope was to attempt to steal out of town on the Martinsburg Pike in the predawn hours of the next morning. The

---

on Saturday evening, as General Milroy told me...." O.R. 1-27-2-102, 165, 175, Elliott, Schenck.

    [4]Beach, pp. 237-238; O.R. 1-27-2-109, 174, McReynolds, Schenck. Exactly whose order was handcarried to Milroy is also subject to speculation. It could have been Lincoln's, or it might have been a copy the following order from Halleck to Schenck, "If you have not executed my orders to concentrate your forces at Harper's Ferry, you will do so immediately...." It may have also been the direct order (of which no copy was produced) from Schenck to Milroy alluded to in Schenck's testimony at the court of inquiry, where Schenck stated, "This telegram [to Tyler requiring a withdrawal to Harpers Ferry] I sent in the apprehension that Milroy might not have received my order to conduct his retreat in the direction of Harper's Ferry...." O.R. 1-27-2-167.

council dispersed and began to spread the word that at 1 a.m. the division would attempt a break-out.[5]

A somber mood permeated the Union forces as their fate was being decided. "It was a moonless, intensely dark night that came down upon Winchester. Those not on guard or picket took what rest they could. The artillery and infantry were in the fort. The cavalry were on the slopes of the hills. If any slept it was by their horses, keeping hold of the reins. No one felt like predicting what the next day would bring forth. All knew that they were surrounded by superior numbers, but hoped that there might be found some opening by which they could break through the lines drawn around them."[6]

Before the retreat could commence, the Federals had several hours of intense preparation still ahead of them. First, all the cannons were spiked because they and the wagons were to be abandoned to the Rebels. The team and artillery horses were gathered together because they were to supply transportation for the teamsters, gunners, and as many infantrymen as could possibly be substituted as their new, barebacked burdens. Whatever ammunition could not be carried was supposed to be thrown into the cisterns of the forts.[7] As all of the preliminaries were commencing in the forts, preparatory orders were spread among the

---

[5]O.R. 1-27-2-47, Milroy. By Sunday night the Union garrison had only one day's rations left as a result of having sent most of their quartermaster's stores to Harpers Ferry on June 11. Further, although his riflemen still had approximately 100 rounds of ammunition apiece, his gunners had only around 30 shells remaining per gun after the fight for West Fort. It is also easy to speculate that Milroy, thanks to his aggressive suppression of Confederate guerrillas in western Virginia the year before, was aware of his potential fate if he fell into Rebel hands as a prisoner. That possibility highlights Milroy's courage, if not his judgement, in staying at Winchester as long as he did. Had his garrison been captured, the Hoosier's reward for lingering might have been a dance at the end of a rope. O.R. 1-27-2- 46, 94, 75, 87, Milroy, Carlin, Alexander.

[6]Beach, p. 240.

[7]O.R. 1-27-2-47, Milroy; O.R. 1-27-2-130, Craven; Beach, p. 241.

men. "When I [Captain Baird of Milroy's staff] approached these regiments I found many of the men asleep in their tents, or in the rifle pits. It was a dark night, and the company officers began at once to wake up their men. Every soldier was given instructions that the evacuation was to be conducted silently, so as not to attract the attention of the enemy, whose sentinels were not more than two hundred yards from the fort."[8]   Next, the "[p]ickets were called in where possible to do silently, and where not possible they were abandoned to fate."[9]   Finally, "...about 12 o'clock Sunday night...the order came to have the men leave their knapsacks and everything of any weight to it and move cautiously and noiselessly out."[10]

For a change, Ares lent the Yankees a small measure of assistance in making their getaway. After the sun was well down behind the western mountains, Confederate General Hays ordered his men to reverse the West Fort redoubt and to dig additional rifle pits and entrenchments in preparation for a possible counterattack. The Johnnies wielded their picks and shovels "...until the small hours of the night..." with so much vigor that their construction noise seems to have drowned out most of the sounds of the Union preparations to flee. Rather than attacking, as they might have done if the Federal retreat had been discovered, the exhausted Butternuts threw themselves "...down on the clover to snatch a few short moments of rest and sleep..." while their adversaries began their exodus.[11]

---

[8]Prowell, p. 74.
[9]Beach, p. 241; O.R. 1-27-2-132, Cravens.
[10]Bruder memoirs, p. 7.
[11]Brachwell, p. 331.

The Confederates on the opposite side of Winchester were not permitted to dream the night away while their comrades dug trenches and their opponents made final preparations to flee. General Ewell recognized that the Federal position was hopeless and, anticipating a retreat rather than a fight or surrender, he deduced the most likely route that the Yankees would follow. Major General Edward Johnson, because of his division's proximity to the likely escape route, drew the assignment to try to interdict Milroy's division if it tried to run.

Pursuant to Ewell's orders, sometime shortly after sunset Johnson and three of the four brigades that comprised his division began to march from the area of the Berryville Pike toward a point on the Martinsburg Pike about two and a half miles northeast of Winchester.[12] Jones' brigade was left behind in order to block an escape attempt out the Berryville Pike. Brigadier General George H. Steuart's brigade, which was comprised of the 1st Maryland Battalion, the 1st and 3rd North Carolina, and the 10th, 23rd, and 37th Virginia Infantry regiments, was assigned to lead the column. Nicholls' Brigade, manned by Louisiana boys from the 1st, 2nd, 10th, 14th and 15th Louisiana regiments under the command of Colonel J. M. Williams, took the middle position. Brigadier General James A. Walker's men of the famed Stonewall Brigade, composed of the 2nd, 4th, 5th, 27th, and 33rd Virginia Infantry regiments were assigned to fill in at the back of the procession.

The order to block a possible Union retreat by way of the Martinsburg Pike was issued after Walker had been ordered to push a skirmish line into town in order to ascertain the location of the Federal perimeter. While Walker made final preparations to carry out that order, the division's medical director, Dr. R. T. Coleman, rode up and advised that the balance of the division was on the march and that the Stonewall Brigade was supposed to take

---

[12]O.R. 1-27-2-331, 500, Johnson.

its assigned position at the rear. Confused by conflicting orders, Walker sent a staff officer to find General Johnson and determine what his brigade was to do. While the staff officer was gone Walker "...ordered the left of my skirmishers to advance into Winchester, and learn whether the enemy still held the place. They advanced into the town, and reported that the enemy had left, and retired to their fortifications soon after dark." The clarification from Johnson did not arrive until 11 p.m., whereupon Walker hurriedly pulled in his skirmishers and rushed to catch up with the rest of his division.[13]

At the head of his attenuated column, Johnson didn't wait very long to exercise some of the independence which his orders necessarily granted. "After moving some distance on the Berryville Road, I was informed by my guide that I would be obliged to cross fields over a rough country in order to carry out literally the directions of the lieutenant-general [Ewell]; and, moreover, that near Stephenson's [Depot], 5 miles north of Winchester, there was a railroad cut masked by a body of woods, and not more than 200 yards from the [Martinsburg] turnpike (along which the enemy would certainly retreat), which would afford excellent shelter for troops in case of an engagement. The night was very dark, and, being satisfied that the enemy would discover the movement and probably escape if I moved to the point indicated by the lieutenant-general, I determined to march to Stephenson's by the road which led by Jordan Springs."[14]

-----

[13]O.R. 1-27-2-501, 517, Johnson, Walker.
[14]Ibid., 1-27-2-501, Johnson.

Carter's Woods
Johnson's Advance

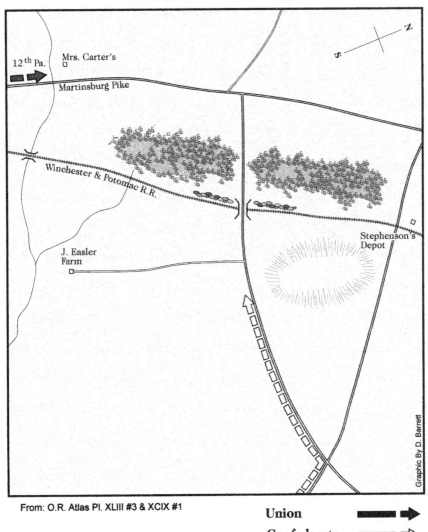

12 th Pa.

Mrs. Carter's

Martinsburg Pike

Winchester & Potomac R.R.

J. Easler
Farm

Stephenson's
Depot

Graphic By D. Barrett

From: O.R. Atlas Pl. XLIII #3 & XCIX #1

Union

Confederate

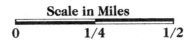

Scale in Miles

| 0 | 1/4 | 1/2 |

Shortly after midnight the Federal column began to take shape, organized by brigade number, with the First Brigade in the lead. General Elliott arranged his regiments with the 12th Pennsylvania Cavalry on the point, followed by the 123rd, 110th, and 122nd Ohio regiments in that order. The 116th Ohio failed to reach the rendezvous on time, got lost in the dark, and fell in behind the Second Brigade. "The artillery and team horses, with their drivers mounted upon them, and all their harness fastened on... and a motley crew they were...," took a position between the Second and Third Brigades about 1,000 yards behind the head of the column.[15] Because Milroy feared an attack from the rear more than from the front, the 13th Pennsylvania Cavalry was detached and positioned at the head of the trailing Third Brigade. The troopers from New York drew the assignment to guard the tail end of the parade.[16]

Then, sometime between 1 and 2 a.m., "...the [Union] column began to move down the hillside. It was a weird procession passing in silence, without a spoken word, through the midnight darkness."[17] In order to avoid the town and hundreds of Confederate sympathizers who would have cheerfully raised an alarm, Milroy led his men for the first mile through a canyon north of the Star Fort and then to the right along a dirt path toward the Martinsburg Pike. The regime of silence was maintained by the jittery Federals except for an occasional clank of a canteen spout against a belted bayonet, a few hushed curses blurted out after stumbles in the darkness, the nickering of nervous horses, the hissing shuffle of thousands of booted feet accompanied by the gentle patter of hundreds of hooves, and Milroy's muted encouragements to his men to "...push along...."[18] Juxtaposed against the strained silence of the soldiers was the racket generated by the

[15]Stevenson, p. 192; O.R. 1-27-2-122, Poore.
[16]O.R. 1-27-2-58, 93, Elliott, Milroy.
[17]Beach, p. 241.
[18]Hewitt, p. 44.

team mules in the center of the column that "...brayed a chorus seldom heard, and as if prompted by a malicious desire to notify the enemy of our departure."[19]

About two hours after the soldiers in blue commenced their march, General Johnson, who was at the head of the Southern column, halted his command on the Harpers Ferry Road at a tiny wooden bridge which crossed the Winchester and Potomac Railroad a few hundred yards from the Martinsburg Pike.[20] "...I [Johnson] rode forward with my staff and sharpshooters to reconnoiter the position and assure myself of the whereabouts of the enemy. I had gone but a short distance when I distinctly heard the neighing of horses and the sound of men moving, and in a few moments ascertained that I had opportunely struck the head of the enemy's retreating column."[21] Those horses undoubtedly belonged to the 12th Pennsylvania Cavalry, who at that instant were about four and a half miles out of Winchester. Moments later the 12th's vanguard collided with Johnson's sharpshooters and the stillness of the night was shattered by shouted challenges followed almost instantaneously by an eruption of rifle and then carbine fire.

As soon as he heard the first spatter of gunfire, Johnson yanked on his reins, spurred his horse, and galloped back to his division with his staff trailing in his wake. Within moments the Confederate division commander rejoined his men and began shouting orders in hopes of being the first to get his regiments into position. "Along the edge of the railroad cut, next to the pike, ran a stone fence, behind which I [Johnson] deployed the three regiments of Steuart's brigade (Tenth Virginia and First and Third North Carolina Regiments) on the right, and three regiments of Nicholls' brigade...on the left. One piece of Dement's battery was placed upon the bridge, one piece a little to the left and rear, the

---

[19]Keifer, vol. 2, p. 13.
[20]O.R. 1-27-2-48, Milroy; O.R. *Atlas*, Plate 43, #3, Hotchkiss; O.R. 1-27-2-501, Johnson.
[21]Ibid., 1-27-2-501, Johnson.

remaining pieces, with sections of Raine's and Carpenter's batteries, the whole under the direction of Lieutenant-Colonel Andrews, on the rising ground in rear of the position occupied by the infantry. Two regiments of Nicholls' brigade were held in reserve as support to the artillery."[22]

While the Confederate commander was rushing back to his men, the Pennsylvanians in the vanguard continued to trade shots with what looked like huge fireflies flickering against the backdrop of a dark sky and an even darker forest.[23] As the Confederate regiments began their deployment, the 12th's Lieutenant Colonel Moss rushed reinforcements from Companies G and F, and perhaps others, to the point of initial contact in hopes of quickly brushing the Rebel skirmishers aside.[24] The newly arrived troopers hastily formed in line for a charge under circumstances that almost certainly evoked disquieting recollections of the rough handling they had received during another nighttime charge at

----

[22]O.R. 1-27-2-501, Johnson. Despite being under his command, Johnson did not mention the 1st Maryland Battalion or the 23rd and 37th Virginia regiments. Perhaps the 23rd Virginia remained with the wagon train while the 37th Virginia continued to escort the artillery reserve pursuant to orders issued on June 13. O.R. 1-27-2-507, Steuart. Without those units, Johnson would have a total of 13 infantry regiments and three batteries of artillery to face Milroy's ordnance-less 10 infantry and three and a quarter cavalry regiments.

[23]On June 15, 1863, at Winchester, Virginia, first light commenced at 4:13 a.m. EST and sunrise occurred at 4:45 a.m. The moon made no visible appearance that morning. U.S. Naval Observatory, Astronomical Applications Department, Http://mach.usno.navy.mil/cgi-bin/aa_pap.

[24]O.R. 1-27-2-70, Titus. The inference that Companies G and F participated in the initial fighting is based upon the account of Private Malden Valentine, a member of Company G, who provided a firsthand account of the initial contact, as well as an article by Sergeant George W. Warfel of Company F, who also related eyewitness accounts of this phase of the action. Although there is no hard evidence, it is also presumed that Lieutenant Colonel Moss remained in command of the regiment and that being closest to the initial contact, he sent the reinforcements.

Manassas Junction 10 months earlier.[25] Despite those memories, when the formation was completed, sabers were drawn, the order was delivered by the shrill bleating call from a bugle, and once again the Curtin Hussars surged forward into the darkness.

At the sound of pounding hooves, the Butternut skirmishers turned and sprinted across the meadow they had occupied, in a desperate race towards the sanctuary of the inky black woods that lay between them and the railroad tracks. Just as the Hussars reached the tree line, barely a saber's length behind the fleeing Confederates, the leading horses nose-dived toward the ground, throwing shocked Bluecoats headlong into the underbrush. Private Malden Valentine, one of the victims, ruefully recalled later that "...the Rebs had stretched telegraph wires from tree to tree...," in preparation for just such an eventuality, "...and we struck it."[26] Private Valentine needed a few moments to gather his wits, but before he could react he found himself staring up the barrel of a .58-calibre rifle. With a carpetbag containing the company records still in his grasp, the dejected Pennsylvanian was escorted to the

---

[25]While patrolling the railroad leading to the supply depot at Manassas Junction after nightfall, about half of the regiment tangled in the dark with Stonewall Jackson's men who were on their way toward seizing the depot on August 26, 1862. At least two men were killed, six were wounded, and between 260 and 319 troopers were captured. Anon., *Philadelphia Inquirer*, 9/1/1862; Bates, *History of the Pennsylvania Volunteers...*, 12th Pennsylvania Cavalry roster.

[26]O.R. 1-27-2-70, Titus; Valentine, *Pennsylvania at Antietam*, p. 206. Perhaps the Confederates learned this trick from the 3rd Pennsylvania Cavalry, who began using telegraph wire to protect videttes from cavalry raids while on picket duty, prior to the battle of Second Manassas. Starr, vol. 1, p. 245. There is also a legitimate question, due to the time factor, about whether Valentine and his comrades struck wire that had been strung by the Rebels. Instead, the troopers may have run afoul of: wire that was strung earlier by the Federals to discourage partisan raiders; farm fences improvised by Mrs. Carter from liberated telegraph wire; or some other impediment such as a rail or stone fence that was hidden by the darkness.

rear as a prisoner. He was soon joined by a goodly number of his dazed and injured comrades.[27]

Those of the cavalrymen who saw the fate of the lead riders before it was too late reined their horses to a stop, quickly sheathed sabers, drew carbines or pistols, and resumed the skirmish with the nearly invisible and well-sheltered Rebel sharp-shooters.[28] It wasn't long before the entire right wing of the 12th Pennsylvania Cavalry galloped onto the scene and began to get into formation for another try at dispersing the enemy. Just when they were almost ready to wager their lives in another charge, the Hussars' right flank was lashed by volleys of rifle fire, to which the troopers responded with as much accuracy as could be obtained in the dark from the backs of skittish and rearing horses. For 15 or 20 long minutes the combatants, who were revealed to each other solely by the spectral yellowish glare of multiple muzzle flashes, exchanged bullets and curses.[29]

As soon as he heard the first outbreak of gunfire, General Elliott deployed his three available infantry regiments for battle. Due to the darkness and the clatter of rifle fire that seemed to stretch across the road in front of him, the Union general assumed that he would have to smash through a Rebel roadblock across the Pike and arranged his brigade accordingly. The column-leading 123rd Ohio was deployed perpendicular to the Pike on the right, the 110th Ohio peeled off and assumed a similar formation on the left flank of their comrades, and the 122nd Ohio was ordered to

---

[27]Valentine, *Pennsylvania at Antietam*, p. 206; Valentine, *National Tribune*, 11/19/1908, p. 7. A total of 156 Hussars were captured during the four-day campaign, most of whom were probably taken either after tumbling over the wire or in the confusion that followed. O.R. 1-27-2-53.

[28]Major Titus, who drafted the 12th's after-action report, maintained that the Rebels fired on his troopers "...from both sides of the road...." It is not clear whether the road in question was the Martinsburg Pike or the intersecting road that the Confederates used to reach the scene of the battle. O.R. 1-27-2-70, Titus.

[29]O.R. 1-27-2-70, Titus.

Carter's Woods
Initial Contact

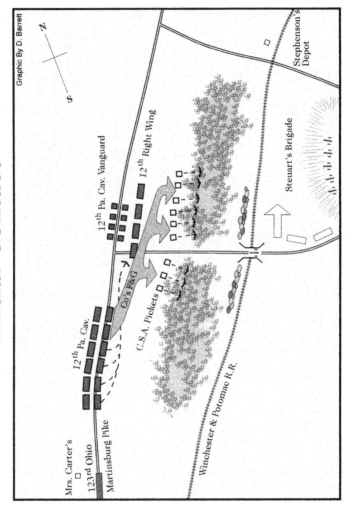

Graphic By D. Barrett

N

S

Mrs. Carter's

123rd Ohio

Martinsburg Pike

12th Pa. Cav.

12th Pa. Cav. Vanguard

Co's F&G

12th Right Wing

C.S.A. Pickets

Steuart's Brigade

Stephenson's Depot

Winchester & Potomac R.R.

From: O.R. Atlas Pl. XLIII #3 & XCIX #1

Scale in Miles

0   1/4   1/2

file into line behind the 123rd.[30]

It is likely that about the time that the Buckeyes were completing their forward-facing line of battle, word arrived via a Pennsylvania trooper, that the road up front had been cleared but that the Pike could only be held open with support from the infantry. Elliott, who was simultaneously hearing the ominous sounds of a Confederate infantry and artillery build-up in the woods on his right flank, responded first by swinging the 123rd Ohio parallel to the right side of the Pike so that their muskets could volley directly into whatever emerged from the darkness. While the 123rd Ohio shuffled to the side of the road, the 110th and the 122nd Ohio began to press toward the sound of gunfire. Perhaps due to the urgency of the situation, rather than maneuver back onto the Pike, the 110th Ohio moved by the left flank on a course about one hundred yards west of, and parallel to, the Pike.[31] Significantly, the departure of the 122nd Ohio was briefly delayed because it was still in the process of forming into a support position behind the 123rd Ohio when its new orders arrived. Critical time was lost as the men of the 122nd Ohio reformed into a marching column so that they could begin to pursue Keifer's 110th Ohio.[32]

The outgunned Hussars tenaciously held their line and kept the Pike open during the time it took the Buckeyes to make their initial faulty alignment and then to march nearly a mile to the point of contact.[33] Just as the harried troopers were beginning to fear that relief would never arrive, the 110th Ohio pounded onto the scene and began forming into a line of battle for the purpose of clearing away the enemy and guaranteeing an avenue of escape. Cognizant that bayonets were preferable to sabers under such circumstances, and having already suffered three killed, a number

---

[30]O.R. 1-27-2-62, 68, 98, Keifer, Ball, Elliott.
[31]Keifer, vol. 2, p. 14.
[32]O.R. 1-27-2-62, 68, 99, Keifer, Ball, Elliott.
[33]Ibid., 1-27-2-62, Keifer.

of men wounded and many more missing in action, the Pennsylvanians moved off a few rods to make way for the infantry. Despite the maneuver, the troopers soon thereafter became the unhappy recipients of artillery fire inadvertently thrown over the heads of the foot soldiers. The screaming and exploding shells whipped some of their horses into a frenzy of fear, and soon the entire regiment was on the verge of chaos. In order to preserve some semblance of order, the regiment moved further to the west out of artillery range.[34]

In their after-action reports, both Milroy and Elliott implied that the 12th Pennsylvania Cavalry abandoned the field without orders as a result of cowardice. Although it is certainly likely that in his own regimental report, Major Titus attempted to put the best possible face on his regiment's performance that morning, it should be recalled that cavalry had almost never been asked to charge artillery, even during daylight, since the British Light Brigade earned its bloody fame in the Crimean War. Further, instances of cavalry charges against infantry were relatively rare up to that point in the Civil War and unheard of in the dark. Most importantly, despite the innuendoes, neither Milroy nor Elliott revealed any plans which they had for the 12th once the infantry became engaged, or that orders were issued to the regiment which went unfulfilled because the Pennsylvanians had disappeared. Finally, it may legitimately be asked, what more might have been expected of the 12th under the circumstances, beyond its accomplishment of holding the Pike open until the infantry arrived?

----

[34]O.R. 1-27-2-70, Titus. Colonel Keifer recorded that the Hussars' efforts to maintain order in the ranks were further impeded by barely controlled team horses and mules that surged through the ranks after fleeing from the artillery fire that also lashed the center of the Union column. Keifer, vol. 2, p. 16. In order to allow the reader to weigh possible bias when evaluating the conflicting interpretations of the performance of the 12th Pennsylvania Cavalry, it must be mentioned that the writer believes that one of his great-great-grandfathers served in the Hussars—a fact that led to a regimental history titled *Leather and Steel: The 12th Pennsylvania Cavalry in the Civil War.*

A more pertinent question to the eventual outcome of the battle may be why Milroy did not, at the first rattle of gunfire, simply turn his entire column to the right, charge the woods en masse, and rout the enemy. The answer is that most of the Hoosier's command was located well beyond where the nearest Rebel was struggling to get into a line of battle. The fighting first erupted at the head of his column nearly a mile from where his leading infantrymen were plodding down the Pike. To compound that disadvantage, at the commencement of the battle Milroy was forced to operate on subjective information gathered in real time from his position near the center of his column. And because of the darkness, Milroy had to rely mostly upon the scant information that could be gathered by ear.[35] That limited sense initially conveyed only the sounds of a minor spat at the head of his division between his cavalry vanguard and just the leading elements of the six regiments that Johnson began to deploy after stumbling upon the Yankee troopers. There was nothing about those first few salvos up front that would have warned Milroy that two Rebel brigades were moving into position from the Union left to right, or that another Confederate brigade of hardened veterans was nearby and straining to reach the action. The scope of the threat only gradually became apparent to Milroy as each successive Rebel regiment or piece of artillery moved into position along his flank and commenced a raking fire into his column. As a result, the battle at Carter's Woods (the local name for the area) evolved incrementally from northeast to southwest. Instead of a combined assault with all his men, the Hoosier was misled into fighting a series of somewhat uncoordinated and overlapping conflicts as he and his brigade commanders responded to the steadily lengthening wall of Confederate fire by engaging, or attempting to flank, newly revealed assailants with the infantry regiments closest at hand.

---

[35]Milroy letter, 6/21/1863.

Back at the head of the column, once the cavalry impediment had cleared away, the 110th Ohio became the first blue-clad infantry regiment to attempt to flank the Rebels out of their chokehold on the Union escape route. After practically running onto the scene, Colonel Keifer hustled his men into a line of battle facing the Pike, despite bearing the brunt of the same artillery and rifle fire that drove off the 12th Pennsylvania Cavalry.[36] Shortly thereafter, the Buckeyes discovered a battle line composed of Virginians and Tar Heels emerging from the woods that filled part of the space between the Pike and the railroad cut.[37] Rather than launch an attack on his own authority, Keifer located Elliott "...some distance in the rear, and obtained his consent to charge them."[38] As soon as their colonel returned, the order to attack was given and a spontaneous cheer erupted from the Ohioans.[39]

"I [Keifer] charged with my regiment upon the enemy, outflanked him on his right, and driving him through the woods upon his artillery, occupying the woods upon the east of the road, opening a destructive fire into the enemy's ranks, throwing him into confusion, and killing large numbers. We also silenced two of the enemy's guns (12-pounders) immediately in our front, capturing one of his caissons." In a few minutes of violence, the Buckeyes were able to clear the Pike and the woods, and to shove the Rebels back into the shelter of the railroad cut.[40]

Unfortunately for the Federals, the need to secure the road had been so urgent that General Elliott did not have time to form his entire brigade for the assault, or even to wait for the 122nd

---

[36]O.R. 1-27-2-62, Keifer.

[37]Keifer, vol. 2, p. 14; O.R. 1-27-2-501, 507, Johnson & Steuart.

[38]Ibid., vol. 2, p. 14.

[39]O.R. 1-27-2-62, Keifer.

[40]Ibid., 1-27-2-62, Keifer; Keifer, vol. 2, pp. 14-15. The Virginians denied suffering any deaths during the entire Winchester campaign, but the 1st and 3rd North Carolina regiments who were positioned on the 10th Virginia's left flank acknowledged nine killed. Steuart's Brigade also reported a total of 32 wounded from June 12 through June 15. O.R. 1-27-2-508.

Ohio to catch up. As a result, the 110th Ohio went in alone with its right flank exposed. Faced with a burgeoning hostile force, supported by two additional pieces of artillery on his vulnerable right flank, Keifer pulled back a short distance and realigned his front to face the enemy more directly.[41]

In the time it took for the 110th Ohio to make its initial foray and realign, the men of the 122nd Ohio were able to double-quick down the road and take a position on the right flank of their comrades. The two Ohio regiments went back to work, "...and in twenty minutes we once more cleared the woods in our front, shooting down the gunners and horses of the enemy's artillery, and bringing off some of the enemy's horses. We were only deterred from taking possession of the enemy's guns by a large body of the enemy again appearing on our right."[42]

As the attack on the Confederate right flank began to make progress, Johnson, perhaps aided by deception and confusion, was able to feed more reinforcements in that direction. "They [the Rebels] got us [the 122nd Ohio] to cease firing by hallooing to us to cease firing for God Sake that we were firing on our own men. And a part of them were dressed in our clothes so that we could hardly tell whether they were our men or not."[43] The resulting Southern numerical superiority on the unsupported right flank of the 122nd Ohio necessitated the withdrawal of both Federal regiments to the western side of the Pike in order to regroup.

Keifer quickly launched his men into the maelstrom for a third time.[44] According to the colonel of the 110th Ohio, "...af-

---

[41]O.R. 1-27-2-62, Keifer.

[42]Ibid., 1-27-2-62, Keifer.

[43]Hartley letter, 6/26/1863.

[44]Both Milroy and Keifer agreed that the latter, rather than General Elliott, assumed functional command of the Union left wing. In his after-action report Keifer implied that he was in control, and overtly made the same assertion in his memoirs. "I found Elliott some distance in the rear, and obtained his consent to charge them [the first time].... Elliott I did not see or receive any order from after the battle began." Keifer, vol. 2, p. 14. Milroy wrote to his wife that "I went up

ter a severe conflict, in which the two lines were engaged in places as near as twenty feet, pouring a murderous fire into each other's breasts, the enemy gave way. Our line then advanced to the enemy's artillery, shooting and driving his gunners from their pieces, and completely silencing them."[45] The immediate goal achieved, Colonel Keifer, allegedly under orders of the "...general commanding...," abandoned the field and marched off toward Harpers Ferry instead of continuing to roll up the enemy's flank.[46] As they pulled out, Milroy was heard to admonish the Buckeyes "...to fall back in good order, and not like damned cowards."[47]

It is puzzling why the Ohioans were ordered to break off contact when, at least according to Keifer's report, they seemed to be on the verge of routing the entire Confederate force. Milroy's report, testimony, and personal correspondence are all silent on that specific point. Perhaps the Hoosier thought that by the time the Buckeyes had managed to clear their own front, what had been the tail end of his column had, pursuant to his orders, already passed behind the fighting and was on its way to safety. That theory is supported by Lieutenant Colonel J. Lowry McGee of the 3rd West Virginia Cavalry who testified at the court of inquiry that "I was ordered by General Milroy to go to the rear, and order Colonel McReynolds and all other troops to pass to the left of

---

towards the left to look after the 110 and 122 O.V.I.... I looked for Elliott, as I had not seen him since the fight commenced and after some time I found him in a deep hollow behind a house standing holding his horse. His whole attention seemed to be occupied in taking care of himself and keeping out of the way of bullets. He was no use to me in all the three days fighting." Milroy letter, 6/21/1863.

[45]O.R. 1-27-2-62, Keifer. Confederate Brigadier General George H. Steuart reported that most of the gunners serving the cannon at the end of the bridge were killed or wounded. O.R. 1-27-2-508.

[46]Ibid., 1-27-2-62, Keifer.

[47]Ibid., 1-27-2-149, Palmer.

where the engagement was going on, and I was ordered to hasten them by."[48]

On the other hand, Milroy may have been convinced that the situation on the Union right flank had already deteriorated to such a point that further fighting would have been useless at best and disastrous at worst. That possibility is supported by the testimony of staff officer F. A. Palmer who related that Milroy sent him to the back of the column to try to find Third Brigade commander McReynolds. After only being able to locate Major Adams and his trailing 1st New York Cavalry, Palmer "...proceeded down the road toward Winchester...until I came to a road that turns to the east, down which I had a view of at least half a mile, and where I had a view of the surrounding country.... As I looked toward Winchester, I saw advancing from that place, I suppose, two sections of artillery, and at the same time I heard what I supposed was a signal gun fired from the direction of Winchester, and I hurried back to General Milroy.... When I told General Milroy that...the enemy was coming up with artillery, he said, 'I must not attempt to fight any longer...[w]e must retreat....'"[49]

---

[48]O.R. 1-27-2-154, McGee.

[49]Ibid., 1-27-2-148, 149, Palmer. Who actually ordered the retreat is also in some doubt. In his somewhat confused account contained in a letter to his wife, Milroy was vague on the question of who gave the order. "I knew it would not do to continue the struggle longer...[i]n spite of all I could do my forces had by this time in the excitement and storm of battle become very much scattered and as the Rebs come howling on after us I could not get my forces together. I come on without the 110th and parts of the 122nd and 87th." Contrary to the assertions contained in his contemporaneous after-action report, in 1900 Keifer implied that he ordered the retreat. "About 5 a.m. therefore, I ordered the whole line withdrawn from the woods, and resumed the march northward...I was soon joined by Generals Milroy and Elliott...." Milroy letter, 6/21/1863; Keifer, vol. 2, p. 15. Keifer's later revised version was supported by Captain Zebulon Baird of Milroy's staff. The staffer testified at the court of inquiry that at Keifer's request he located Milroy with the Second Brigade, but without reaching the Hoosier, he "...returned with all possible expedition to Colonel Keifer...[but] I met...the [Buckeyes] falling

Yet a third, or ancillary, possibility is suggested by a somewhat ambiguous reference in a letter from a lieutenant in the 122nd Ohio. "After we cut our way through and got past them...they sent a shower of bullets after us which appeared to fly almost as thick as hail in any hail storm that I ever seen and we had more men killed and wounded then than in all the rest of the battle."[50] Finally, at about that same time, a Rebel shell burst close enough to the Hoosier to fracture the thigh bone of the horse he was riding.[51] It may have been the heavy and well-directed volley from even more newly arrived Southern reinforcements, coupled with the jolt to his senses from the shell concussion, that dampened Milroy's usual ardor for battle and convinced him that self-preservation for himself and the Ohioans trumped further efforts to save the balance of his command. For whatever the reason, Milroy headed for Harpers Ferry close on the heels of Elliott's Buckeyes.

Before they had gone very far, Milroy almost halted his First Brigade in order to resume the fray. Lieutenant Colonel McGee, who apparently reached Milroy after Palmer did, later testified that "I reported [to Milroy] the four regiments that I had found [at the rear of the column] in good condition, and told the general that they were very near, and we had better halt until they come up. The general called General Elliott, Colonel Keifer, and several other officers about him, gave them the substance of my report, and suggested that they halt there. They were unanimous, I believe, in opposition to that suggestion. The general consented, and moved on."[52]

-----

back." O.R. 1-27-2-136, Baird.
[50]Hartley letter, 6/26/1863.
[51]Milroy letter, 6/21/1863.
[52]O.R. 1-27-2-155, McGee.

About an hour before he gave up the fight and seemingly ceded management of his division to a committee, Milroy took control of the fighting in front of his Second Brigade.[53] First, he had to reorient the leading 87th Pennsylvania toward the right, since it, like the 123rd Ohio, had originally formed facing down the Pike rather than toward the Confederates in the woods.[54] Then, the Hoosier "...had them [a skirmish line comprised of Company A, 87th Pennsylvania] go into the forest to see what was there it being still dark or rather just breaking day."[55]

As soon as the realignment was completed and his skirmishers were headed toward the woods, Milroy launched an attack. Pursuant to orders, Colonel John W. Schall and his 87th Pennsylvania, "'...advanced and the one to my left [probably the 122nd Ohio on its first assault] moved forward at the same time. We both moved toward Carter's Woods, and had gone only a few steps when skirmishing began. It was still dark, and we could see but a short distance. We continued nearly to the woods, when the enemy opened upon us with artillery, posted about one hundred yards in our front. While we were thus engaged with the enemy, the 18th Connecticut was stationed in our rear. They opened fire almost through us. This brought confusion into the ranks of my regiment and I ordered it to fall back.'"[56]

The inexperienced Connecticut boys mistook the 87th Pennsylvania for the enemy due to the darkness and the latter's location in a "...stream of pine along the edge of the forest...." The friendly fire, that mortally wounded at least Pennsylvania Private Peter Free, continued until Milroy personally intervened. "I dashed along in front of them and by the fiercest yelling and knocking up their guns with my sword I got their firing stopped

---

[53]Milroy letter, 6/21/1863.
[54]Prowell, p. 75.
[55]Milroy letter, 6/21/1863; Prowell, p. 75.
[56]Schall, as quoted in Prowell, p. 75.

Carter's Woods
Keifer's & Ely's Assaults

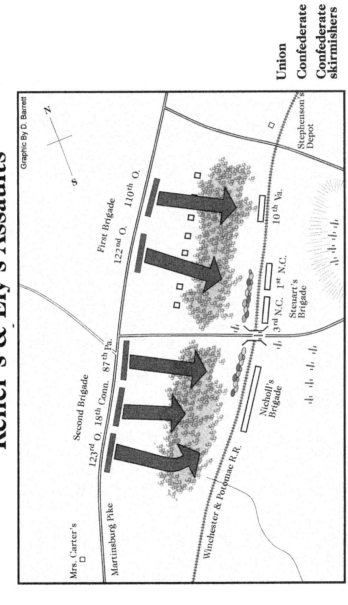

Graphic By D. Barrett

Mrs. Carter's

Martinsburg Pike

Second Brigade

123rd O. 18th Conn. 87th Pa.

First Brigade

122nd O. 110th O.

Winchester & Potomac R.R.

Nicholl's Brigade

3rd N.C. 1st N.C.

Steuart's Brigade

10th Va.

Stephenson's Depot

N

S

Union

Confederate

Confederate skirmishers

From: O.R. Atlas Pl. XLIII #3 & XCIX #1

Scale in Miles

0   1/4   1/2

and got them to understand that they were firing on their friends and that the enemy was beyond them...."[57]

While the Pennsylvanians struggled in the dark to get back into proper alignment, they undoubtedly offered their own explanation to the boys from Connecticut, in less than dignified terms, about who the enemy was and where they were located. Milroy used the delay to summon the 123rd Ohio, that had been left standing alongside the road when Elliott sent his two leading regiments down the road to relieve the cavalry. As the Buckeyes marched onto the scene Milroy ordered them to pass behind his battle line, so as to extend the right flank of the 18th Connecticut.[58] Despite a passage made harrowing by Rebel shells seemingly flying around their heads "...in every direction...," the Ohioans finally ducked and stumbled into place on the right flank of Milroy's patchwork line of battle.[59]

Within moments after the last of the Ohio riflemen took their places in line and fixed their bayonets, the three-regiment assault force went back to work with a yell and "...though grape and canister ploughed great lanes through our poor ranks, not a man faltered or turned back." Even though they didn't run, "...the flashes of musketry in the darkness, casting a sickly glare all around; the roar of artillery, the crashing of grape shot through the brush; the cheers of the charging troops, and cries of the dying..." surely made them want to, and left them with memories which would haunt them until their last days.[60]

The advance remained steady and firm for a time but soon became confused in the dark. "We [the 123rd Ohio] found in the charge that we had lapped over the 18th Connecticut, our left on

---

[57]Prowell, p. 85; Milroy letter, 6/21/1863.

[58]O.R. 1-27-2-48, Milroy; O.R. 1-27-2-62, Keifer. What happened to the 123rd Ohio between the time that Elliott left them beside the road until its involvement in the fight remains a mystery.

[59]Bruder, Memoirs, p. 8.

[60]Keyes, p. 47.

their right. The 18th fell back and becoming mingled together also ordered our Regt. to fall back. We had got close enough to their battery for me to discover their position...[which was] in the woods on the opposite side of a deep rail road cut. There was a small bridge over this cut for a wagon road that ran along the south side of these woods. At the end of this bridge they had two pieces planted and the cut was full of rebs which they used as an entrenchment."[61]   Undoubtedly somewhat intimidated by the strength of the Southern position, the beleaguered and disorganized Federals fell back into the shelter of a ravine about 150 yards from the woods.[62]

Not all of the 87th Pennsylvania's infantrymen had fallen back when their regiment began to be pelted by friendly fire during their first charge.   Privates Sylvester Golding, L. J. Klinedinst, and John C. Hoffman, who had nearly reached the Rebel artillery during that first advance, failed to take notice when the rest of their comrades withdrew into the darkness. After the trio had lain in the dew-covered morning grass shooting at the Confederate gunners for a shorter time than it probably seemed, it gradually occurred to them that the Minié balls sizzling over their heads were coming from both east and west. As the three measured the odds of surviving a retreat compared to holding their ground, the second assault commenced. The courage engendered by the approach of three friendly regiments and the temptation offered by a stranded Confederate caisson spotted on the Rebel side of the no-man's-land overcame the riflemen's concern for life and limb. With a rush the three daredevils leapt out of the night and seized the caisson. The Yankees strained and heaved the stubborn piece through the brush and trees as fast as possible so as not to be left behind for a second time. They got the thing almost back into their lines but were finally forced to abandon the prize

---

[61]Bruder, Memoirs, p. 9.
[62]Prowell, p. 76.

out of a reasonable fear that it, and they, would be blown to pieces if the caisson were struck while being dragged across the open field which lay between them and the Pike.[63]

After falling back and reorganizing again (at approximately the same time that the First Brigade began pulling out in order to begin its retreat) the plucky Federals in Milroy's Second Brigade sucked up their courage and launched a third assault against the dim and deadly woods.[64] The 87th Pennsylvania was only able to force its way about 40 yards into the thicket before being bludgeoned to the ground by a storm of lead and iron. Unable to advance, Colonel Schall's men had to be satisfied with peppering the Rebel line for nearly a half hour with as rapid rifle fire as they could deliver under the encumbrance of trying to load their rifles in the semidarkness while lying on their backs.[65] Thirty casualties stopped the 18th Connecticut in its tracks.[66]

The Buckeyes, who were either more resolute or blessed with lighter opposition, were able to press ahead. "We...charged up to the railroad cut where we came to a stand-still. The only thing the men could do was to load and fire and shoot down the gunners, and they stood nobly up to the work, killing at one time all of the gunners except one man, but they were immediately manned again by taking men from the ranks."[67]

At this point the Yankees' situation quickly began to unravel. In another accident of timing favorable to the Southern cause, General Johnson's trailing unit, the famed Stonewall Brigade, came rushing onto the scene. "Advancing at once with the Second and Fifth [Virginia] Regiments through the fields on

---

[63]Prowell, pp. 85-86.
[64]O.R. 1-27-2-120, Schall.
[65]Prowell, p. 76.
[66]O.R. 1-27-2-77, Peale.
[67]Bruder, Memoirs, p. 9. In Lieutenant C. S. Contee's section of Dement's Confederate battery, 13 of his 16 gunners were either killed or wounded. O.R. 1-27-2-451.

the right of the woods in which General Steuart's brigade was posted, we crossed the railroad, and reached the turnpike without encountering the enemy."[68] The added weight of Stonewall's former brigade would soon prove to be too heavy for the sagging Federal line.

Colonel Schall of the 87th Pennsylvania saw that his regiment was being flanked on the left either by Butternuts who were no longer occupied by fighting Elliott's men or, more likely, by some of the Stonewall Brigade. He attempted to withdraw his men from the vice but when confusion and perhaps some panic spread through the ranks, unit cohesion evaporated. Many of his men scattered toward any apparently safe direction while the rest surrendered.[69]

At least one of the York Countians refused to succumb to panic, however. "'Tiney' Grove, the innocent man of Company G, thought it unwise that so many overcoats should be left on the field. After falling out of ranks on one of the charges, he threw over his back a dozen coats and began to retreat alone. But he was halted by an officious 'Johnny' who caught him by the arm, saying 'Yank, I want you and your coats.' 'Tiney' obeyed the command, and marched back with his coats."[70]

After launching Ely's Brigade on its third assault, and before Private Grove began to police the field, Milroy moved to the head of his column. Undoubtedly influenced by the success of Elliott's men, the Hoosier sent orders to Colonel Ely directing that he pull the balance of his Second Brigade out of the fight and to follow the First Brigade up the road toward Martinsburg.[71] Only the 18th Connecticut, where Ely was located when the order arrived, seemed to have gotten the order. The ill-timed command broke the Yankees' resolve and sent a rapidly disintegrating 18th

---

[68]O.R. 1-27-2-517, Walker.

[69]Prowell, p. 76.

[70]Ibid., p. 88.

[71]Milroy letter, 6/21/1863; O.R. 1-27-2-130, Craven.

Carter's Woods
Stonewall Brigade's Attack

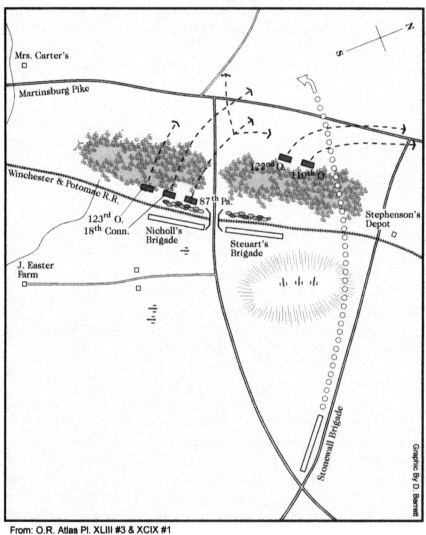

Mrs. Carter's

Martinsburg Pike

Winchester & Potomac R.R.

122nd O.

110th O.

87th Pa.

123rd O.
18th Conn.

Nicholl's
Brigade

Steuart's
Brigade

Stephenson's
Depot

J. Easter
Farm

Stonewall Brigade

Graphic By D. Barrett

From: O.R. Atlas Pl. XLIII #3 & XCIX #1

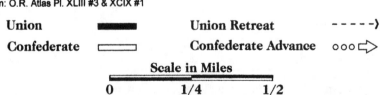

| Union | ▬▬▬ | Union Retreat | - - - -) |
| Confederate | ▭▭▭ | Confederate Advance | ooo ⇨ |

Scale in Miles

0   1/4   1/2

Connecticut, along with some residual fragments of the 87th Pennsylvania, directly into the grasp of the hard hands of the Stonewall Brigade.

The results were predictable. "The smoke and fog was so dense that we [Brigadier General James A. Walker's Stonewall Brigade] could only see a few steps in front, and when, on reaching the Martinsburg turnpike, I saw a body of men about 50 yards to the west of that road, moving by the flank in the direction of Martinsburg, it was with difficulty I could determine whether they were friends or foes, as they made no hostile demonstrations, and refused to say to what brigade they belonged. Being satisfied at last that it was a retreating column of the enemy, I ordered the command to fire. The enemy gave way, and retreated back from the pike in disorder at the first fire, returning only a straggling and inaccurate fire. Pressing them back rapidly to the woods west of the road, they made no stand, but hoisted a white flag, and surrendered to the two regiments [2nd and 5th Virginia] before the others came up."[72]

Unaware that they had been abandoned, the men of the 123rd Ohio stood alone and continued to bang away until they were "...compelled to fall back by overpowering numbers. So soon as we emerged from the edge of the woods we discovered that we were surrounded, or nearly so and that the 18th Conn. had already raised the white flag...the balance of our forces having passed forward on to the right flank of the rebs along with Gen. Milroy, [and having] made their escape...leaving us no other alternative but to surrender."[73]

---

[72]O.R. 1-27-2-517, Walker. In another curious reversal of fortunes, 11 months later at almost the same hour, the Stonewall Brigade, along with most of Johnson's division, would be captured en masse by the Union Second Corps at the Muleshoe at Spotsylvania. Matter, p. 199.

[73]Bruder, Memoirs, p. 9.

Had Milroy been able to thrust his remaining five un-bloodied infantry regiments into the contest, the Rebels might still have been driven away and the entire command saved. Unfortunately for the Yankees, the potential firepower carried by the balance of the division's riflemen was squandered, either as the result of Milroy's hope that the rest of his column could safely pass behind the combatants on the front line, or through the "fog of war." When the fighting erupted at the head, and then the center of the column, those five trailing regiments (one from the First Brigade, and two each from the Second and Third) halted to wait for orders to be sent from officers who were becoming totally engrossed by the fighting up ahead. For what may have been as long as an hour the Bluecoats in the 116th Ohio, 12th West Virginia, and the 5th Maryland, who were located at the tail end of the Second Brigade, stood in column in the middle of the road and waited for orders. As they marked time, stampeding team horses plowed through the formation crushing several lead-footed Yankees against the fences which lined the road, while occasional artillery shells either screamed over their heads or burst in their ranks.[74]

Finally, either on their own initiative or at the direction of a staff officer, part of the 116th Ohio and all of the 12th West Virginia formed a battle line on the west side of the Pike. After a few more minutes of being helplessly abused by Confederate artillery, the two regiments marched off to "...attack the enemy in the rear of the woods on the left of the pike, which I [Colonel

---

[74]O.R. 1-27-2-152; O.R. 1-27-2-81, Klunk.

James Washburn, 116th Ohio] did by marching up the lane that lies to the left of the pike and runs at right angles with it."[75]

It is unclear from Colonel Washburn's report whether he was ordered to attack enemy troops in the woods on the left (west) of the Pike or to form a line of battle on the left of the road and then attack the enemy troops that were already in the woods on the right of the road. If the former interpretation is correct, the enemy troops remain unidentified, but were either part of the same group that purportedly sniped at the 12th Pennsylvania Cavalry's vanguard from the left side of the road at the beginning of the fight, or were a portion of the Stonewall Brigade which was in the process of flanking and capturing the 18th Connecticut and the 123rd Ohio.[76]

That Washburn was ordered to form on the left and attack toward the right is supported by the following: "Having proceeded up this lane some distance, I filed to the right, and marched in toward the rear of the woods as ordered."[77] Before an assault could be launched from the new location however, Washburn "...received an order from a staff officer [probably Lieutenant Colonel McGee] to fall back to the lane and make my retreat the best way possible, as the firing had nearly ceased, and to attack the enemy at that time and place would effect no good."[78] The

---

[75]O.R. 1-27-2-66, Washburn. Colonel Washburn's account differs from that of General Milroy, who reported that he gave orders to the unengaged troops at the rear of the column that they should follow the Pike northward behind the fighting but that those troops went in the wrong direction. O.R. 1-27-2-48, Milroy.

[76]Ibid., 1-27-2-70, Titus.

[77]Ibid., 1-27-2-66, Washburn.

[78]Ibid., 1-27-2-66, Washburn. Except for the following, the *Official Records* provide nothing about what happened to the 5th Maryland during the fight at Carter's Woods: "...I [Lieutenant M. Poore, division ordnance officer] saw a body of men to the left of the road, perhaps amounting to two companies. They belonged to the Fifth Maryland Regiment...I brought them back to where the line had been formed, and just as we got there, the order had been given to move forward [to the 87th Pennsylvania, 18th Connecticut and 123rd Ohio]...." O.R. 1-27-2-122, Poore.

powder and lead carried by nearly a quarter of the Union infantry marched off without ever having been given the opportunity to contribute to what could have been a crushing assault on the Confederate left flank.

The trailing Third Brigade added little toward the salvation of the Federal division during the entire engagement. Moments before the commencement of the initial sparring match between the Hussars and the Rebel skirmishers, Milroy was riding past the middle of his Second Brigade toward the head of his column. On the way, the Hoosier encountered Colonel McReynolds and demanded to know the location of the Third Brigade, what its condition was, and why McReynolds wasn't with his men. McReynolds replied that the Third Brigade was "'...all right.'" Not surprisingly, Milroy found that answer unsatisfactory and curtly reminded McReynolds that "You ought to be with your brigade...'" As Milroy reined his horse around to continue toward the front of the column, the faint popping of rifle and carbine fire startled everyone. At the sound of gunfire, Milroy spurred his horse into a gallop, shouted back over his shoulder to McReynolds, "'Hurry up your brigade, colonel,'" and then disappeared into the darkness.[79]

---

[79]O.R. 1-27-2-154, McGee. Staff officer Cravens recalled the order to McReynolds as "'Move up rapidly with your command, colonel.'" O.R. 1-27-2-130. Historian Stevenson, McReynolds' loyal chief of staff, remembered Milroy's orders somewhat differently. "The general then directed us to place it [the infantry] in line on the east side of the road, along a stone fence running at right-angles thereto." Stevenson, p. 192. This version is neither supported by McReynolds nor the timing of events, since the alleged order was given well before the Rebels had deployed in that direction and at a time when the only fighting involved the 12th Pennsylvania Cavalry and Confederate skirmishers.

Pursuant to his orders, McReynolds rushed back to his men and ordered that they accelerate their pace to the double quick, which shortly brought them to a point where they could see the muzzle flashes from the Rebel artillery. At first the only effects from the cannon blasts were visual—purple and orange disks floating in the darkness in front of their eyes. Soon, however, the riflemen became acutely aware that they had been noticed, thanks to the yellowish trail of burning fuses that arched in their direction, the almost instantaneous flash and thunderclap from shells that exploded nearby, the acrid smell of sulfur, and the whir of solid shot that sailed overhead.

Possessed with only a sketchy idea of the course of developments at the front of the column nearly a mile ahead, and suffering under the fire from a six-gun Southern battery, Colonel McReynolds made a decision reminiscent of the behavior of his commander. The New Yorker shrugged off, or at least reinterpreted, his orders to come up to the aid of the rest of the division and concocted his own plan to attack the Confederates and save the column.[80] In his mind's eye McReynolds envisioned a "...pretty opportunity for a charge..." wherein the 67th Pennsylvania and 6th Maryland Infantry regiments would pitch into the Rebel left flank as the 13th Pennsylvania Cavalry swooped around and pounced on the Confederates from behind.[81]

"I [McReynolds] ordered the two regiments of infantry [6th Maryland and 67th Pennsylvania] in a flanking position to the battery, while I moved with the Thirteenth Pennsylvania Cavalry, for the purpose of charging."[82] As ordered "...[w]e [the 6th Maryland and the 67th Pennsylvania] filed off [to the right of] the Martinsburg road about 3 miles from Winchester...then, to a stone

---

[80] O.R. 1-27-2-110, McReynolds.

[81] Ibid., 1-27-2-110, McReynolds.

[82] Ibid., 1-27-2-110, McReynolds. McReynolds said that he left the 1st New York Cavalry standing alongside the road without orders because he had "...no confidence in them." O.R. 1-27-2-113.

wall that was running from the road, and facing toward the battery that was firing on us."[83]   Next, McReynolds "...put the Thirteenth Pennsylvania Cavalry immediately in motion, and moved along some distance from the stone wall with them, intending to get in the enemy's rear and attack the enemy simultaneously with the infantry."[84]   Perhaps if a coordinated and resolute punch would have been landed by McReynolds' men, the Rebel batteries might have been over-run and their left flank "rolled up like a wet blanket." The blow never landed.

Whether the fault was to be found with McReynolds, with the individual regiments, or perhaps with fate, remains a matter for debate. During the after-battle court of inquiry, and in its final report, there was quite a bit of criticism directed toward McReynolds for his alleged failure to follow Milroy's orders to bring the Third Brigade into the fight and for his supposed disappearance from the field. In particular, Lieutenant Colonel J. Lowry McGee of the 3rd West Virginia Cavalry, who had been pressed into staff duty, provided a particularly damning version of events. "I was ordered by General Milroy to go to the rear, and order Colonel McReynolds and all other troops to pass to the left of where the engagement was going on....   I heard nothing of him [McReynolds] until I got to a run across the road, about three-quarters of a mile from the battle-ground, where I learned that some troops had filed to the west of the road....   I came to the First New York Cavalry. I found Major Adams, and inquired if he knew anything of Colonel McReynolds. He replied that he had been hunting him for the last half hour, and could get no tidings of him. He said he had sent two orderlies, one of whom had returned, and the other had not....   I could not find Colonel McReynolds at all. I inquired of the commanding officers of four regiments, one of which belonged to his command, and none of

---

[83]O.R. 1-27-2-150, McKellip.
[84]Ibid., 1-27-2-110, McReynolds.

them could tell me where he was, or had seen him since the fight commenced."[85]

Lieutenant E. D. Spooner, of the 5th U.S. Artillery, an observer without an agenda (with his guns captured at West Fort, he had no other duties), provided an explanation as to the whereabouts of the Third Brigade's commander as various staffers and aides frantically searched for him. The gunnery officer testified that he was with McReynolds on the morning of the battle and that McReynolds was attempting to help the Union cause, although perhaps not in the way his commander intended. "He was giving instructions to his brigade, and not only to his own brigade, but to a portion of General Elliott's, the Thirteenth Pennsylvania Cavalry [repositioned at the head of the Third Brigade], that was drawn up in line of battle to the right of the Martinsburg road. He went to its [the 13th Pennsylvania Cavalry's] commanding officer, Major [Michael] Kerwin, and told him that he wished his regiment to take a battery, and that it was to be a desperate charge. He also gave him instructions how to do it. After he had done so, he turned around to give some instructions to one of his orderlies. I am pretty sure he intended to accompany this regiment in the charge, but before he turned around they started off...."[86]

The other cavalry regiment from Pennsylvania failed to rise to the challenge. As they attempted to move around the Confederate far left flank, the troopers of the 13th Pennsylvania Cavalry were subjected to intense artillery fire similar to that which had battered the rest of the Union line, including one blast that allegedly slaughtered, but probably only scattered, almost an entire company.[87] Whether it was artillery, or a volley of rifle fire

---

[85]O.R. 1-27-2-154, McGee.

[86]Ibid., 1-27-2-147, Spooner.

[87]Ibid., 1-27-2-71, Kerwin. Michael Kerwin was a major in the 13th Pennsylvania Cavalry, which was commanded during the action at Winchester by Colonel James A. Galligher. Kerwin, who authored the 13th's after-action report, claimed that "[a]t one fire, Company A, composed of 62 men, lost every man

from approaching enemy infantry as claimed by one of the troopers in the ranks, the regiment's horses were thrown into a panic. Faced with this new threat, the 13th's officers became confused about what to do next. The dilemma was resolved when "...an [unidentified] officer dashed in among us and gave orders for every man to get away as best he could. This order ended all discipline, and away we went, everyone looking out only for himself...and as we left the field of battle farther and farther behind us, the noise became less and less until it died out altogether. We thus continued to madly dash on, but to where we knew not. We had only one object in view, and that to escape from our enemy."[88] Major Kerwin chose a more delicate explanation for the behavior of his regiment, "Seeing no other cavalry on the field, we withdrew toward Charlestown...."[89]

Ares was even less kind to the Third Brigade's foot soldiers. Before their battle formation could be completed "...the command was given, 'By the right flank, march!' We [the 6th Maryland and the 67th Pennsylvania] moved on, then, in quick time, and in perfect order, until we reached the Winchester railroad, and there a battery opened on us. We moved to the railroad and halted, the battery in the meantime playing on us. From there we passed through the tunnel or arch, and down by a ravine, that protected us from the enemy's battery."[90]

---

excepting 9, including 2 commissioned officers," but this assertion is refuted by the casualty reports.

[88]Erskine, *Grand Army Scout & Soldiers Mail*, 3/14/1885. The claim that they received an order similar to "every man for himself" was supported by at least one other member of the regiment. McElhenny, *National Tribune*, 5/20/1909. Another member of the 13th claimed that the charge was aborted because of telegraph wire strung in front of the enemy identical to that which was encountered by the Hussars. Averill, *National Tribune*, 6/6/1895.

[89]O.R. 1-27-2-71, Kerwin. For its behavior the regiment won the sobriquets of the "Skedaddling 13th" and the "Galloping 13th." Averill, *National Tribune*, 9/16/1909.

[90]Ibid., 1-27-2-150, McKellip.

Darkness, which had earlier interfered with Federal dispositions, now removed its sheltering cloak and exposed the Yankee maneuvers to full view. "Riding to the front, I [Colonel J. M. Williams, commander of Nicholls' Confederate brigade] observed that the line of the enemy, which was moving on the pike, was changing direction so as to flank my left. To meet this movement of the enemy, I ordered the Second Louisiana...and the Tenth Louisiana...to change front, and move perpendicularly to the Martinsburg pike and attack the flanking force."[91]

It was their own misbehavior, rather than fate, that finally delivered the Third Brigade's leading regiment into the clutches of their adversaries. "When we [the 6th Maryland] got to the house that stands on the left-hand side, a great many of the regiment in advance of us [the 67th Pennsylvania] went into the yard and buildings....," ostensibly to quench their thirst at the well or springhouse in the farmyard.[92] Since no exculpatory after-action report was filed by anyone from the 67th Pennsylvania, it may be concluded that the men of that regiment degenerated from a fighting force into a mob that crowded around the water sources (and perhaps also indulged in a little foraging for chickens, eggs, bread, etc.). Or, as Lieutenant Colonel McKellip of the 6th Maryland put it, "From that point the regiment in advance of us...ceased to be an organized regiment."[93]

Disobedience proved to be a capital offense for many of the infantrymen from Pennsylvania. "These regiments [the 2nd and 10th Louisiana], having met the enemy, moved by the left flank on parallel line with the enemy's line until he had discovered about 1,000 of his [the Union] men; then opened fire on his [the Union] line...."[94] Adding to the slaughter, "Raine's battery was faced

---

[91]O.R. 1-27-2-512, Williams.
[92]Ibid., 1-27-2-150, McKellip.
[93]Ibid.
[94]Ibid., 1-27-2-512, Williams.

Carter's Woods
McReynolds' Attack

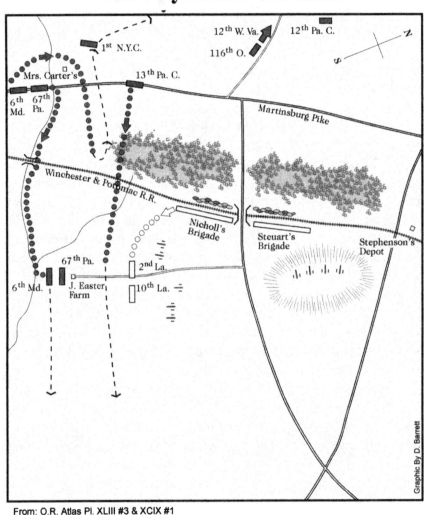

12th W. Va.   12th Pa. C.

116th O.

1st N.Y.C.

Mrs. Carter's

13th Pa. C.

6th 67th
Md. Pa.

Martinsburg Pike

Winchester & Potomac R.R.

Nicholl's
Brigade

Steuart's
Brigade

Stephenson's
Depot

67th Pa.

6th Md.   J. Easter
           Farm

2nd La.

10th La.

Graphic By D. Barrett

From: O.R. Atlas Pl. XLIII #3 & XCIX #1

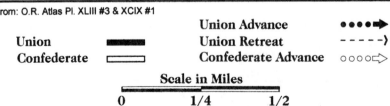

		Union Advance	●●●●➡
Union	▬▬▬	Union Retreat	- - - -)
Confederate	▭	Confederate Advance	○○○○➪

Scale in Miles

0   1/4   1/2

to the left, and played upon them with fine effect...."[95] Within moments the barnyard was littered with 17 dead or dying, and over 30 wounded, Bluecoats. Too disorganized to regroup or respond with a covering fire, the survivors of the 67th Pennsylvania were captured almost to a man.[96]

Despite almost certainly having witnessed the fate of their brigade mates, the Marylanders resisted the urge to lay down their arms and surrender. "The colonel went in front of the regiment, and gave the command, 'By the left flank, guide center.' We moved up the crest of that hill in line of battle. There we found the enemy in position, with artillery, and too strong for us to cope with."[97] Conceding to reality, discretion prevailed, and the 6th Maryland fled around the Rebel left flank and hustled off to Harpers Ferry where it arrived almost intact.[98] On their way, as they crossed the Opequon Creek, the Marylanders were treated to the sight of McReynolds and some of his companions riding east in such a determined and rapid fashion that they were unable to respond to calls from Lieutenant Colonel McKellip.[99]

The men of the 1st New York Cavalry, who had originally been detailed to act as the rear guard, and who sat atop their horses and watched at least part of the disintegration of the rest of their brigade, held the Federals' last hope for liberating the

---

[95]O.R. 1-27-2-502, Johnson.

[96]Ibid., 1-27-2-49, Milroy; O.R. 1-27-2-512, Williams; Bates, *History of the Pennsylvania Volunteers...*, 67th Pennsylvania.

[97]Ibid., 1-27-2-150, McKellip.

[98]Ibid., 1-27-2-49, Milroy. The Maryland boys were fortunate that only 130 of their number were captured, mostly while straggling on the retreat. The Third Brigade's flanking movement was discovered at about the same time that the Stonewall Brigade arrived on the scene. Walker initially dispatched the 4th, 27th and 33rd Virginia regiments to intercept the Marylanders, but when an adjutant ordered him to bring his entire command to the right flank, the three regiments had to be recalled before they could "gobble up" the Marylanders. O.R. 1-27-2-517, Walker.

[99]Ibid., 1-27-2-151, McKellip.

column.[100] Minute after agonizingly long minute dragged by as Lieutenant Colonel Alonzo W. Adams and his troopers chafed under artillery fire that delivered shell after exploding shell over their heads while they waited in column for orders from the elusive McReynolds.[101] Probably fearing that if he didn't attack soon that his men would break and flee, the lieutenant colonel moved his regiment "...forward [up the Pike] at a trot until we reached a point from a quarter to a half mile in advance of my former position on the left of the road [and probably behind the rest of the brigade which was moving toward the railroad], and, as I believe, within 500 yards of the enemy, where I found an open field...and where I formed a line of battle...."[102]

When the formation was completed "...the order rang out, 'Draw sabres! Forward! Trot!' The men gathered their reins, grasped firm hold of their sabres, fixed themselves firmly in their saddles, clenched their teeth, and spurred their horses into a gallop.... They came within range of the infantry firing. But that line was too strongly posted. It would have been a grand charge, like that of the Light Brigade at Balaklava, but at a fearful sacrifice of life, with nothing to gain but the name.... But just then some one with some sense, either a staff officer or some junior officer of the regiment, appeared at the head of the column and ordered it off to the left."[103]

Lieutenant Colonel Adams offered his own explanation why the New Yorkers were ordered to peel off to their left rather than

---

[100]O.R. 1-27-2-142, Adams.

[101]Both McReynolds' and Adams' reports confirm that the former never made contact with the latter during the entire engagement despite one of Adams' orderlies making a frantic search for the errant brigade commander. Although not supported by hard evidence, it may be inferred that McReynolds was not far behind the "Galloping 13th." O.R. 1-27-2-110, 142.

[102]O.R. 1-27-2-142, Adams.

[103]Beach, p. 243. Lieutenant Colonel Adams described this abortive charge in his official report but neglected to mention it in his testimony before the court of inquiry.

"do and die." In his original report, Adams wrote that "I [Adams, or more likely the whole regiment] charged down the lines to the front, but just before reaching the position of the enemy's guns, I came in contact with a perfect barricade of telegraph wire wound together and stretched from tree to tree across roads and through woods and fields, so as to completely obstruct the farther progress of cavalry in this direction."[104]

After the charge was aborted, Adams' maneuvers, at least according to his chief critic William Beach, nearly provoked a mutiny. "The column moved rapidly across the fields with the enemy's firing on its right flank, but was soon out of range of the infantry, but not of the artillery. It was getting light and Adams here halted the regiment, as if he wanted to see all that was to be seen. Someone urged him to go instead of waiting longer where nothing could be done. But he replied, 'I am in no hurry to get out of here.' Quinn [the junior major primarily responsible for Adams' arrest on June 13] retorted, 'I noticed you were in a hurry to get out of where you were a few minutes ago.' 'Hurrah for Major Quinn!'...'Quinn take command and lead us out, and let the other major stay if he wants to!' The men had no confidence in the commanding major's strategy.... The loud protests against waiting there for nothing induced the self-important major to move on."[105]

It is doubtful that the series of movements that Adams ordered next, allegedly in response to the dissension in his ranks, did anything to restore his men's confidence. The lieutenant

---

[104]O.R. 1-27-2-85, Adams. The quotation was contained in Adams' after-action report which was filed on June 26, 1863, from Bloody Run, Pa., where the 12th Pennsylvania Cavalry was also posted at the time. Perhaps the reference to telegraph wire confirms the report from the 12th's Private Valentine. It is also possible that Adams learned of the Hussars' experience and inserted the story in his report as a handy explanation.

[105]Beach, p. 244, emphasis in original. Beach's history leaves little doubt that he was not one of Adams' admirers.

colonel led the New Yorkers back into a field on the left of the Pike.   When the Rebel gunners once again found the troopers' range, the regiment was moved 100 yards to the left.   Still without orders, the hapless horsemen were made to shift position three more times.   The bobbing and weaving only ended after the 116th Ohio and the 12th West Virginia were ordered to retreat to the northwest, and the troopers from New York were sent along to guard their rear.[106]

Practically speaking, the battle at Carter's Woods, and/or Second Winchester, was over when the New Yorkers aborted their charge, leaving only the desperate flight of the Federals who managed to escape and the rounding up of those who had not. Colonel Keifer of the 110th Ohio provided a sad postscript to the battle when he described the final, futile fight of the day. "Lieutenant Weakley with 60 men was left upon picket [on Apple Pie Ridge], in consequence of his whereabouts not being known to me, and a false report that he was with the wagon train.   The lieutenant, with most of his men, were left at their post on picket, and alone engaged the enemy at Winchester on the morning of the 15th.   After a most gallant resistance, they surrendered."[107] Weakley's men would not feel lonely and abandoned for long.

---

[106]O.R. 1-27-2-142, Adams. It is possible that McReynolds and Adams lost contact because the latter's maneuvers on the left of the road were taking place at approximately the same time that McReynolds was trying to get his infantry and the 13th Pennsylvania Cavalry into line. If so, the 1st New York Cavalry would have been almost directly behind the balance of the Third Brigade, rather than on its right flank. Given that the New Yorkers started at the rear of the column, Adams' orderly probably went down the Pike to find McReynolds rather than toward the railroad tracks.

[107]Ibid., 1-27-2-64, Keifer.

8

MILROY'S WEARY BOYS

Major General Schenck,
Don't give General Milroy any command at Harper's
Ferry; we have had enough of that sort of military genius.
—Henry W. Halleck[1]

The rising sun and the slowly dissipating gun smoke unveiled the shattered wreckage of Milroy's division. The Union dead were strewn over the battlefield: some lay in contorted positions impossible during life; others, except for a crimson stain, looked as if merely napping; while a few consisted of little more than clotted gore and dismembered pieces. Four thousand dazed and demoralized Yankee prisoners either ministered to wounded comrades or mutely waited for instructions. Scattered about them was the detritus of battle: discarded rifles and equipments, hats, blouses, blankets, haversacks, canteens, a random shoe, and dead or dying horses. The mist that clung to the air above the battlefield reeked of sulfur and freshly spilled blood. And, for those who paused to listen, the morning was filled with the sounds of suffering and defeat, surly orders barked to d____d Yankees, the deep-pitched murmur of wounded men who were able to restrain the expression of their agony to low moans, the occasional scream

---

[1]O.R. 1-27-2-171.

or curse from those poor souls who could not, and the buzz from flies beginning to reconnoiter the carnage.[2]

Unfortunately, the *Official Records* do not provide a sufficiently detailed account of Union casualties to allow an accurate tally of how many Federals were killed or wounded in Mrs. Carter's woods. For the entire four-day campaign, the Union losses, provided as killed, wounded, and captured (ranked by killed and wounded) were: 123rd Ohio- 21, 62, 466; 18th Connecticut- 18, 46, 534; 67th Pennsylvania- 17, 38, 736; 110th Ohio- 4, 51, 210; 12th West Virginia- 6, 36, 191; 116th Ohio- 8, 29, 141; 87th Pennsylvania- 4, 21, 87; 122nd Ohio- 8, 25, 380; 12th Pennsylvania Cavalry- 4, 12, 156; 6th Maryland- 1, 6, 167; Alexander's Maryland battery- 0, 5, 34; 5th Maryland- 0, 5, 315; 5th U.S. Artillery (Battery L) 3, 1, 77; 1st New York Cavalry- 1, 3, 56; 1st Massachusetts Heavy Artillery- 0, 3, 40; 1st West Virginia Light Artillery (Battery D)- 0, 3, 80; 13th Pennsylvania Cavalry- 0, 1, 247; 1st West Virginia Cavalry (Co. K) 0, 1, 11; 3rd West Virginia Cavalry (Cos. D & E) 0, 1, 71. The total Union casualties were 95 killed, 348 wounded, and 4,000 captured.[3] On the other side of the line, General Lee acknowledged 252 casualties (42 killed and 210 wounded) during the entire Winchester campaign, of which 88 were suffered by Hays' Brigade and 66 by Gordon's.[4]

Whatever the exact numbers of their losses, there were immediate tasks and responsibilities for both the victors and the vanquished that morning, with the foremost being care for the wounded. The blue and butternut casualties limped or were

---

[2]O.R. 1-27-2-53.

[3]Ibid., 1-27-2-53. For unknown reasons the official tally does not seem to include the 1st New York Cavalry's losses suffered at the Opequon Creek.

[4]Ibid., 1-27-2-335. There has been some speculation that General Lee understated all of the casualty counts for the Gettysburg campaign. For example, in his report, Gordon claimed that his brigade suffered 75 casualties on June 13. O.R. 1-27-2-491, Gordon.

carried to local homes which were impressed into service as field hospitals. Captain Bruder of the 123rd Ohio, who suffered a severed vein in his thigh from a ball in the hip, was taken to a brick house along the road, where he remained unconscious for two days.[5] He would survive his ordeal intact, but many others would leave the makeshift hospitals incomplete, while a few would give up their last breath on a dining room/operating table.

As the surgeons from both sides struggled to do the wounded more good than harm, small details of Yankee prisoners, including Private Valentine of the 12th Pennsylvania Cavalry, buried the dead.[6] After the wounded and dead had been attended to in their fashion, the Federal prisoners were sent shuffling and staggering off toward Winchester. At that moment, portions of Milroy's exhausted and broken division were headed toward almost every point on the compass. They were also well on the way toward earning the stigma of being among "Milroy's Weary Boys."[7]

Upon arrival at Winchester, the Federal prisoners were herded into the same forts which they had recently defended. The commissioned officers were culled from their men and herded toward Staunton, Virginia, almost immediately after arrival. Shortly thereafter, about half of the 3,856 noncommissioned and

---

[5]Bruder, Memoirs, pp. 11-13.

[6]Valentine, *National Tribune*, 11/19/1908.

[7]When, and from whom, the pejorative nickname "Milroy's Weary Boys" originated has not been conclusively determined. It is probable that Milroy supplied that albatross himself in an official dispatch of June 16, 1863, where he wrote in part, "We were pursued by a large cavalry force who picked up a number of my weary boys." *The New York Times*, 6/17/1863, p. 1. Five days later, in a telegraph to his wife, the Hoosier also referred to those of his men who retreated to Bloody Run, Pennsylvania, as "...my weary worn out boys...." Civil War historian Shelby Foote has written however (without attribution) that the nick-name became attached following Milroy's retreat after the battle of McDowell. Foote, vol. 1, p. 465. Given the personality revealed in his letters, it is doubtful that Milroy, who was devoid of a sense of irony, would have used the phrase in an official dispatch if it already had such a negative connotation.

enlisted prisoners were driven south in pursuit of their officers, while the others, who no doubt slept on the dirt floor of the fort as if on a feather mattress at home, moved out the following morning.[8]

The first group of enlisted prisoners was formed into ranks of fours and then surrounded by Butternuts from the 58th Virginia. Before the procession started down the Pike on the 90-mile march to Staunton, Virginia, the Confederate regiment's Colonel Board admonished his soldiers, "'Men, these Yankees have fallen into our hands by the fortune of war. I want them treated as gentlemen as long as they behave themselves. If I know of any abuse or insults they shall be punished.'"[9] With that warning still ringing in their ears, the Rebel infantrymen began shepherding their prisoners toward the ultimate destination of Southern prison camps. "...[W]e [the Federal prisoners] began our journey to the rebel Capital. Passing thru the silent streets of Winchester, we swung out onto the broad white turnpike...."

"At first the prisoners were silent. Later, the cool evening breeze sprang up and the novelty of the situation wore away, a subdued conversation arose, gradually increasing into passing jokes and quips, chaffing each other and, even the guards, until, when at the end of about eight miles, we filed into a field near the village of Newtown for the night bivouac, a tone of cheerfulness, even hilarity, prevailed in the blue-clad ranks.

"The 'bivouac' was simply to lie down upon the wet grass. The prisoners were packed closely together to make the work of the guards safer and easier. Most of us Yanks were thinly clothed...some had blankets and a few had overcoats.... The cordon of sentinels drew closer around us; a bugle sounded 'Taps,'

---

[8]O.R. 1-27-2-53; Sawyer, *National Tribune*, 10/23/1913. Private Valentine recalled that both groups of enlisted men moved out the next morning. Valentine, *National Tribune*, 11/19/1908.

[9]Sawyer, *National Tribune*, 10/23/1913.

and the thousand and a half prostrate forms settled down to get as much comfort as they could from the situation. "

"About dawn those not already awake were brought to their senses by reveille played by the Drum corps. The Orderly-Sergeants stepped around among the captives shouting: 'Fall in! Turn out, you Yanks! Fall in lively thar!' Long before sunrise the column was in motion and marched steadily till about 7 o'clock when it turned into a field to the right. Going about a quarter of a mile we halted in a beautiful grove, thru which ran a stream of clear, cold water.

"Soon the banks of the stream were lined with prisoners and guards making their morning toilets. A small ration of bacon and hardtack had been issued to us before we left Winchester, and this we proceeded to eat, our friends the Virginians taking their own breakfast at the same time. After resting there about an hour the line was formed, the column moved out upon the pike again and settled down to a long day's work.

"Before us lay a succession of low undulating hills, crossing the road at right angles.... The broad, white, macadamized turnpike could be seen rising and falling over these hills a long distance ahead. On the left, 10 miles or so away, arose the outline of the Blue Ridge Mountains.... The sky was deep blue, a cool breeze was blowing and all nature looked fresh and lovely. The captive train, prisoners and guards, started off in good spirits, talking and joking.

"But as the sun mounted higher the breeze fell away. The many trampling feet stirred up the white lime dust, which overhung the column in a choking cloud. The pangs of thirst began to torment. The steady, monotonous tramp was held hour after hour...over clear brooks, where there would be a short, struggling halt for water.... A couple of short halts for rest in the forenoon; half an hour at noon, two halts in the afternoon, were the only breaks in the steady, onward movement. At the noon halt about every man had exhausted his store of rations.

"Sometimes, going over a rise far ahead, we would see another detachment of prisoners. These were the captured officers of Milroy's command who had left Winchester a few hours ahead of us.... At other times a squad of cavalry would appear, and, riding along on the flanks of the column, have a good-natured talk and chaff with the Yankees. Farmers and their laborers in distant fields would leave their work and hasten to the roadside to see the passing show. Once we met a battery of six guns on its way to join Lee's army. It was said that this was a brand-new outfit, just landed from a blockade runner. Everything, excepting the horses and men, was furnished by the British Government, it was said. The long, bright Napoleons, mounted upon elegant carriages; the fine horses in russet harness, the men in neat gray uniforms, made the best appearance of anything we had yet seen stamped with the C. S. A. brand....

"Very frequently the unsodded mounds in the fence corners or beside the road showed where some soldier lay—it might be Gray, it might be Blue—who had fallen exhausted and died, or had been killed in some [earlier] skirmish. Everywhere were sad evidences of war's cruel work.

"Late in the afternoon the white-tipped thunder clouds appeared above the western mountains. The threatening clouds, rising higher and blacker; the pealing thunder, the swift lightning darting from cloud to cloud and to the earth, showed that a storm of no ordinary power was rapidly advancing. Soon came the sound of many waters, and we saw the oncoming line of the cloudburst charging down upon us. It overwhelmed us in one of the worst deluges of wind, rain and hail I ever experienced. For some minutes we stood there in the road, soaked by the rain and beaten by the hail. When the fury of the storm had passed it settled into a drizzling rain. Saturated completely, we splashed onward the rest of the afternoon, passing thru Strasburg, across Cedar Creek...and, further on, over Fisher's Hill....

"As night began to fall we turned into a field and halted upon a side hill at the foot of which ran a small stream.... On this hillside, wet, cold, tired and hungry, we made our bivouac—the dripping rain above and the wet grass beneath.

"Towards midnight the wagons with the rations came up, and we were routed out to receive the allowance which was to make our supper that night and breakfast and dinner the next day. A pint of raw flour and a small piece of bacon were given to each man. Then in darkness and rain we started fires, mixed our flour with water, without salt or rising, and cooked it on tin plates and half canteens. To the Yankees this was a new experience, and the product—well, just imagine! Still, it was all we would have to eat for the next 24 hours. The guard had a like ration, but they had salt and rising and Dutch ovens in which to bake their dough.[10]

By June 23, all of the foot-sore Yankee prisoners had shuffled up to the railhead at Staunton in preparation for transportation to Richmond. Their duty completed, the 58th Virginia turned the captives over to the Richmond Home Guard and rushed north toward Pennsylvania. The Home Guard apparently did not share the same noble attitude toward their prisoners as had Ewell's veterans, prompting Sawyer to cryptically remark that in Staunton "...the screws were put on..." by the Guards.[11] In addition to whatever indignities the prisoners were subjected to by the Guards, they were "...piled into freight cars, and after a long weary night ride we arrived in Richmond..." on June 25.[12]

The next day, the entire sorry lot was transferred to Belle Isle, Virginia, where most would spend a month or two waiting to be exchanged. The enlisted prisoners from the 12th Pennsylvania Cavalry seem to have been particularly fortunate since 143 of their 156 prisoners were transferred to Camp Parole, Annapolis, by July 25, 1863. The officers of that regiment were not so fortunate. Several, including the 12th's chaplain, Graves B. Hammer,

---

[10]Sawyer, *National Tribune*, 10/23/1913, p. 5.
[11]Ibid., 10/23/1913.
[12]Valentine, *National Tribune*, 11/19/1908.

remained in captivity until mid-autumn.[13]   On the other end of the spectrum, a number of the officers of the 67th Pennsylvania were not exchanged for a year, and several officers of the 87th Pennsylvania did not attain their freedom until the war ended.[14]

The most unusual Union prisoners were "apprehended" between the battlefield at Carter's Woods and the town of Winchester. "In the grove just mentioned an unusual sight met our [Confederate soldier's] eyes.   All the bright colors of the rainbow, all the finery displayed in the most fashionable shops of a city seemed assembled there in that strip of woods.... In a few minutes they started toward us, two and two, led by a gray-clad soldier. When they reached us, we found they were the wives and sweethearts of our enemies, who, in their haste to follow the army, had put on their most costly attire and mounted the army wagons and horses in an effort to escape. As they passed us all were in tears and excited our sympathy by their hasty inquiries as to what had become of Lieutenant or Captain or Colonel So and So."[15]

The fact that the Federal officers were apparently so cavalier about the fate of their wives and daughters speaks volumes about Northern confidence in the chivalry of their Southern adversaries. The Yankees were not disappointed, because the 17 women who were "captured" outside of Winchester after they abandoned the futile effort to keep up with their fleeing men, endured the shortest stay at Confederate expense, and there is no indication that any of them were molested. It is unclear, though,

---

[13]O.R. 1-27-2-182; *Pennsylvania Daily Telegraph*, 10/12/1863.

[14]Taylor, p. 82; Prowell, p. 82. At least one member of the 67th Pennsylvania was shipped to the Confederate prison at Salisbury, North Carolina. White, Harry, *Pennsylvania at Salisbury*, p. 49.

[15]Brackwell, *Confederate Veteran*, vol. 30, p. 331. Although mostly related to Federal officers, at least two of the female captives were wives of Union enlisted men who were able to remain with their husbands by serving as washer-women. Prowell, p. 89.

why the Southerners thought it necessary to place the women in captivity.[16] Whether from spite or concern for their safety, the women were also shipped to Richmond and there spent 10 anxious days as prisoners in Castle Thunder until arrangements were made for their release.[17]

The half of Milroy's division that did not surrender on June 15 made a desperate effort to avoid capture. General Milroy shared amply in that ordeal. Immediately prior to the collapse of Federal resistance, Milroy attempted to extricate, rather than fight, his unengaged men by ordering the tail end of his column to pass behind the protection of the five fighting regiments and for Colonel Ely's force to follow immediately thereafter. Those may have been the last orders issued by the Union major general, who allegedly became distracted by his efforts to secure a replacement mount when "...my black horse which I was riding was struck by a piece of shell which exploded by me and his thigh bone fractured...."[18] When a substitute horse was located, Milroy galloped off after the men of the 110th and 122nd Ohio regiments, who had already commenced their escape, rather than attempting

---

[16]A possible reason for the women being held captive for a time appeared in the *Richmond Sentinel* on June 20, 1863. "What shall be done with Mrs. Milroy, if indeed, she has been captured, as is believed? A common sentiment is that she ought to be tried for stealing. She took possession of a lady's house, who was driven out of her accommodation, but she stole the wearing apparel and the ornaments, and the household effects of all those whom her husband's tyranny placed in her power." *Philadelphia Inquirer*, 6/24/1863. Perhaps, if the Confederate authorities actually believed the foregoing, they held the Union women until it was conclusively established that Mrs. Milroy was not among the captives.

[17]Prowell, p. 81.

[18]O.R. 1-27-2-49, Milroy; Milroy letter, 6/21/1863.

to lead the balance of his embattled troops to victory or safety.[19]

After the disintegration of 87th Pennsylvania, a few of the York Countians crawled away from the fight behind the cover of a stone fence which ran toward the Pike. Those fugitives claimed to have encountered The Old Gray Eagle, as Milroy was called by some of his men, soon after he had departed the battlefield. The leader of the Weary Boys was apparently so exhausted that he slept on his horse, a perch that was maintained only through the assistance of aides who propped him up in the saddle.[20]

Although the most prominent, Milroy was far from being the only member of the Winchester garrison who earned the designation of being a "Weary Boy." His soldiers had endured an abbreviated night's rest on June 13, a day's fighting on the 14th, and a sleepless night and another battle during Monday's predawn hours. For those Bluecoats who chose northeast as the direction of their flight, 35 hot and dusty miles separated them from the relative safety offered by the big guns at Harpers Ferry. Those with the will and the stamina completed the journey by the end of the day, a testament to the power of sufficient motivation to overcome aching feet and leaden muscles.[21]

For some of the Federals, particularly the troopers of the 13th Pennsylvania Cavalry the journey was even longer. After hearing the command "[e]very man for himself...[the 13th] struck to the right, making Berryville our objective point; but we did not go far until we captured a Confederate dispatch bearer on his way

---

[19]O.R. 1-27-2-49, Milroy.

[20]Prowell, p. 87. Milroy wrote to his wife that he had not slept at all during the Saturday or Sunday nights which preceded the battle at Carter's Woods. He may also have been suffering from a concussion or mild shock caused by the shell which exploded near him and which injured his horse. Milroy letter, 6/18/1863.

[21]For distance traveled in a continuous march, the flight of the Weary Boys to Harpers Ferry placed them at the same level of ambulatory accomplishment as the Stonewall Brigade that marched 37 miles on May 31, 1862, and the men of the Union Sixth Corps who marched approximately the same distance on their way to Gettysburg on the night of July 1-2, 1863. Tanner, p. 338; Maier, p. 79.

from Berryville, who told us that the town was in the hands of the enemy. We then headed for Charlestown, but discovered we were too late again, and we then made for Harper's Ferry."[22]

A few of the Yankee regiments dragged into Harpers Ferry as shrunken but organized units: the 110th Ohio arrived with 323 men; the 13th Pennsylvania Cavalry with 321 troopers; the 122nd Ohio with about half a regiment; and the 6th Maryland mostly intact.[23] Other regiments were represented by only tattered fragments: 155 infantrymen from the 87th Pennsylvania; about one-third of the 116th Ohio; and 30 men from 18th Connecticut.[24] It may be assumed that the physical discomforts of the march quickly passed once the refugees were secure within the fortifications surrounding Harpers Ferry, but it certainly took longer to heal their psychological injuries. It would take them even longer to erase the stigma of having served under Milroy at Winchester.[25]

While that morning's killing, surrendering, or fleeing was unfolding a short distance to the southeast, the troopers of the 12th Pennsylvania Cavalry sat patiently in their saddles waiting for

---

[22]McElhenny, *National Tribune*, 5/20/1909.

[23]O.R. 1-27-2-62, 71, 72, Keifer, Kerwin, Hanson.

[24]Prowell, p. 82; O.R. 1-27-2-78, Peale.

[25]Many of Milroy's Weary Boys would eventually return to the Shenandoah Valley. About half the division was attached to the Army of West Virginia that remained in the area during most of the balance of the war. A few regiments were assigned to garrison duty in the lower Valley to guard against guerrillas. The rest eventually joined the Third Division of the Sixth Corps. For the latter group, after the Wilderness, Spotsylvania, Cold Harbor, Third Winchester, Fisher's Hill, Cedar Creek, Petersburg and Sailor's Creek, few people had the nerve to mention the time spent with Milroy at Winchester.

orders and listening to the sounds of the ebb and flow of battle. After a time, they were joined by the infantrymen of the 116th Ohio and the 12th West Virginia, who had earlier set off up a back road to the left of the Pike. Shortly thereafter, the Pennsylvanians' position became the rallying point for the survivors of the battle who had neither been captured nor fled toward Harpers Ferry.

Along with the flotsam from almost every regiment in the division came orders either to proceed to Harpers Ferry, as Milroy recalled it, or to flee toward Hancock, Maryland, as others remembered.[26] Because retreat to Harpers Ferry was impossible due to the rapid approach of Confederate infantry from the direction of the Martinsburg Pike, the impromptu, hodgepodge brigade headed into the interior to the northwest on what was to become a 28-mile flight to Bath, West Virginia.

"We [what will hereafter be referred to as the hodgepodge brigade] then quickly moved to the left, westward, through a piece of woods, skirmishing with an unseen foe as we went, until we reached an open field beyond, where we halted and reformed. We found we had the two regiments named [116th Ohio and 12th West Virginia], besides fragments of several others...and about half of the 12th Pennsylvania cavalry. A course of retreat was soon settled upon. The infantry moved out in advance, the cavalry covering the rear. Colonel Washburn [of the 116th Ohio] was in command of the infantry, and Major Adams [of the 1st New York Cavalry] of the cavalry...."

"[W]e were enabled in the confusion following the engagement, aided by the mist of early dawn, to get well on our way before we were discovered by the rebels. When they did discover us, they followed with a considerable force, determined to cut us off from a gap in the mountains, which we were aiming, with all speed, to reach. The detachment of the 1st New York

---

[26]O.R. 1-27-2-49, Milroy; Wildes, p. 59.

cavalry did splendid service now in protecting the rear of our column, and preventing the enemy's cavalry from obstructing our march. The 12th Pennsylvania cavalry went forward to possess and hold the gap that we were endeavoring to reach. They performed their work well. By dint of hard marching, and considerable maneuvering and skirmishing, we reached the gap, and entering the narrow mountain pass, we were safe against further successful pursuit by almost any amount of force...."[27]

After beating their pursuers to the gap, the hodgepodge brigade divided into two contingents. "The First New York and a part of the Twelfth Pennsylvania Cavalry were with us until afternoon, when they left us, and went directly through to Hancock the same night."[28] Lieutenant Colonel Wildes' account seems to indicate that he and at least some of the Buckeyes from the 116th Ohio accompanied the cavalry. "As we were about starting again, we learned that a force of rebel cavalry was trying to get possession of certain mountain roads ahead of us a short distance, in order to cut us off from the ford of the Potomac at Sir John's Run. Hastily throwing a few companies forward, to command these roads, we moved out quickly, and crossed the ford without molestation, but we were scarcely across before the enemy appeared on the opposite bank of the river. From here we sent our regimental horses and mules to Cumberland, in charge of Captain Powell's [1st New York Cavalry] company of cavalry."[29]

At first light on Tuesday, June 16, Colonel Washburn and the rest of his accidental command left the vicinity of Bath and resumed their retreat. At 10 a.m. his Bluecoats also reached the crossing of the Potomac at Sir John's Run and then, after four more weary hours of marching, reunited with the cavalry at Hancock, Maryland. "Here (at Hancock) I [Colonel Washburn] found the Twelfth West Virginia, part of the Eighty-seventh

---

[27]Wildes, p. 59.
[28]O.R. 1-27-2-66, Washburn.
[29]Wildes, p. 59.

Pennsylvania, and detached companies, stragglers from every infantry regiment in the division, together with the First New York, Twelfth Pennsylvania, and Colonel [James A.] Galligher of the Thirteenth Pennsylvania Cavalry, who assumed command of all the forces then at Hancock...."[30]

Bone tired, hungry, dirty, demoralized, and probably frightened as well, the entire contingent settled down in the Maryland village for some desperately needed rest. Fate had other plans however, and at 10 p.m., after life had just begun to creep back into their exhausted muscles, a rumor reached the Federals that not only was a train being prepared to meet them at Little Orleans Station on the B & O Railroad, but that the Confederates were advancing on Hancock. Colonel Galligher of the 13th Pennsylvania Cavalry, who had somehow managed to straggle into Hancock with few, if any, of his own regiment, ordered the hodgepodge brigade up and onto the road towards Cumberland.[31]

Probably with equal measures of enthusiasm and confusion, the 2,000 infantry, 1,000 cavalry, and 300 team horses under Colonel Galligher's command filled the Cumberland Pike and moved off in hopes of evading the Rebels and reaching supplies and safety.[32] Approximately 10 hours and 18 to 20 exhausting miles later, the Federals turned right, off the Cumberland Pike, in the direction of Little Orleans Station. That destination was attained at noon, "...but, greatly to the disappointment of the men, who were nearly worn out, we found no train in waiting for us."[33] The Yankees had more disappointments coming.

"During the afternoon, while waiting for a train, I [Washburn] received a dispatch from Colonel Galligher—the cavalry having kept the pike toward Cumberland instead of following us to the station—that the enemy [cavalry under Brigadier General

---

[30]O.R. 1-27-2-66, Washburn.
[31]Ibid.
[32]Ibid., 1-27-2-154, 183.
[33]Ibid., 1-27-2-66, Washburn.

John D. Imboden] occupied Cumberland, and were coming down the canal and railroad in the direction of the station. I accordingly retraced my steps toward the pike, and bivouacked for the night about 1 and 1/2 miles from the station. At 3 o'clock the next morning [June 18], we started again toward the pike, and reached it soon after sunrise. After reaching the pike, we marched up the pike about 4 miles, and then took a road over the mountains, leaving the pike to the left, and moved toward Chaneyville, which point we reached the same evening. Here we bivouacked for the night, and the next day (Friday, 19th instant) we reached this place (Bloody Run [Pennsylvania]) and reported to General Milroy in person, who arrived here from Hopewell about the same time."[34]

For some of the troopers in the 12th Pennsylvania Cavalry, arrival at the tiny village of Bloody Run (now Everett) near Bedford, Pennsylvania, was more or less a homecoming. The men of that regiment who had grown up amid the mountains and valleys of central Pennsylvania, along with rest of the Weary Boys who accompanied them, were lavished with a reception that offered some compensation for the previous days' privations. "...[U]pon hearing of our coming, the people of that place [Bloody Run] prepared a glorious feast for us. Long tables were placed in the middle of the principal street, which were loaded with warm and cold meats, potatoes, bread, pickles, splendid hot coffee, and great bowls and pails of milk. We were nearly starved, and no meal we ever ate was so heartily relished...."[35]

Probably more weary of soul than body by that time, General Milroy also received a much needed lift when he rejoined his men at Bloody Run soon after their arrival. "It was a sad meeting. The 'Old Grey Eagle' looked gloomy and broken-hearted, but we drew up in line to receive him, and, as he approached, presented arms, and cheered him loud and

---

[34]O.R. 1-27-2-66-67, Washburn; O.R. 1-27-2-183, Schenck.
[35]Wildes, p. 61.

long...."[36] Some of the general's perceived depression may have been generated by the condition of the men who were required to stand in formation in order to cheer him. "Nearly all the infantry had their feet badly blistered. In some cases their boots and shoes which they had not had off for over a week were filled with blood and matter."[37]

Milroy would only be permitted to remain in command of his Weary Boys for one more day. On June 20, the 12th Pennsylvania Cavalry's Colonel Lewis B. Pierce reappeared as if from thin air, apparently having conveniently recovered from one of his suspiciously timed sick leaves. With orders in hand from Major General Darius N. Couch, in whose district, and under whose command, the hodgepodge brigade found itself, Pierce unceremoniously replaced the fallen Eagle.[38]

One of Milroy's last orders before being sacked was to dispatch the 12th Pennsylvania Cavalry to the strategic village of McConnellsburg, Pennsylvania, which was located to the east of Bloody Run astride a pass through the Cove Mountain Ridge.[39] From there, it was hoped that the Pennsylvanians, along with the balance of the hodgepodge brigade (hereafter Pierce's Brigade), which remained at Bloody Run, could launch an attack against Jenkins' cavalry, who had captured Chambersburg, Pennsylvania.

---

[36]Wildes, p. 60.

[37]Milroy letter, 6/21/1863.

[38]Regimental records, 12th Pennsylvania Cavalry, National Archives. There are no references in the regimental papers or the *Official Records* indicating any participation by Colonel Pierce in the battles of Second Winchester or Carter's Woods. Pierce's military records indicate that in mid-March he requested a 30-day leave of absence due to illness but do not include a reference to the date on which he actually returned to duty. The Hussars' muster sheets list Pierce as having been present during June.

[39]The 12th left for McConnellsburg, a 24-mile march, on the morning of June 21. *Philadelphia Inquirer*, 6/24/1863.

Failing that, the crippled brigade was expected to at least block further Confederate depredations in the center of the state.[40]

It is doubtful that Pierce's beleaguered command had any realistic hope of seriously threatening the Rebel cavalry. Although the Federal force at Bloody Run boasted 110 officers and 2,236 enlisted men, the boast was hollow. Lieutenant Colonel Piatt, who apparently inspected the force at Bloody Run, reported that "...many are without arms or shoes, and the whole in generally bad condition."[41] Several days later, Colonel Pierce added "...about one-third of the men without arms, all somewhat demoralized, and desiring to get to their regiments.... We have two pieces of artillery here, not effective; cannot be used out of point-blank range. They are smooth-bore guns, without scale or harness."[42] Even worse, only about 20 rounds of small arms ammunition remained for each of the men who had managed to retain a weapon.[43]

Although it seems that Colonel Pierce had justifiable reasons for his reluctance to commit his new command to battle, at least one unabashedly biased source alleged that timidity, rather than realism, dictated Pierce's lack of aggression. Later in 1863, the 12th's Major Darius Titus, who had already made one legal assault on his colonel, would make another attempt to purge Pierce from the regiment and, not coincidentally, to clear his own path toward promotion. In charges intended to secure Pierce's dismissal from the service, Titus alleged that "...on or about the 25th day of June 1863 upon receiving an intimation that the Rebels were approaching, he [Pierce]...did become so excited and confused as to be incapable of giving intelligible and necessary commands to his subordinate officers..." and "...that he did there appear in the presence of officers and men talking in a loud and

[40]O.R. 1-27-2-237, 295, Schenck, Piatt.
[41]Ibid., 1-27-3-295.
[42]Ibid., 1-27-3-389.
[43]Ibid., 1-27-3-506.

excited manner and that he did evince other signs of confusion and fear such as walking hastily to and fro in his office in and out of it, ordering his staff officers and orderlies here and there and instantly ordering them to stop and hold on, shaking of the hand, tremulous of voice, indecision and loss of presence of mind."

Not content with shaming his commander with the allegations about June 25, Titus threw in another anecdote which he hoped would support a conviction for conduct prejudicial to good order and military discipline. "...[O]n or about the 27th day of June 1863 at Bloody Run Pa. Colonel L. B. Pierce...did order his command to retreat to Bedford Pa. upon an intimation being received that the Rebels were approaching, without making any effort to first ascertain the strength of the attacking party, which party afterwards proved to be a force of thirty-three of our own men under Capt Jones, 1st N. Y. Cavalry coming in with about 60 Rebel prisoners captured at McConnellsburg, Pennsylvania.[44] Before he countermanded his orders the infantry had marched in the rain and mud towards Bedford about 8 miles...."

Finally, the vindictive major described a third incident, this time on July 12, where Pierce allegedly lost his nerve and ordered another retreat from an undetermined number of Rebels. Not only did the retreat prove unnecessary, but Pierce "...gave orders for the disposition of his command in an excited, turbulent and incoherent manner that he did order Col Klunk [12th West Virginia] 'to hide' certain prisoners...." When Klunk and his prisoners came into view, Pierce apparently mistook them for the enemy and ordered "...the cavalry of his command to retreat and form line of battle in a narrow street where few of the cavalry could be brought into action at once in case they were attacked...."

---

[44]Major Titus may have been mistaken about the date of this incident. One historian for the 1st New York Cavalry reported that his regiment was still in Everett on June 27, but also recorded that on June 29 the 1st's Captain Jones captured 30 or more prisoners during a skirmish in McConnellsburg. Beach, pp. 259-261.

Then, in front of his command, the allegedly rattled colonel "...exclaimed in a loud and beseeching tone of voice, 'Are there not some citizens here that will show us where to go, are there not some citizens here that will show Col. Klunk where to hide these prisoners,' or words to that affect."[45]

Although reluctant, for whatever reason, to lead his infantry into battle, Pierce was not correspondingly hesitant to order his cavalry and the subordinates who commanded them into harm's way. Almost from his first day in command, Pierce thrust his former regiment into close proximity with the enemy that occupied Chambersburg, which is only a short distance from McConnellsburg. From the latter village the Pennsylvanians conducted numerous reconnaissance missions in hopes of obtaining intelligence on the strength, location, and movements of Lee's army. On June 24, scouts acting upon the orders of the regiment's temporary commander, Lieutenant Colonel Moss, reported from McConnellsburg that the Southerners were advancing on Mercersburg and Loudon in force.[46] The next day, it was reported that a "...detachment [probably of the 12th Pennsylvania Cavalry]...charged strong picket of enemy...at McConnellsburg, and drove them into town, creating great commotion in a large force of the enemy, mostly infantry—about 2,000."[47]

---

[45] Pierce Military Records, National Archives. Some punctuation supplied.

[46] O.R. 1-27-3-297.

[47] Milroy's report attributed the attack to Major Adams and the 1st New York Cavalry rather than to the 12th Pennsylvania Cavalry, despite the fact that it was the Hussars who were stationed in McConnellsburg on June 25. William Beach, a historian of the 1st New York Cavalry who consistently claimed as much credit as possible for the New Yorkers, placed his regiment at Bloody Run on the day of the attack. Milroy may either have received inaccurate information or was so preoccupied with his own future that he made an error. It is also possible that Milroy deliberately diverted credit from the 12th in order to maintain the impression that it was unreliable, and therefore that his decision to ignore the warning of its commander on June 12 was justifiable. O.R. 1-27-2-279, 280, Milroy; Beach, p. 259.

Four days later, on June 29, another scouting party from the 12th disappeared somewhere beyond McConnellsburg. Perhaps the missing Hussars belonged to Sergeant John H. Black's Company G, that was driven out of McConnellsburg (along with the rest of the 12th Pennsylvania Cavalry) at about that time. "...[W]e [Company G] joined the regiment, moved on to Bloody Run, and from there to McConnellsburg, where we remained for several days, until a strong force of 'Rebs' moved on towards the place. Our troops all left the place leaving our company in the rear. We went up the mountain with 14 men and met the 'Rebel' advance and had a pretty brisk skirmish with them, finding they were too many for us. We fell back slowly firing all the while. Sorry to say we had three men wounded in the affray, among which was my highly esteemed friend Sergeant Stiffler."[48]

Thirty-one New Yorkers under the command of Captain Jones, who were dispatched to find the missing Pennsylvanians, cantered into McConnellsburg around 8:30 a.m. At the village they had a chance encounter with another Union cavalry company that was so new that they had not yet been issued all their equipments. While the two contingents tried to sort out who was whom and which captain was in command, a force of Rebels, described as not over 200 strong, was spotted descending towards the village from a nearby mountain.

Jones quickly took charge and headed for the street with the words, "'Get on your horses and get to your places; I'll fight them.'" The partially equipped rookies rode north toward safety but the New Yorkers formed into a battle line. "The rebel cavalry could be heard coming in from the east. In a few minutes they came up the hill on a smart gallop, but slackened at sight of Captain Jones and his trim command, not more than three hundred yards off.... The Confederates came to a dead halt just as the

---

[48]Black letter, 7/1/1863. William J. Stiffler survived the wound he received at McConnellsburg.

head of the company reached the alley between the Fulton House and Greathead's store. Not more than thirty seconds before this Captain Jones had wheeled by file, and as the sabres went up it seemed as if a bright sheet of steel, about two and a half feet wide by one hundred long, had been suddenly turned up on its edge, the sight of which struck the rebels with fear and confusion."

The Butternuts were obviously startled by the Federal show of confidence. As they paused to weigh the implications, one of their number spotted the bluecoated rookies on their way to safety and mistook that column for the source of the Union backbone. With the new information tossed into the equation, the entire Southern contingent "...broke up in a wild dash in retreat, with Captain Jones leading in pursuit." Jones and his troopers kept the Confederates on the run with some well-directed carbine fire that left several dead Johnnies in their wake. The Empire Staters returned with 32 prisoners who were either too intimidated to continue their flight or whose horses had failed them.[49]

Jones' triumph was not the first contact that the 1st New York Cavalry had with Lee's invaders. Almost immediately after he had escorted McReynolds' fleeing wagon train from Berryville to safety, Lieutenant William H. Boyd, Jr., began to lead his men in a crusade against the Rebels. On June 22, Boyd's troopers encountered a contingent of the 14th Virginia Cavalry under the command of Captain J. W. Wilson, who was acting under instructions to attempt to draw any Federals they could find into an ambush. According to his orders, when Wilson's men saw the bluecoated troopers, they fell back upon their main column with the New Yorkers in hot pursuit. Thirty-five Federals charged headlong into Wilson's men who, thanks to the security engendered by a large number of Jenkins' cavalry in close proximity, were able to dismount and lay their trap. Boyd's men were slammed by a blast of gunfire that claimed the life of Corporal

---

[49]Beach, pp. 259-261.

William H. Rihl and converted Sergeant Milton Cafferty into a wounded prisoner.[50] Before the Confederates could increase their harvest, the Federals withdrew at a gallop and quickly reported the location of their adversaries to headquarters.

Perhaps chastened by that unpleasant surprise, Boyd's party assumed responsibilities more commensurate with their size—scouting and reporting on the Rebels' progress. For the next four days, until June 29, the New Yorkers rode the crest of the Confederate wave, maintaining contact but avoiding battle. On that day, however, a dozen of the Yankees surprised and captured a Rebel force three times larger than their own. The next day an isolated Confederate foraging party was "gobbled up" by Boyd's troopers and on July 1 they repeated the feat. After Lees' defeat, the New Yorkers nibbled at the tail of the retreating Southern column, skirmishing occasionally and claiming a number of hungry Johnnies caught while trying to steal food to fill their bellies.[51]

Unlike Boyd's men, who required no prodding, Colonel Pierce apparently needed a shove from his commander to commit his brigade to aggressive action. On June 27, Couch sent this telegraphic advice to Pierce, "You may have to exercise large powers as regards your command. You understand that you hold in check the rebels, and cover the country. Harass them, and do not be cut off."[52] The next day Pierce received more cajoling, "In case the enemy march on Mount Union or Hollidaysburg, by falling on their rear or flanks you will demoralize their whole command. Attack them in small parties at night."[53]

Instead of reports from Pierce about lightning raids on the enemy's flank, the pugnacious department commander received

---

[50]Corporal Rihl is generally accepted as the first Union soldier killed in Pennsylvania during the Gettysburg Campaign. A monument has been erected at the site of his death.

[51]Beach, pp. 248-253.

[52]O.R. 1-27-3-363.

[53]Ibid., 1-27-3-389, Couch.

only useful, but uninspiring, dispatches concerning the disposition and strength of the Rebel forces west of Gettysburg. Couch, who transferred out of the Army of the Potomac in disgust over Fighting Joe Hooker's performance at Chancellorsville, was apparently feeling so stifled by his backwater assignment to the Department of the Susquehanna, that he pressed even harder for Pierce to take some aggressive action. On July 3, Couch finally gave a direct order for an attack. "...Make every exertion to harass, and show of force. I think Meade will whip them tomorrow, and we must help him every way. Push on at all hazards." Later in the day though, Couch, who seems to have spent some time at the Henry W. Halleck school for avoiding accountability, appended a note of caution onto that order, "Of course, you will not obey literally any order I send to you as regards moving, if it is manifestly unsafe; otherwise I take the responsibility of the movement."[54]

Finally, on July 5, Colonel Pierce made a limited effort to satisfy Couch's demands for action. The reliable Captain Abram Jones of the 1st New York, along with 120 troopers from his regiment and 80 from the 12th Pennsylvania Cavalry, was sent on a raid toward Williamsport, Maryland, which was located on the northern bank of the Potomac. The expedition pushed eastward down a country lane towards Cunningham's Crossroads, which was located a few miles into Maryland on the road between Chambersburg, Pennsylvania, and Williamsport. Near the intersection some loyal civilians advised Captain Jones that there was a huge Rebel wagon train rumbling south on the main road. Jones took a few scouts and crept close enough to see some of the 2,100 Butternut cavalry who, in groups separated by half-mile intervals, were guarding the wagon train which stretched from one horizon to the other.

---

[54]O.R. 1-27-3-506, Couch.

Bloody Run/Cunningham's Crossroads

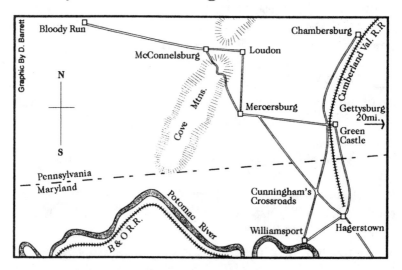

From: O.R. Atlas Pl. CXXXVI

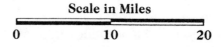

Choosing robbery rather than aggravated assault, Jones sent one portion of his command up the road to block a rescue attempt from the north, left a second portion on the lane as a reserve, and hid the rest near the intersection. When the closest Rebel troopers passed out of sight to the south, the audacious Yankees sprang out of the bushes. The startled teamsters were induced, by threats of death reinforced with brandished sabers and pistols, to silently change course and head west on the country lane towards the waiting Federal reserve. Approximately 100 wagons filled with Confederates who had been wounded at Gettysburg were received by the reserve, which was led by the 12th's Captain David A. Irwin and manned by some of his troopers from Company E.

The Yankee raiders snatched as many wagons as their strained nerves, and the approach of another squad of Rebel cavalry from the north, permitted. Fully aware of the risk of losing his newly acquired booty, Captain Jones "...arranged his men so as to make as large a show of force as possible facing toward the rear of the train, and waited for the guard to attack, his object being to give as much time as possible for the captured wagons to get away. It seemed a long time before the enemy could make up their mind what to do. Finally they got together a large force in line and throwing out skirmishers, began to move forward. The captain waited as long as he thought prudent, when he wheeled his command and galloped away."[55]

The prize came cheaply but not for free. In the ensuing running skirmish the Union raiders suffered three killed and several wounded. In return for their sacrifice, the Federals netted over a hundred wagons, several hundred horses, two pieces of artillery, and 653 mostly wounded prisoners, including four staff officers and 28 field officers.[56] Couch sent Pierce a congratulatory wire, "Your brilliant conduct has quite electrified

---

[55]Beach, pp. 264-266.
[56]O.R. 1-27-3-580, Pierce.

us."[57] The raid's success probably electrified Colonel Pierce as well.

After the delivery of the Confederate prisoners captured at Cunningham's Crossroads, a few minor brushes between Lieutenant Boyd's troopers and Lees' strays and rear guard, and reports from the 12th Pennsylvania Cavalry who continued to dog the Rebel retreat, the involvement of Milroy's former division in the Gettysburg Campaign came to an end. During that time, however, there was an abortive effort to combine militia regiments from Reading, Pennsylvania, with Pierce's Brigade for a strike at the Rebel flank. The militia movements were so slow that an exasperated President Lincoln was prompted to write this typically insightful comment: "...forces now beyond Carlisle to be joined by regiments still at Harrisburg, and the united force again to join Pierce somewhere, and the whole to move down the Cumberland Valley, will, in my unprofessional opinion, be quite as likely to capture the 'man in the moon' as any part of Lee's army."[58]

For the Hoosier, the battle to salvage his reputation commenced as the Gettysburg Campaign drew to a close. First, Halleck placed him under arrest, but the charges expired because no written specifications were filed. Not content with dodging that bullet, Milroy demanded a court of inquiry in hopes of proving that the fault for the disaster rested on other shoulders. While the Old Gray Eagle attempted to salvage his career, his former charges commenced the task of trying to survive the balance of the war while attempting to live down the stigma of having been among Milroy's Weary Boys.

---

[57]O.R. 1-27-3-581.
[58]Ibid., 1-27-3-583.

EPILOGUE

Major General Milroy,
*   ...[Y]ou have just lost a division and, prima facie, the*
fault is upon you. And while that remains unchanged, for me
to put you in command again, is justly to subject me to a
charge of having put you there on purpose to have you lose
another....

—Abraham Lincoln[1]

The outcome of the second battle of Winchester was neither the result of brilliant Confederate generalship nor merely the product of ineptness on the part of the Federal commander as he attempted to fend off overwhelming numbers. Rather, the Union disaster was the inevitable product of a series of events and circumstances sown together by the personality of Robert H. Milroy.

For his part, Richard S. Ewell was the fortunate recipient of that patchwork quilt which was delivered to him like a gift on Christmas morning. Old Bald Head, when he reached Winchester, was relatively new to both the duties of corps commander and to the responsibilities of independent command. Fortunately for the South, Ewell was able to follow the template for capturing Winchester that had been crafted by the great Stonewall Jackson during the summer of 1862 when he smashed Banks' army and drove the Bluecoats out of the town in a rout. That formula was followed closely and competently by Stonewall's loyal protégé.

---

[1]Lincoln letter to Milroy, 6/29/1863 as quoted in Beach p. 245.

Unfortunately for the Southern cause, Ewell's inexperience may have lost the other half of Milroy's division.

Although there is some question about whether Ewell believed that his mission parameters included only the obligation to push Milroy's garrison out of the way, on the afternoon of June 13 the Confederate commander squandered several opportunities that his mentor would have ruthlessly seized.[2] By mid-to-late afternoon, 20 of Allegheny Johnson's hardhanded regiments faced three novice Federal ones on the relatively accessible plain on the southeast side of Winchester. Ewell never ordered what would presumably have been a crushing assault.[3]

Overwhelming Ely's depleted brigade was not the only opportunity that the Virginian passed up that Saturday. While Johnson's men waited in hiding, the one cavalry and three infantry regiments that Elliott initially employed for the sortie to Kernstown were permitted to back down the Valley Turnpike with their left wing in the air, without any interference from Johnson's division except for a few artillery rounds thrown at the Union flank.[4] Under the circumstances, even one of Johnson's regiments might have been able to rout Elliott's entire force with a hard-hitting flank attack, and one brigade should have been able to nab the entire force before it got behind Abraham's Creek. Despite the potential for a quick and decisive victory, Ewell apparently sacrificed those two golden opportunities in favor of waiting until his divisions could unite their flanks and present a consolidated front.

---

[2]Early on June 13, before the day's march commenced, Ewell told Johnson, "You are the operator now...I am only a looker on." Ewell as quoted in Pfanz, *Richard S. Ewell*, p. 283. It is not clear why Ewell delegated his authority in that manner, but because he was with Johnson when the division commander deployed his men and then later restrained them, Ewell retained ultimate responsibility.

[3]O.R. 1-27-2-500, Johnson; Coddington, pp. 590-591. Johnson's total division totaled 22 regiments, but General Steuart left the 23rd and 37th Virginia behind to guard the division's trains and the reserve artillery. O.R. 1-27-2-507, Steuart.

[4]Ibid., 1-27-2-500, Johnson.

Inexplicably, Ewell continued to tolerate Johnson's passivity while the grossly outnumbered Federals on Winchester's southwestern side fended off Early's assault long enough to reorganize behind Abraham's Creek and the millrace. At the close of the day, Ewell held a numerical advantage of at least 34 infantry regiments to eight.[5] Even allowing for the late hour, the geographic advantages held by the Yankees, and the fact that Early's men were blown, a concerted assault would seem to have offered a golden opportunity to finish off the Federals. Instead, Ewell hesitated until darkness resolved the issue, thereby leaving his corps with the possibility of having to storm Milroy's forts on Apple Pie Ridge the next day.

It is possible that Ewell's apparent lack of a killer's instinct was the result of war weariness that seems to have gripped him after completion of the Valley Campaign and the struggle on the Peninsula. In a letter to his niece written in July of 1862, the Virginian wrote: "It may be all very well to wish young heroes to be in the fight, but for my part I would be satisfied never to see another field. What pleasure can there be in seeing thousands of dead and dying in every horrible agony—torn to pieces by artillery; so many times the wounded being left on the field for hours before they can be cared for. I wish this war could be brought to a close, but except by the hands of Providence I can see no way of its coming to an end.... Since March I have been almost constantly within hearing of skirmishing, cannon, etc., and would give almost anything to get away for a time so as to have a little quiet. I don't know that I ever lived so hardly or so much

---

[5]Although the Yankees also had two cavalry regiments, the troopers were of little value for defensive operations. The number of rifles that the Federals could bring to bear on their southern front was further diminished by the necessity to maintain at least a scratch force in the forts and at the picket posts on the roads leading into the eastern side of the town. Thanks to sympathetic residents, Ewell was apparently fully aware of the size of the Federal garrison in Winchester as well as basic strength and location of the fortifications. Pfanz, *Richard S. Ewell*, p. 281.

exposed to everything disagreeable as during the last few weeks."[6]

That battle fatigue may have somewhat eroded Ewell's belief in the Cause as well. "I fully condole with you over the gloomy prospect in regard to the war. Some 100,000 human beings have been massacred in every conceivable form of horror, with three times as many wounded, all because of a set of fanatical abolitionists and unprincipled politicians backed by women in petticoats and pants and children. The chivalry that you were running after in such frantic style in Richmond have played themselves out pretty completely, refusing in some instances to get out of the state to fight. Such horrors as war brings about are not to be stopped when people want to get home. It opens a series of events that no one can see to the end."[7]

As the campaigning season of 1863 loomed over the horizon, and his stump continued to plague him, the Virginian also penned the following in a letter to his subordinate Jubal Early: "...I don't feel up to a separate command...I was in hopes that the war might be brought to a close before the end of the spring, but I have lost all hopes of that. I don't want to see the carnage and shocking sights of another field of battle, though I prefer being in the field to anywhere else as long as the war is going on."[8] Perhaps as June 13 played itself out, Ewell secretly hoped that the Yankees would run away during the night so that he could be spared the sight of another gore-strewn field.

On Sunday, despite what his personal feelings may have been, Ewell tried to emulate the basics of the Jackson plan by taking Winchester from the west. Fortunately for Milroy's division, because Stonewall was able to rout Banks' men before they could hunker down in their forts, he did not leave a plan

---

[6]Ewell letter, 7/20/1862, from Hamlin, pp. 111-113. Hereafter quotations from Ewell's letters taken from Hamlin will be cited by reference only to the letter and the date it was written.

[7]Ibid., 8/14/1862.

[8]Ibid., 3/8/1863.

detailing how to trap and capture the town's garrison once it had pulled into a defensive shell. It is arguable that luck rather than skill saved Ewell's endgame from being botched as well.

By 9 p.m. on June 14, three Rebel divisions, each nearly comparable in size to Milroy's, were within relatively close proximity to Winchester. Early's division was firmly entrenched on the town's western flank and controlled the roads to the Allegheny Mountains. Johnson's division held the east and southeastern fronts and the roads to and beyond Berryville, while Rodes' division was just completing the capture of Martinsburg about 12 miles (six-hours' march) northeast of Winchester. If Milroy had a way out, it was to march down the Martinsburg (Valley) Turnpike and then turn east somewhere between Winchester and Martinsburg, a fact that should have been obvious to everyone on the field.[9]

Although Rodes controlled the Pike, and the route to Williamsport, Maryland, he had not entirely choked off Milroy's possibilities for escape. Between Winchester and Martinsburg a number of decent roads branched off toward Harpers Ferry through Smithfield, Leetown, and Charlestown, while dozens of farm lanes and country paths provided additional alternate, albeit difficult, avenues for retreat. The only way to totally bar the door was to close the Pike near the outskirts of Winchester. If Ewell erred in administering the coup de grâce, it was in failing to do so promptly.

---

[9]Colonel (later Speaker of the United States House of Representatives) J. Warren Keifer claimed in his 1900 history, that he suggested to Milroy that the Second Division should try to retreat in the direction of the town of Bath, which is northwest of Winchester. Although the plan might have been successful as late as Sunday morning, by late Sunday evening Early's division was too close to what would have been the flank of a column heading directly from Winchester in that direction. Further, at that point such a route would have been even more dangerous than the Martinsburg Pike, since by use of the former, the Federals would have forfeited the excellent paved surface of the Pike, which provided both speed and the ability to rapidly concentrate if attacked.

Ewell's first option could have been to order Rodes to close down on Winchester from the north, a choice that was probably not seriously considered for several reasons. The Virginian could not have been sure about exactly what Rodes' situation was, the men of Rodes' division were undoubtedly exhausted from having spent the entire day marching from Berryville, and if they left immediately after capturing Martinsburg they would not have reached Winchester until 2 a.m. at the earliest, which might have been too late.

Ewell still had two other divisions to manipulate. He must have known that Milroy could not chance an attack against either Early or Johnson because both held strong physical positions and a Union attack against either would have immediately brought the other Rebel division smashing into the Union rear. Therefore, the Southern commander could either have sent some of Early's men around the top of Winchester to seal the Pike, or he could have ordered Johnson to do the job. The use of Early's division would have been impractical because it was already spread from the eastern side of Bowers Hill to just north of West Fort, a distance of nearly five miles. In addition, a movement to the Pike would have been difficult for lack of a good road and cumbersome because units would have been required to shuffle along the front to assure full coverage and safety. Almost by default the task fell to Johnson.

Around dusk Ewell ordered Johnson to seize the Pike about two and a half miles northeast of town. Allowing some time to get in motion, and for a slower march due to having to slog cross-country part of the way, Johnson should have been on the Pike with his first units no later than midnight—at least an hour before the Federals commenced their own march. Had Johnson followed orders, Milroy probably would have marched headlong into several fully formed and relatively well-emplaced Confederate brigades. The outcome would have been short and complete.

Instead, Johnson chose to disregard his orders and follow better roads towards a point that was four and a half miles down the Pike, but nearly seven miles marching distance from his point of departure. The chosen route nearly tripled his marching distance. Not only did Johnson add extra miles when time was possibly critical, but his march was also inexplicably slow, even allowing for the darkness. By his own account it took the lead elements of Johnson's division approximately seven hours to tramp six or seven miles.[10] Johnson is extremely fortunate that he did not enter the history books as the goat of the story.

If Milroy's column had departed Winchester an hour earlier (the time originally intended), Johnson's Butternuts would only have been able to capture "road apples" deposited by the horses of the 1st New York Cavalry. Even worse, had the Federals begun their march only a half hour earlier, Johnson would have delivered his column into the middle of Milroy's division. Given the Old Gray Eagle's propensity for impetuous attack, it is likely that the Union division would have faced to the right, at least secured the railroad cut as a bastion, and probably smashed Johnson's column in detail as it struggled to change from a column into a line of battle in the dark. As it was, Johnson was extremely lucky that the two columns met at their points, that he was able to secure the railroad cut ahead of Milroy's infantry, and that his rapidly dwindling supply of ammunition held out just beyond the last Yankees' assault. Once on the scene Johnson responded intelligently and aggressively, but winning hides most mistakes.

With the benefit of hindsight, a better strategy is evident. It appears that Ewell could have safely moved at least a brigade of Johnson's division across the Martinsburg Pike under the cover of the assault on the West Fort. Had he done so, and then dispatched two of Johnson's remaining three brigades at dusk, it is doubtful that anyone from Milroy's division would have escaped. Perhaps when he discovered that the back door had been closed, Milroy would have capitulated. If not, in the time that would have been

---

[10]O.R. 1-27-2-501, Johnson.

available until the Federals could have arrived on the scene in force, that first Rebel brigade on the Pike would have had ample time to erect emplacements that would have been virtually impregnable in the dark. Milroy probably would have conceded after his lead elements tested such an impediment. Had the Hoosier pressed the issue, in the time it would have taken to deploy his division and to try to smash through a determined defense, the balance of Johnson's division would have fallen upon the Yankee flank, and Early's men could have passed through town and assaulted from the rear.

Perhaps Ewell thought that his orders to Johnson allowed sufficient time to accomplish the foregoing scenario and it was Johnson's improvisation that nearly allowed the cup to slip. Another possibility, although not claimed in his report, was that Ewell preferred to allow Milroy an apparent escape route so as to draw him out of his fortifications for a stand-up fight, rather than forcing the Hoosier to defend the Union emplacements to the last man (which he might have done rather than surrender).

The latter possibility was clearly dreaded by every Johnnie with an imagination, including the normally fearless Brigadier General John B. Gordon, who fully expected to have to lead his brigade against the "...frowning fortress in front...." The prospect of the "...dreadful slaughter that awaited my men..." in front of the Yankee works caused the Confederate general to have his only presentiment of his own demise.[11] Fate allowed the Southerners to attain most of the prize without that bloody assault. If Milroy had managed to slip away unmolested instead, the literature would now be filled with aspersions that not only was Ewell no Stonewall at Gettysburg, but that he missed the measure at Winchester as well.[12]

---

[11]Gordon, p. 68.

[12]Ewell's military career followed a trajectory somewhat similar to that of Milroy's. On May 29, 1864, after having been compelled to admonish Ewell about his lack of self-control two weeks earlier at Spotsylvania, Lee relieved Ewell of

Unlike Ewell, who, through inexperience (or perhaps compassion), may have somewhat mishandled the opportunities offered to him, Milroy deliberately orchestrated his own downfall. He could have joined with Halleck during the late spring of 1863 and encouraged a pullback of his division to a less exposed position. Or, he could have at least taken a neutral position and refrained from the braggadocio that made a withdrawal away from a hypothetical enemy seem like a gross act of cowardice. Almost certainly, had he followed either course, his division would have been safely ensconced at Harpers Ferry when Ewell's corps plunged into the central Valley.

Even when the Confederate threat changed from hypothetical to actual, Milroy continued to press his agenda through additional bombast and what could most charitably be labeled as a purposeful interpretation of intelligence. On June 12, upon receiving a report from Lieutenant Colonel Moss that the 12th Pennsylvania Cavalry had encountered Confederate infantry and artillery, in addition to the usual ragtag Butternut cavalry, Milroy could have supplied Schenck and thereby Halleck with a detailed report. Instead, because he undoubtedly anticipated that an unvarnished report would most likely have resulted in a recall order, Milroy sent a dispatch that was both deceptive and seductive. Schenck was told that the Pennsylvanians had "...had a slight skirmish..." with only 500 cavalry. That assertion misrepresented Moss's report and provided a number that was neither mentioned in Milroy's after-action report nor corroborated by staff officer

---

command of the Second Corps. Ewell spent the balance of the war in Richmond in charge of garrison troops while trying without success to obtain a new field command. On April 6, 1865, Ewell, along with the Richmond garrison, a hodge-podge of other units, and a handful of other generals, was captured at the battle of Sailor's Creek. Ewell finished his days as a gentleman farmer. On January 24, 1872, the Virginian died from the same illness that claimed his wife two days earlier.

Cravens, who allowed that Moss was accurate at least in regard to an encounter with 1,500 riflemen.

Milroy was not satisfied with massaging the composition and the numbers of the Rebel force. After slipping in an innocuous warning (that might prove useful later) that the Confederates were "...probably approaching in some force...," the Hoosier reiterated his refrain that he was "...entirely ready for them..." and that he could "...hold this place...." Given the balance of the telegraph, even Milroy's request that Schenck "...state specifically whether I am to abandon or not...," was probably calculated to both pressure his corps commander and to signal that Schenck would be solely responsible for an order to withdraw that might soon thereafter appear as cowardly.[13]

The fact that Moss was not placed in arrest impeaches the veracity of the information that Milroy gave to Schenck. Milroy's failure to send a force to confirm or debunk the Pennsylvanian's report provides strong evidence either that the Hoosier was certain that the force at Cedarville could have at worst only been J.E.B. Stuart's long anticipated cavalry raid, or that Milroy didn't really want to know the truth. From Milroy's perspective, knowing the truth could have had extremely unfortunate consequences because if Moss's observations were confirmed and withheld from Schenck, Milroy would have been chargeable. If he reported the facts instead, he had to expect that he and his division would be dragged back to Harpers Ferry. Ignorance fit the Hoosier's agenda and his subsequent actions and decisions support the

---

[13]O.R. 1-27-2-163, Milroy to Schenck. No adequate explanation has been discovered to explain why, given the context of the preceding month, that the combination of a dispatch from Pleasonton regarding reports of Ewell's advance and Milroy's telegraph did not generate an immediate, preemptory order from Halleck to abandon Winchester. Perhaps he was otherwise engaged on that fateful Friday evening, or possibly he either assumed Milroy's division was already in motion or that the future of his own career dictated that he take a pass on a difficult decision.

conclusion that Milroy was totally focused upon remaining in Winchester regardless of almost any cost.[14]

If Colonel Keifer's memoirs are credible, as the clock moved from Friday into Saturday Milroy continued to prefer subjective reality over potentially unpleasant facts.[15] Even though the Buckeye colonel reported that his scouts could not penetrate more than a few miles south of town, which strongly supported Moss's earlier report, Milroy both ignored the intelligence and withheld it from headquarters. Rather than consider that the Rebels might somehow have slipped an army into the Valley undetected, Milroy fretted over the possibility that he might be branded a coward if he retreated from an imaginary threat. When Keifer pressed the issue, he was shown the door. It would seem that to Milroy, humiliating a fellow officer was preferable to a prolonged discussion that put into question the Hoosier's desires or his assessment of the situation.[16]

Based upon the available intelligence, which also included newly arrived reports of significant contacts between the

---

[14]It is impossible at this point to make a definitive judgment on whether Milroy deliberately chose to avoid learning the truth (although it seems so), or was merely enthralled by the logic of his own assumptions that if any force other than Stuart's was coming, Hooker would have discovered the fact and headquarters would have supplied a warning.

[15]There is no specific reason to question Keifer's veracity except that stories which portray the teller as having imparted prescient but unheeded advice, in a private meeting with someone who has been silenced by death, are always subject to healthy skepticism. The account has been included because it is consistent with other information about Milroy and has not been contradicted by any discovered source.

[16]Keifer, vol. 2, pp. 6-7. Keifer also related that earlier in the week, based upon intelligence he had gathered, that he ordered all the wives of his regiment's officers who were in Winchester to go home to Ohio. The women protested the order to Milroy, who countermanded it with a comment that Keifer was "...too apprehensive of danger...." Keifer added that he derived some satisfaction when he greeted those same ladies after they returned from their sojourn to Castle Thunder in Richmond.

Confederates and the 1st New York Cavalry south of Berryville, Milroy could have chosen to slip out of town in the predawn hours of June 13, a decision that would seemingly have delighted General Halleck. He also had the more cautious option of sending his infantry and most of his artillery to an intermediate location closer to Harpers Ferry such as Martinsburg or Charlestown. With a battery in support, his two cavalry regiments would have been strong enough to hold the town against an inconsequential threat (whereupon his infantry could have quickly reoccupied the town) and nimble enough to escape a serious one. Instead, the Union commander pushed his foot soldiers up the Front Royal and Valley Turnpikes toward the enemy.

Perhaps Milroy's aggressiveness on Saturday morning was simply a manifestation of a feisty personality. It is also possible that his decision may instead have been a deliberate attempt to complicate his ability to easily extricate his division from Winchester. That is, if a direct order to retreat arrived during the day, the Hoosier could have pleaded that his men were engaged with the enemy and could not immediately withdraw. Perhaps in confirmation of such a hidden agenda, instead of making some effort either to make preparations to flee or to disengage, in the afternoon the Hoosier committed even more troops to a conflict miles from his forts and sent another telegraph with the same chorus, "[I] [a]m perfectly certain of my ability to hold this place."

Milroy would later seek to justify his decisions by referring to Schenck's order of June 12 that required that he stay until ordered to do otherwise. Despite orders (for which Milroy had never before shown slavish adherence), the Hoosier was certainly aware that the military practice of the time would have excused disobedience of any order short of "hold at all hazard" if he, the commander in the field, had any justification for believing that the order had been rendered obsolete by new information not available when it was made.[17] But even if he had mistakenly believed the order to be mandatory, there was no justification for committing the bulk of his forces (rather than just his cavalry) to a fight on an open plain miles from his fortifications—unless his intention was to accomplish more than just to "hold the place."

By the close of June 13, Milroy had a prisoner from the Louisiana Brigade, a day's worth of listening to the din of battle drawing progressively closer on two fronts, reports that the Berryville garrison had barely escaped capture on a third, and a good view of a myriad of campfires from two Rebel divisions bivouacked barely outside the streets of Winchester. Nevertheless, instead of making plans to sneak off that night, or early Sunday morning, he issued a stream of orders contracting his lines and moving units into the best possible defensive positions.

Failing to leave during the night of June 13-14 deprived the Hoosier's division of a safe and virtually certain route of escape, the existence of which should have been obvious. In addition to the location of a large number of Confederates that he had personally observed on the southern side of town, by dusk on Saturday, Milroy probably had been advised by dispatch that Bunker Hill was under attack by Confederate cavalry. By 9 p.m. he knew that Rodes' infantry had captured Berryville and could have been sealing the Martinsburg Pike at Bunker Hill at that moment, if the Confederates had marched there with determination.[18] On the other hand, Milroy had not received any intelligence indicating that the Rebels had penetrated far enough to threaten the route to toward Bath. Although the roads between Winchester and Bath were narrow, indirect and unimproved, the

---

[17]The court of inquiry acknowledged that Milroy could have acted on the new information available to him on June 13 without censure. O.R. 1-27-2-195.

[18]Rodes captured Berryville sometime before noon on June 13 and could have reached Bunker Hill, approximately 15 miles away, by 8 p.m. There was no way that Milroy could have known that Rodes was headed for Martinsburg, a destination that would not be reached until mid-day on Sunday.

difficulty in making a nighttime passage would seem to have been more than outweighed by the probable absence of opposition.[19] One can legitimately argue that the hypothetical dangers inherent in a flight to Bath during the predawn hours of June 14 would have been significantly less than the known threats posed by two Confederate divisions to the south and another possibly astride the Martinsburg Pike.

Milroy stayed and fought because he wanted to, not because he felt he had to. And if the foregoing arguments are not conclusive, there is also the dispatch that came into Winchester on Saturday afternoon that modified Schenck's June 12 order. "Instruct General Milroy to use great caution, risking nothing unnecessarily, and to be prepared for falling back in good order if over-matched...."[20] Milroy made a calculated decision to ignore both an expressed grant of discretion and an order to act prudently.

The most intriguing question to arise from the entire Winchester debacle is why Milroy acted so rigidly and resisted the demands of reality with so much vehemence that his actions now appear to have been beyond stupidity. It is submitted that it was the Hoosier's tragic flaw, a nearly overwhelming hubris, that compelled him to cling to Winchester until disaster was assured. That assessment is based upon Milroy's dispatches to headquarters, his military biography, his actions at Winchester which defied reason or blind obedience to orders, and the content of his letters to his

---

[19]Colonel Keifer alleged that at an unreported council of war convened at 11 a.m. on Sunday, he suggested a retreat by the Back Creek or Apple Pie Roads that would have carried the division west of Martinsburg and on to Pennsylvania. Keifer, vol. 2, p. 13. By then, such a retreat would have been extremely hazardous, requiring an undetected disengagement from Johnson's division on the southeast and from Early's troops on Bowers Hill. Further, because such a plan would have taken several hours to organize, if not discovered and attacked by Johnson from the rear, they might have been intercepted by Early's troops, who would have been moving in that direction up the western flank of Little North Mountain (although the Federals would not have been aware of the latter risk).

[20]O.R. 1-27-2-165, Schenck to Piatt.

wife. All of the foregoing point inexorably to the conclusion that Milroy sincerely believed that he was smart and skilled enough, and that his defenses were "...so very perfect and scientific...," that his garrison could hold out against any Confederate force, or as he put it, even "...in spite of fate."[21]

Given human nature it is also very likely, although he never wrote anything that directly supports the conclusion, that Milroy's extravagant self-confidence was bolstered by recollections of past successes. In the fight at McDowell, he won glory and greater responsibility by attacking a grossly superior force rather than making a prudent withdrawal. At Second Manassas, his brigade's stubborn refusal to run on the last day of the battle indisputably led to an interview with President Lincoln and, from Milroy's unique prospective, probably to the salvation of the entire Federal army. If fighting rather than running worked so well for him before, it is not surprising that he firmly believed he could make it work again at Winchester.

Milroy was proud, physically courageous, naturally pugnacious, and extremely patriotic—all traits that would have made the idea of flight instinctively abhorrent. He believed that those in command should have shared his desire to press the fight at every opportunity. Instead of receiving the encouragement and support he felt was appropriate, the Hoosier was convinced that the proponents of "West Point science" had, in an often insulting manner, repeatedly throttled his aggressive instincts and thereby spared the Rebels from a number of whippings. It may also be legitimately surmised that Milroy nourished the opinion that facing the enemy in battle at Winchester, instead of running, would have provided a golden opportunity to show Halleck and the president that aggression rather than caution was the way to stamp out the rebellion—and that he was the general best suited for the job. Perhaps more importantly, a victory in Winchester would have

---

[21]Milroy letter, 9/4/1862; O.R. 1-27-2-166, Milroy to Schenck.

repudiated Halleck's military philosophy, his leadership abilities, and his treatment of Milroy. Manipulating the chain of command to permit him to stay at Winchester was the key. Achieving a victory there was, apparently at least as far as Milroy was concerned, a foregone conclusion.[22]

Not only may we presume that the Hoosier's ego led him to believe that if given the chance he could outshine the West Point clique—we may also safely be assumed that he developed a substantial ego stake in his own rhetoric. Milroy had repeatedly proclaimed that he could hold Winchester no matter what. A person with a normal self-image might have been able to accept that a change in circumstances would excuse a change of heart. Hubris such as Milroy's demanded that he prove he was right, rather than concede that he wasn't. And with his opinion of his own abilities, the consequences of failure seem never to have crossed his mind.

That same hubris may have also inflated Milroy's career concerns to a point that logic and his sense of responsibility to his men were obliterated. Remaining at Winchester was more important to the Hoosier's self-image than merely doing his duty as an officer and a man. Since commanding the Cheat Mountain District at the end of 1861, Milroy had been more or less independent from direct, day-to-day supervision. He was permitted discretion at McDowell and even at Second Bull Run he had the illusion (or perhaps delusion) of semiautonomy at the head of his Independent Brigade. As he candidly observed to his wife, while in command of the garrison in Winchester he enjoyed the closest approximation to the role of an emperor that America could

---

[22]A deeper psychological need, beyond this writer's professional competence to evaluate, may also have come into play. A psychiatrist might conclude that Milroy was intensely insecure and that his rash courage and braggadocio were merely a facade intended to convince the world, and perhaps himself, that he was as worthwhile a man as his father expected him to be.

provide, with virtually the power of life and death over the town's residents and near absolute authority over his own men.

A retreat would have ended all that, taking him back to Harpers Ferry where much of the balance of his corps was quartered and where he would have been under much more direct supervision. Taking daily, direct orders would have been, in his opinion, a gross waste of his superior military talents. He also knew full well that being second in command, like being vice president, was "not worth a pitcher of warm spit." Even worse, because Schenck would still have needed to protect the B & O Railroad somehow, the Second Division might have been broken up in order to guard bridges and miles of deserted track, which might have left Milroy with little or no division to command.

Finally, Milroy, who was enthusiastically pro-Union and almost fanatically abolitionist, was truly loath to abandon the town which he rightfully viewed as the heart of the anti-Union, pro-slavery rebellion in the Shenandoah Valley. He knew that so long as he held Winchester, he kept a stake in that heart. Nearly as significant, as long as he commanded the garrison in Winchester, he enjoyed the power to torment the recalcitrant secessionists among the population and to punish them for their slights, insults, and insubordinations which had, on an almost daily basis, stung his personal dignity, and that of the country he loved. Conversely, if forced to withdraw, he and his men would have been subjected, without the ability to respond, to the jeers, curses, and laughter of the town's secessionist harpies, who had plagued him for months. It is doubtful that Milroy would have felt as great a threat to his pride and dignity if Winchester had been just another sleepy Southern village that could have been vacated without those considerations.

Milroy was totally comfortable with his subjective perception of his own superior intellect, courage, and military ability. From that perspective it would have been foolish to: willingly free the traitors in Winchester; risk being labeled a coward; surrender his power and independence, with the concurrent possibility of advancement and glory; and acquiesce to a subordinate position in Harpers Ferry. Rather, filled with blind confidence that he could manage any situation, the Hoosier meant every word of his challenge "[l]et them come."²³ When the Rebels picked up the gauntlet, Milroy was granted the opportunity to put substance behind his bluster. History's verdict has not been kind.

Just as victory obscured questionable judgments on the Confederate side, the decision to stay at Winchester, and his eventual defeat, obscured any positive actions taken by Milroy. If one is willing, for argument's sake, to accept Milroy's contention that he stayed because he had been ordered to do so, the Union commander's performance was uneven, but not totally without merit. There can be little excuse for his failure on June 12 to send a force to confirm what had probably been discovered by the 12th Pennsylvania Cavalry on the Front Royal Road. Because he failed to uncover the full extent of the threat faced by his garrison, had Ewell's plans been different, Winchester might have been taken by storm on Friday evening. Given that the initial sighting occurred around 1:30 p.m., and that the point of contact was only eight to 10 miles south of Winchester, it would have been possible for the lead Confederate division to have arrived virtually undetected on the outskirts of Winchester in line of battle by as early as 6 p.m. Such a surprise appearance might have resulted in an outcome worse than that actually suffered.

Milroy's performance on the thirteenth was somewhat better. Although his early reconnaissance efforts were arguably appropriate, the Hoosier courted disaster when he shoved the majority of Elliott's brigade five miles up the Valley Turnpike to Kernstown. Milroy later claimed that he only anticipated a cavalry raid by J.E.B. Stuart. If the vulnerable Federal brigade had been intercepted by the cavalry force the Hoosier claimed to have been expecting, they would probably have been cut to pieces as they

---

²³O.R. 1-27-2-164, Milroy to Piatt.

struggled to retreat over a relatively open plain that was suitable, if not ideal, for mounted operations. Alternatively, Elliott was fortunate that his brigade wasn't dismembered by a surprise assault on its vulnerable left flank. Although it was important for Milroy's force to locate and maintain contact with the approaching Confederates, the job could have been just as adequately, and much more safely, performed by either of the two cavalry regiments then at Milroy's disposal.

As commander, Milroy was entitled to credit for Elliott's determined fighting retreat, the repulse of Early's division at Abraham's Creek, and for putting together two defensive lines which held the significantly larger Confederate force in check for another 24 hours. Within the assumed context of an order to hold the post, Milroy's actions considerably delayed the Rebel advance and, at least for the day fended off a crushing defeat, which, considering the disparity in numbers, was no mean feat. Under the circumstances, although Ewell's caution certainly was a factor, the Hoosier managed his division fairly well on June 13.

For most of Sunday, June 14, Milroy's performance remained mired in inconsistency. His defensive dispositions and aggressive deployments kept the town clear from repeated, albeit limited, Rebel incursions. From a strategic perspective though, the Hoosier stumbled again. As the morning progressed, Milroy had the use of three unemployed cavalry regiments. Although it was appropriate to dispatch a contingent of the 12th Pennsylvania Cavalry for a scout to the west of town, it was not a wise decision (as hindsight illustrates) to rely solely upon that single patrol for definitive intelligence on the location of the Confederates. It would have been much more prudent to have pushed a battalion from one of his idle cavalry regiments out to picket Little North Mountain. Had more of the bluecoated troopers been employed for the type of duty for which they were suited, Milroy would have had ample warning of Early's approach.

Milroy's nonchalance concerning his western flank may be partially excused by the strength of his fortifications on that side of town. Further, Milroy's suspect judgment in failing to string videttes along the crest of Little North Mountain was offset by the enormous physical courage he displayed above the walls of the Main Fort. Additionally, since there are no reports of serious Union casualties as a result of the two-hour Rebel bombardment from Little North Mountain and West Fort, but there were ample reports of casualties among the Southerners, it may be concluded that West Fort was not nearly as important to the Federal defensive scheme as Jubal Early claimed. In fact, it is entirely plausible that the Union-hating Early emphasized the significance of West Fort because it was the only one he captured.

Had Milroy not been so focused on discrediting the 12th Pennsylvania Cavalry so as to justify ignoring their discovery on June 12, he might have justifiably crowed about the effectiveness of his dispositions at West Fort. The force positioned in that tiny emplacement revealed the Confederate attack well in front of the main fortifications, broke their formation, and exposed them to a two-hour artillery pummeling—all at a relatively minimal cost. Viewed objectively, West Fort served admirably as an effective tripwire.

Milroy's best work (if he can be excused for lingering in Winchester so long) was provided by his preparations for the evacuation of Winchester and in fighting the battle at Carter's Woods. First, it was not an easy task to extricate his infantry, cavalry, and nearly a thousand assorted team horses and mules from the Confederate noose without being discovered. Had it not been for Milroy's refusal to grant multiple supplications from his cannoneers to take their guns, the clatter of artillery, limbers and caissons would almost certainly have given the movement away before it had hardly commenced. Although extremely hard to predict, it is likely that if discovered early on, the Union division would have suffered a much worse fate as Early attacked from the rear and Johnson came in from their front.

Given the circumstances, Milroy fought the battle of Carter's Woods fairly well, and was ultimately defeated by fate, darkness, the "fog of war," and the untimely arrival of Confederate reinforcements, rather than by poor generalship. As discussed earlier, the Yankees nearly got away, an accomplishment that would have made Milroy a hero. As it was, his initial deployment worked well. His cavalry vanguard found the enemy, fixed them in position, and held the escape route open in the process. When the seriousness of the threat became apparent, Milroy threw one brigade to the front and led another in a series of assaults that stole the initiative from the Rebels. Had the Union commander's instructions been received and obeyed in a timely fashion, the balance of his Second Brigade, the team animals, and all of the Third Brigade would have passed down the Pike behind the fighting regiments. Then the engaged troops could have peeled off and made their escape as well.

Unfortunately for Union arms, the trailing units didn't get their orders in time because of darkness and the fact that Milroy's staff officers couldn't find Colonel McReynolds, who was off trying to organize and lead an attack of his own. Despite the confusion, Milroy still came within a whisker of winning a stunning victory because General Johnson admitted (perhaps with a dash of dramatic effect) that because his men were down to one round of ammunition apiece, another Federal attack would have swept them away.[24]

It appears that the final Federal disintegration resulted from a misperception of fact rather than an error of judgment. From his position in front, where the First Brigade had beaten the Rebels back into the railroad cut, the battle seemed well in hand if not won. Justifiably believing that the back half of his division had already passed by, Milroy sent orders for the Second Brigade to disengage and follow him up the Pike. With the benefit of hindsight, it might have been better if he had launched one more assault with the First Brigade to assure that the Second could

---

[24]O.R. 1-27-2-501, Johnson.

disengage (and perhaps to have blocked the advance of the Stonewall Brigade). However, from Milroy's point of view, which did not include knowledge of the approach of Confederate reinforcements, to have done so would have necessarily entailed considerable, and from his perspective unnecessary, casualties. But for the sudden and unexpected appearance of the Stonewall Brigade in the small gap between the first two Federal brigades, both would have probably gotten away without further significant losses. Milroy cannot be faulted because the fortunes of war overcame what were otherwise solid tactical decisions.

Finally, at least one author has speculated that the entire command could have escaped if Milroy had sent his men northward on the country lane toward Bath over which half of his refugees eventually escaped. While this is a possibility, it was probably not an option available to the Union commander on the scene for several reasons. First, it is not clear that Milroy was even aware that the lane existed, or that it led to safety. More importantly, for that tack to have been successful, the vanguard and then the rest of the column would have had to have started up the lane immediately. The fighting did not start, and the need for an alternate route did not become apparent, though, until at least a portion of the column was already past the lane. Once the fighting started it would have been extremely difficult to arrange a retreat from the middle of the column, and Johnson, if not pinned in his railroad cut, would have undoubtedly gobbled up the Federal column from behind.

Milroy's leadership at Carter's Woods rescued his division from annihilation, and thereby allowed the Hoosier a crumb of self-respect. A tally of the facts shows that it was only a modest dispensation. Ninety-five Federals sacrificed their lives, 348 took a bullet, a canister ball, or a piece of shrapnel, and another 4,000 spent time in Southern prison camps, thanks to Milroy's hubris.[25]

---

[25]O.R. 1-27-2-53.

On a strategic level the picture was nearly as bleak for Federal arms, despite the best efforts of Milroy's apologists to spin the outcome. Those loyalists maintained, with varying degrees of ardor, that the delaying action in the Shenandoah Valley allowed the Army of the Potomac to catch up with, and eventually defeat, Lee's army at Gettysburg. That argument maintained that if Confederate General Ewell had been able to tramp northward for the two days he spent surrounding and capturing Winchester, the Southerners might have been able to add 40 or 50 miles to their incursion. That extra reach might have facilitated the capture of Harrisburg, the fall of which was imminent when Lee pulled his men back to Gettysburg, or perhaps resulted in the decisive battle having been fought at Lancaster or Reading, Pennsylvania, rather than at the crossroads in Adams County.[26] Milroy's defenders ignored the alternate possibility that Ewell might have spent the two extra days living off the fertile valleys of Pennsylvania and Maryland while waiting for the balance of the Army of Northern Virginia to catch up with him. Either result is, of course, pure speculation.

At a minimum, though, it would have been reasonable to claim that Milroy's ill-conceived stand at Winchester delayed the Confederate advance into Pennsylvania by at least one full day. Had General Rodes had that extra day, he probably would have been able to wrest Harrisburg from the disorganized and ill-trained militia that defended it. The damage that would have been inflicted to property, and Union morale, by the sacking of the capital of the Keystone State are incalculable. Had Milroy gained that same day, and thereby rescued Harrisburg, by a Winchester-like delaying action on the outskirts of Harrisburg instead of Winchester, he would have been proclaimed a hero even if his division

---

[26]Had the Rebels crossed the Susquehanna River first, it is even possible that they would have had an unmolested route to Philadelphia while the Federals were forced to backtrack to a port large enough to facilitate their transfer by water across the Chesapeake Bay.

had suffered identical casualties in the process (as was General Lew Wallace after the battle of Monocacy). Timing, if not everything, is certainly important, and Milroy's career paid a heavy price for that important day having been purchased in the middle of June instead of at the end of the month.

What is not subject to speculation is that one full Federal division was smashed to pieces at an admitted cost to the Confederates of only 252 dead and wounded.[27] In addition to 200,000 rifle and carbine cartridges, Milroy also donated two 24-pounder howitzers, four 20-pounder Parrotts, and seventeen 3-inch ordnance rifles, all of which were repaired and available to the Confederate war effort a day after they were taken.[28] One need not have too vivid an imagination to conclude that additional Union blood was poured into the soil around Gettysburg because of that extra ammunition and ordnance.[29]

With a little more imagination, the consequences of Milroy's hubris grow even worse.[30] What would the outcome of the battle at Gettysburg, and the entire war, have been if Milroy's

---

[27]O.R. 1-27-2-336.

[28]Coddington, pp. 14, 89.

[29]The captured field pieces were eventually assigned to Jenkins' cavalry brigade where they became engaged, but did little harm, in the Confederate probe to the outskirts of Harrisburg, Pennsylvania. Nye, p. 123. Although only peripherally involved in the cavalry fight on July 3, Milroy's guns may have claimed some of Major General Alfred Pleasonton's troopers. Longacre, p. 227. It may also be assumed that the availability of those extra cannons spared Lee from having to transfer some of his original artillery reserve to his troopers. The disposition of the four 20-pounder Parrotts has not been discovered.

[30]On June 9, Schenck reported that he had 17,400 troops in the vicinity of Winchester besides Milroy's division. O.R. 1-27-2-124. The Eighth Corps also included a force of undetermined size at Baltimore. Although Piatt maintained that the June 9 numbers were somewhat inflated, and that the troops in Baltimore were of the lowest quality, it is conceivable that the strength of the balance of Schenck's corps would have been considered sufficient for its defensive role so as to allow the Hoosier's intact Second Division to be temporarily attached to the Army of the Potomac.

intact division had been available: to extend the exposed right flank of the Union Eleventh Corps on July 1; to counterattack after the repulse of the Confederate assault on Little Round Top on July 2, or after Pickett's charge the following day; or if it had been on hand to delay or perhaps block Lee's crossing of the Potomac River at Williamsport, Maryland, during the Confederate retreat?[31]

Perhaps as a result of his legal training and experience on the bench and in front of the bar, Milroy enjoyed more success at the court of inquiry than he did on the field of battle. His defense commenced with the after-action report that he delivered on June 30, 1863. It was a document that was clearly intended as much as a brief for his defense as it was a recapitulation of the engagement. Milroy asserted four points as justification for his actions: that he was forced to stay in Winchester because of Schenck's order of June 12; that the 12th Pennsylvania Cavalry's claim to have discovered what later proved to be Ewell's advance on that same day was not credible because the regiment was unreliable; that the failure of that same regiment to spot Early on his way to Little North Mountain cost him the West Fort (and further confirmed their incompetence); and finally that Colonel McReynolds was responsible for the loss of the rear half of the column at Carter's

[31]This latter possibility is the most intriguing. If an intact Second Division had been retained at Harpers Ferry and the First Division had been consolidated, Schenck would have had nearly 25,000 troops on the Potomac. Lee probably had about 50,000 men capable of fighting when his retreating column reached Williamsport, and as it was he only escaped by a whisker. It is easy to speculate that Schenck's forces could have held the southern shore and blocked Lee's crossing of the Potomac long enough for Meade's army to catch up and either starve the Rebels into submission or crush them in a vise.

Woods.[32] Milroy's testimony, and that of his staff, during the
court of inquiry carefully hewed to those basic positions.

After 15 days of testimony, the court gave Milroy a tepid
exoneration. Most of the responsibility for the disaster was laid
upon General Schenck for failing to heed Halleck's wishes and
upon the War Department for providing little worthwhile intelligence.[33] The court mildly admonished Milroy for misleading
Schenck because the Hoosier "...had, in the most confident and
extravagant terms, repeatedly made [representations] as to his
ability to hold the post against a large force of the enemy."[34]
Regarding Carter's Woods, the court wrote that "...the evacuation
of Winchester by general Milroy was as well ordered as could

----

[32]For perspective, although it is this writer's opinion that Milroy's attacks on
the 12th Pennsylvania Cavalry were premeditated and unjustified, the regiment's
staff did have its problems. In 1862 the regiment's original colonel resigned under
a cloud of scandal and its second in command was dismissed for shooting some of
his own troopers while in a drunken rage. Colonel Pierce, who was apparently
absent at the battle, Major Titus, and Lieutenant Colonel Bell (after he assumed
command) were all cashiered later for incompetence. In 1864, probably in part
because of Milroy's efforts, but also because of its own officers, the Hussars'
division commander at the time labeled them as one of the worst regiments in the
service.

[33]The court of inquiry wrote the following about Schenck: "That the General-in
Chief, prior to the attack...had repeatedly instructed General Schenck to maintain
only a small force at [Winchester]...and that General Schenck had disregarded these
instructions, viewing them as suggestions merely.... That it was owing to General
Schenck that at the time of the attack and evacuation there were at Winchester any
more troops, munitions, &c., than would have been sufficient for a mere
outpost...." O.R. 1-27-2-196. President Lincoln added, "Some question can be
made whether some of General Halleck's dispatches to General Schenck should not
have been construed to be orders to withdraw the force, and obeyed accordingly;
but no such question can be made against General Milroy." O.R. 1-27-2-197.

[34]The court, in its findings of fact also wrote, "This last assertion of General
Milroy [on June 14, that he could hold Winchester for five more days], made at a
time when he must have known that his provisions and ammunition were nearly
exhausted, shows that he had an overweening confidence in the strength of his
position and his own ability to defend it." O.R. 1-27-2-190.

have been expected under all the circumstances...." The court also found that "...during the retreat the troops of General Milroy were not kept well in hand, but were very much dispersed, but that this was in great part owing to the sudden attack made upon them in the darkness of the night, and to their being obliged to force their way through a body of troops superior in numbers, and in some part also (in the opinion of the majority of the witnesses) to a want of active co-operation on the part of Colonel McReynolds...."[35]

With a velvet touch, President Lincoln administered a crippling wound to Milroy's career through his endorsement to the report dated October 27, 1863. "Serious blame is not necessarily due to any serious disaster, and I cannot say that in this case any of the officers are deserving of *serious* blame. No court-martial is deemed necessary or proper in the case."[36]

Although spared from being cashiered, Milroy nevertheless paid a heavy price in mental anguish and humiliation. "...I feel deeply grieved at having so many good Union people at Winchester in the power of the demons.... They all had so much confidence in my ability to hold the place and it pains me deeply to think I had to disappoint them.... I see the newspapers and writers are abusing and lying on me most horribly about the Winchester affair. This is terribly annoying."[37] The Hoosier

---

[35]O.R. 1-27-2-196-197. Neither the 12th Pennsylvania Cavalry nor any of its officers were censured for their performance at Winchester.

[36]Ibid., 1-27-2-197, Lincoln. Emphasis supplied.

[37]Milroy letters, 6/21/1863 and 6/25/1863. Milroy's feelings of persecution did not come solely from a complex. For example, New York City's (and perhaps the North's) most widely read newspaper editorialized that Winchester "...ought to have been held...if there had been generalship and pluck at the head...." Worse, it attacked the Hoosier personally, asserting that the loss of men and material was due to "...the want of cool courage and capacity in the commanding general. Unfortunately, Milroy is one of the political generals, appointed not for his military abilities, but for his violent abolition opinions. Such men, being fanatical, have not the brains to lead armies.... Milroy's frantic conduct [at Second Manassas] showed

even hinted at suicide. "The first time I was ever out of command or away from my command a day or night since the war commenced, and this too under such humiliating circumstances to myself and under the present terrible circumstances of my country. I have never in my life been so entirely wretched and miserable. Life has never had many attractions for me and were it not for you and the children would not long endure its agony."[38]

Despite his apparent depression, Milroy continued to press the administration for reinstatement and a new command. In response to the letter he received from President Lincoln quoted at the beginning of this and previous chapters, Milroy responded with another letter to Lincoln begging for help. In that plea he revealed the depth of his desperation by writing that "[e]ven...a crowd of

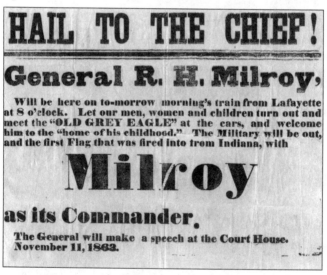

Milroy Broadside

(Courtesy of Rensselaer Public Library)

---

that he had no presence of mind in battle.... His own report...shows how extravagant...he is in his language and how illogical his mind." New York *Herald*, 6/22/1863, p. 4; Faust, pp. 532-533.

[38]Milroy letter, 6/30/1863.

raw niggers [presumably a reference to command of a colored regiment] would be preferable to this agonizing inactivity...."[39] On September 13, 1863, Milroy sent another letter to the chief executive, apparently after the usually patient Lincoln had cut short an interview with the Hoosier that must have been extremely uncomfortable for both men. After writing that the president should be wary of officers who drank too much and aware of the strategic importance of the Shenandoah Valley, Milroy included that the officers of his division had petitioned for his reinstatement. The deflated major general then offered that if their petition could not be granted, that he would be willing to accept a command in Texas. The letter ended with a plea that his fate not be left to Henry Halleck.[40] It was.

For over a year, Milroy floated in military limbo without a command. The only discovered mention of the Hoosier during this period was a rather unflattering reference in a dispatch from Lieutenant General Ulysses S. Grant to Major General William T. Sherman on April 9, 1864, after the latter had apparently requested that he be assigned additional generals. Grant wrote, "I do not think any more generals will be sent to you unless you want Milroy, McCook or Crittenden."[41] Sherman preferred to do without the help, rather than accept any of the tainted trio.

Eventually the need for generals and the likely perception that if kept on a tight leash, Milroy could make a decent division commander, allowed the Hoosier's career to surface for air. On August 31, 1864, he received an assignment to command two

---

[39]Milroy letter, 7/13/1863. O.R. 1-51-1-1076.

[40]O.R. 1-51-1-1087.

[41]Ibid., 1-32-3-305. Both McCook and Crittenden were blamed for the Union disaster at Chickamauga, but both were exonerated at courts of inquiry similar to the one given Milroy. McCook never held a field command again during the war. Crittenden resigned after a brief stint with the Army of the Potomac. Faust, pp. 192, 457.

brigades as part of the defenses of Nashville, Tennessee.[42] Within days, Milroy's truncated division participated in repulsing an attack by Major General Joseph Wheeler's gray-clad cavalry on September 3, 1864.[43]

After two more months of garrison duty, Milroy's new command, under Major General Lovell H. Rousseau in Murfreesboro, was put on full alert as the result of the advance of the Confederate forces who would soon thereafter precipitate the battles of Franklin and Nashville, Tennessee. Following the battle at Franklin, Major General Nathan Bedford Forrest led his butternut riders against a number of blockhouses that guarded the Nashville & Chattanooga Railroad. According to Milroy, he and three of his regiments relieved one of those beleaguered outposts on December 4, 1864. The Hoosier's troops suffered 64 casualties while claiming 8 to 10 dead Confederates and 20 prisoners from the seemingly invincible Forrest.[44]

Three days later a Rebel force comprised of Forrest's horsemen and a division of infantry under Major General William B. Bate took a swipe at Fort Rosecrans, an imposing fortress that sat along the Wilkenson Pike near the site of the earlier battle of Stone's River. Milroy's command was dispatched to fend off the raid. Probably deterred by the size of the Yankee force, and perhaps having heard about Milroy's impetuous style, the Southerners attempted to draw the Bluecoats into an ambush rather than confront them line to line.

True to form, the Hoosier sent his men smashing into the Confederate formation. Intimidated by the violence of Milroy's assault, and still skittish after the bloodletting at Franklin, Bate's riflemen broke and fled the field in a rout. Forrest, who was practically Ares incarnate, rode into the center of the terrified foot soldiers and tried to stem the retreat by encouragement and

---

[42]O.R. 1-39-2-328.
[43]Ibid., 1-52-1-631.
[44]Ibid., 1-45-1-615, 616.

example. That didn't work—so he resorted to shooting a fleeing color-bearer who refused to halt. When even that draconian measure failed, Forrest resorted to pummeling the refugees with the flat side of his sword. Eventually order was restored, but the Confederates had no choice except to make a strategic withdrawal from the field. Milroy claimed that his men captured two cannons, a battle flag, killed two lieutenant colonels and took 197 prisoners at a cost of 28 killed and 208 wounded or missing.[45]

The Hoosier was thrilled and gratified because he had been given the opportunity to help his country—and to bask again in the glow of success. Gushing with gratitude, but unable to suppress his resentment, Milroy wrote to Rousseau, "I...tender...my most grateful acknowledgement of his [Rousseau's] kindness in affording me the two late opportunities of wiping out to some extent the foul and mortifying stigma of a most infamously unjust arrest, by which I have for near eighteen months been thrown out of the ring of active, honorable and desirable service."[46] It wouldn't be long before that gratitude began to wear a little thin.

Neither Milroy nor his men participated in the crushing defeat delivered to the Confederates at Nashville in mid-December. During the balance of the war, the Hoosier carried out his mundane assignment to protect the Nashville & Chattanooga Railroad as far as Stevenson, Alabama.[47] Despite four years of war and many months of numbing garrison duty, Milroy lost none of his hatred for his adversaries. On March 1, 1865, he reported, "I have about 200 men...under very efficient officers, who are

---

[45]O.R. 1-45-1-617-620; Wills, pp. 287-288; Foote, p. 677.

[46]Ibid., 1-45-1-619.

[47]Milroy obtained his authority pursuant to General Order 12 of 1865, dated 2/28/1865. During this time the units in his mini-division changed regularly, presumably as they gained some military training they were pulled away for more important duty. During this period Milroy commanded the 54th, 148th and 152nd Illinois, the 143rd Indiana and the 184th and 188th Ohio. O.R. 1-49-1-633, 785, 778, 882.

actively engaged in scouting and sending guerrillas and their friends to hell."[48]

It also appears that Milroy gained very little insight from the disaster at Winchester and his ensuing precipitous fall from grace. In early April the Hoosier began to enroll local men into a home guard. When Rousseau revoked the order, Milroy wrote a petulant letter justifying his order and explaining that his commander must have misunderstood the situation. For good measure Milroy added, "With all due deference, I do not think that reasons against my order...should have been heard without at least giving me a hearing before striking."[49]

Then, despite all that he had suffered as a result of his own hubris, one of Milroy's last-recorded dispatches at the very end of the war confirmed that he remained certain that no one's judgment could be superior to his own. Unhappy with what he perceived to be a stupid order to grant amnesty to certain ex-Confederates, Milroy penned a response to his commanding officer that reeked of thinly veiled sarcasm. "Am I to understand that I am directed to send flags of truce to all bands of guerrillas, horse-thieves and other armed out-laws that may be within reach of my command? ...All will gladly go through the motions of accepting the terms offered."[50] It is safe to assume that on his last day in the service, Milroy shook his head in disgust over all the mistakes that others had made during the war—and a fist in the direction of West Point.[51]

---

[48]O.R. 1-49-1-809.

[49]Ibid., 1-49-2-219, 291.

[50]Ibid., 1-49-2-570.

[51]After the war Milroy served for a time as a trustee for the Wabash and Erie Canal. In 1872 he moved to Washington State, where he first served as that state's superintendent of Indian affairs and then as an Indian agent in Olympia, Washington, where he died in 1890.

On February 13, 1864, on their way from Winchester to camp at Martinsburg after having failed to intercept a band of Confederate partisans, Corporal John Service and what remained of the 18th Connecticut passed over the battlefield at Carter's Woods. What he saw there moved him to make the following entry in his diary. "As I stand here upon this sacred spot, my mind is full with thoughts of the past...here is the field where the army gathered and made charge after charge upon the Rebels, who were stationed over in that woods just beyond. These trees, and the ground, still shows marks of the contest.... [T]he most sadest sight to see are the graves of those soldiers who fell on that day...they were not buried like a person would do a friend, no, they were simply laid on the ground and the green sod turned over them.

> No useless coffin enclosed their hearts,
> Nor in sheet, or in shroud, did lay them
> But they lay, like soldiers taking their rest
> With not any clothes around them.

As I look at these graves, what do I see, nothing but bones. The hogs that run at large in Virginia have made sad havock among them. Yes, those bones, which were once animated with life now lay scattered over the ground. A fit emblem of our existence."[52]

---

[52]Service diary, 2/13/1864.

Order of Battle

Units comprising the Second Division
of the Union Eighth Corps
Major General Robert H. Milroy commanding

First Brigade
Brigadier General Washington L. Elliott commanding

110th Ohio	116th Ohio
122nd Ohio	123rd Ohio
12th Pennsylvania Cavalry	13th Pennsylvania Cavalry

Battery L, 5th United States Artillery

Second Brigade
Colonel Willilam G. Ely commanding

18th Connecticut	5th Maryland
87th Pennsylvania	12th West Virginia

1st West Virginia Cavalry (Co. K)
3rd West Virginia Cavalry (Co. D & E)
1st West Virginia Artillery, Battery D

Third Brigade
Colonel Andrew T. McReynolds commanding

6th Maryland	67th Pennsylvania

1st New York Cavalry
Baltimore Battery, Maryland Light Artillery

Heavy Artillery
Captain William F. Martins commanding
14th [1st] Massachusetts Heavy Artillery

Units Comprising the Confederate Second Corps
Army of Northern Virginia
Lieutenant General Richard S. Ewell commanding

Early's Division
Major General Jubal A. Early commanding

Hays' Brigade
Brigadier Harry T. Hays commanding

5th Louisiana	6th Louisiana
7th Louisiana	8th Louisiana
	9th Louisiana

Smith's Brigade
Brigadier General William Smith commanding

31st Virginia	49th Virginia
52nd Virginia	58th Virginia

Hoke's Brigade
Colonel Isaac E. Avery commanding

6th North Carolina	54th North Carolina
21st North Carolina	57th North Carolina

Gordon's Brigade
Brigadier General John B. Gordon commanding

13th Georgia	26th Georgia
31st Georgia	38th Georgia
60th Georgia	61st Georgia

Artillery
Lt. Colonel H. P. Jones commanding

Charlottesville (Virginia) Art.	Courtney (Virginia) Art.
Louisiana Guard Art.	Staunton (Virginia) Art.

Johnson's Division
Major General Edward Johnson commanding

Steuart's Brigade
Brigadier General George H. Steuart commanding

1st Maryland Battalion	1st North Carolina
3rd North Carolina	10th Virginia
23rd Virginia	37th Virginia

Stonewall Brigade
Brigadier General James A. Walker commanding

2nd Virginia	4th Virginia
5th Virginia	27th Virginia

33rd Virginia

Nicholl's Brigade
Colonel J. M. Williams commanding

1st Louisiana	2nd Louisiana
10th Louisiana	14th Louisiana

15th Louisiana

Jones' Brigade
Brigadier General John M. Jones commanding

21st Virginia	25th Virginia
42nd Virginia	44th Virginia
48th Virginia	50th Virginia

Artillery
Major J. W. Latimer commanding

1st Maryland Battery   Alleghany (Virginia) Art.
Chesapeake (Maryland) Art.   Lee (Virginia) Battery

Rodes' Division
Major General Robert E. Rodes commanding

Daniel's Brigade
Brigadier General Junius Daniel commanding

32nd North Carolina   43rd North Carolina
45th North Carolina   53rd North Carolina
2nd North Carolina Battalion

Dole's Brigade
Brigadier General George Doles commanding

4th Georgia   12th Georgia
21st Georgia   44th Georgia

Iverson's Brigade
Brigadier General Alfred Iverson commanding

5th North Carolina   12th North Carolina
20th North Carolina   23rd North Carolina

Ramseur's Brigade
Brigadier General Stephen D. Ramseur commanding

2nd North Carolina   4th North Carolina
14th North Carolina   30th North Carolina

O'Neal's Brigade
Colonel Edward A. O'Neal commanding

3rd Alabama   5th Alabama
6th Alabama   12th Alabama
26th Alabama

Artillery
Lt. Colonel Thomas Carter commanding

Jeff. Davis (Alabama) Art.   King William (Virginia) Art.
Morris (Virginia) Art.   Orange (Virginia) Art.

Cavalry
Jenkins' Brigade
Brigadier General Albert G. Jenkins commanding

14th Virginia Cav.   16th Virginia Cav.
17th Virginia Cav.   34th Virginia Batt. Cav.
36th Virginia Batt. Cav.   Jackson's Virginia Battery

BIBLIOGRAPHY

MANUSCRIPTS

Bruder, W. H. 123rd Ohio Journal, U.S. Army Military History Institute, Civil War miscellaneous collection.

Congdon, James A. Letters, 12th Pennsylvania Cavalry, Historical Society of Pennsylvania.

Crowl, Thomas. 87th Pennsylvania, Letters, U.S. Army Military History Institute.

Detwiler, George W. 12th Pennsylvania Cavalry, Pension Records and Papers, National Archives, Washington, D.C.

Graham, William P. Letters, 12th Pennsylvania Cavalry, private and unpublished.

Kesses, John C. Letters, *Civil War Times Illustrated* Collection, U.S. Army Military History Institute.

Lee, Mrs. Hugh. Diary, Handley Regional Library, Winchester, Virginia.

McMillen, Jefferson O. 122d Ohio, Letter dated June 9, 1863, U.S. Army Military History Institute, Gregory A. Coco Collection.

Michaels, James David. Letters, n.d., U.S. Army Military History Institute.

Milroy, Robert H. Collection, Rensselaer Public Library, Rensselaer, Indiana.

O'Brady, James. Letters and Pension Records, 12th Pennsylvania Cavalry, National Archives, Washington, D.C.

Powell, David. 12th West Virginia Infantry, Memoirs, *Civil War Times Illustrated* Collection, U.S. Army Military History Institute, 1904.

Service, John. Unpublished Diaries, Letters, and Memoirs. Private Collection.

Seymour, Capt. William J. Diary, U.S. Army Military History Institute, Gregory A. Coco Collection.

Stewart, James. Letter dated November 2, 1862, U.S. Army Military History Institute.

Twelfth Pennsylvania Cavalry, Individual Military and Pension Records, National Archives, Washington, D.C.

Twelfth Pennsylvania Cavalry, Regimental Records, National Archives, Washington, D.C.

Twelfth Pennsylvania Cavalry, Regimental Records, Pennsylvania Archives, Harrisburg, Pa.

Weirich, Charles. Letters, 12th Pennsylvania Cavalry, U.S. Army Military History Institute.

ARTICLES

Coles, David J., and Stephen D. Engle, ed. "Powder, Lead and Cold Steel: Campaigning in the Lower Shenandoah Valley with the Twelfth Pennsylvania Cavalry—The Civil War Letters of John H. Black." *The Magazine of the Jefferson County Historical Society.*

Wells, Dean M. "Ewell Seizes the Day at Winchester." *America's Civil War*, March 1997.

BOOKS -- Primary Sources

Allan, William. *Stonewall Jackson, Robert E. Lee, and the Army of Northern Virginia, 1862.* New York: De Capo Press, 1995.

Beach, William H. *The First New York (Lincoln) Cavalry: From April 19, 1861 to July 7, 1865.* New York: The Lincoln Cavalry Association, 1902.

Cassler, John O. *Four Years in the Stonewall Brigade.* Guthrie, Oklahoma: Scotts Capitol Printing Company, 1893.

Colt, Margaretta Barton. *Defend the Valley: A Shenandoah Family in the Civil War.* New York, New York: Oxford University Press, 1994.

Early, Jubal A. *Narrative of the War Between the States.* New York: De Capo Press, Inc., 1989.

Gordon, John B. *Reminiscences of the Civil War.* Baton Rouge, Louisiana: State University Press, 1993. (First published in 1903 by Charles Scribner's Sons)

Grant, Ulysses S. *Personal Memoirs of U. S. Grant.* New York: Charles L. Webster & Company, 1885.

Hamlin, Captain Percy Gatling, ed. *The Making of a Soldier: Letters of General R. S. Ewell.* Richmond, Virginia: Whittet & Shepperson, 1935.

Hartley, James J. *The Civil War Letters of the Late First Lieut. James J. Hartley, 122nd Ohio Infantry Regiment.* Edited by Garber A. Davidson. Jefferson, North Carolina and London: McFarland & Company, Inc., 1998.

Hay, John. *Inside Lincoln's White House: The Complete Civil War Diary of John Hay.* Edited by Michael Burlingame and John R. Turner Ettlinger. Carbondale and Edwardsville, Illinois: Southern Illinois University Press, 1997.

Hewitt, William. *History of the 12th West Virginia Volunteer Infantry: The Part it Took in the War of the Rebellion 1861-1865.* 12th West Virginia Infantry Association, 1898.

Hotchkiss, Jedidiah, and William Allen. *The Battlefields of Virginia — Chancellorsville.* D. Van Nostrand: New York, 1867. (Butternut & Blue, reprint).

Jones, Virgil Carrington. *Ranger Mosby.* McLean, Virginia: EPM Publications Inc., reprint.

Keifer, J. Warren. *Slavery and Four Years of War: A Political History of Slavery in the United States, Together with a Narrative of the Campaigns and Battles of the Civil War in which the Author Took Part: 1861-65, Volumes 1 and 2.* New York: G. P. Putnam's Sons, 1900. (Reprinted by Mnemosyne Publishing Company, Inc., 1969.)

Keyes, Charles M., ed. *The Military History of the 123d Regiment of Ohio Volunteer Infantry.* Sandusky, Ohio: Register Steam Press, 1874.

Leon, L. *Diary of a Tarheel Confederate Soldier.* Charlotte, North Carolina: Stone Publishing Company, 1913.

Mosby, John S. *Mosby's Memoirs.* Nashville, Tennessee: J. S. Sanders & Company, 1995.

Mosby, John S. *Mosby's War Reminiscences.* Camden, South Carolina: John Culler & Sons, 1990.

Prowell, George R. *History of the Eighty-Seventh Regiment, Pennsylvania Volunteers.* York, Pennsylvania: Press of the York Daily, 1903. (Reprinted by Windmill Publications, 1994.)

Reed, Thomas Benton. *A Private in Gray.* Camden, Arkansas: T. B. Reed, 1905.

Rowe, Alfred Seelye. *History of the First Regiment of Heavy Artillery Massachusetts Volunteers, formerly the 14th Regiment of Infantry, 1861-1865.* Boston, Massachusetts: Commonwealth Press, 1917.

Scott, John. *Partisan Life with Col. John S. Mosby.* New York: Harper & Brothers, Publishers, 1867.

Stevenson, James H. *Boots and Saddles, A History of the First Volunteer Cavalry of the War, Known as the First New York (Lincoln) Cavalry.* Harrisburg, Pennsylvania: The Patriot Publishing Company, 1879.

United States War Department. *The War of the Rebellion: A Compilation of the Official Records of the Union and Confederate Armies.* 70 vols. in 128 parts. Washington, D.C.: Government Printing Office, 1880-1901.

United States War Department. *Atlas to Accompany the Official Records of the Union and Confederate Armies.* Board of Publication: George B. Davis, Leslie J. Perry, Joseph W. Kirkley. Compiled by Capt. Calvin D. Cowles, Washington, D.C., 1891-1895.

Valentine, Malden. *Pennsylvania at Antietam, Report of the Antietam Battlefield Memorial Commission of Pennsylvania.* Harrisburg, Pennsylvania: Harrisburg Publishing Company, 1906.

Walker, William C., Chaplain. *History of the Eighteenth Regiment Connecticut Volunteers in the War for the Union.* Norwich, Connecticut: Regimental Committee, 1885.

Wild, Frederick W. *Memoirs and History of Captain F. W. Alexander's Baltimore Battery of Light Artillery.* Baltimore, Maryland School for Boys, 1912.

Wildes, Thomas F. *Record of the One Hundred and Sixteenth Regiment, Ohio Infantry Volunteers in the War of the Rebellion.* Sandusky, Ohio: O.I.F. March, 1884.

Williamson, James J. *Mosby's Rangers: A Record of the Operations of the Forty-Third Battalion Virginia Cavalry from its Organization to the Surrender.* New York: Ralph B. Kenyon, 1896. (Time-Life, reprint 1982.)

BOOKS -- Secondary Sources

Ackinclose, Timothy. *Sabres & Pistols: The Civil War Career of Colonel Harry Gilmore, C.S.A.* Gettysburg, Pennsylvania: Stan Clark Military Books, 1997.

Barnett, Louise. *Touched by Fire.* New York: Henry Holt & Co., 1996.

Bates, Samuel P. *Martial Deeds of Pennsylvania.* Philadelphia, Pennsylvania: T. H. Davis & Co., 1875.

--------. *History of the Pennsylvania Volunteers, 1861-1865.* Vol. 4. Philadelphia, Pennsylvania: B. Singerly, 1870.

Beck, Brandon H., & Charles S. Grunder. *The Second Battle of Winchester, June 12-15, 1863*. Lynchburg, Virginia: H. E. Howard, Inc., 1989.

Burton, William L. *Melting Pot Soldiers: The Union's Ethnic Regiments*. Second Edition, New York: Fordham University Press, 1998.

Coddington, Edwin B. *The Gettysburg Campaign, A Study in Command*. New York: Charles Scribner's Sons, 1968.

Delauter, Roger V., Jr. *Winchester in the Civil War*. Lynchburg, Virginia: H. E. Howard, Inc., 1992.

Faust, Patricia L. ed. *Historical Times Illustrated Encyclopedia of the Civil War*. New York: Harper Perennial, 1986.

Furgurson, Ernest B. *Chancellorsville 63: The Souls of the Brave*. New York: Alfred A. Knopf, 1992.

Foote, Shelby. *The Civil War, A Narrative*. New York: Vintage Books, 1986.

Hearn, Chester G. *Six Years of Hell: Harpers Ferry During the Civil War*. Baton Rouge, Louisiana: Louisiana State University Press, 1996.

Hennessy, John J. *Return to Bull Run, The Campaign and Battle of Second Manassas*. New York: Simon & Schuster, 1993.

Jannett, J. H., George W. F. Vernon, and L. Allison Wilmer. *History and Roster of Maryland Volunteers War of 1861-65*. Baltimore, Maryland: Guggenheimer, Weil & Company, 1898.

Jones, Terry L. *Lee's Tigers: The Louisiana Infantry and the Army of Northern Virginia, Doctoral Dissertation*. Texas A&M, 1983.

Keen, Hugh C., and Horace Mewborn. *43rd Battalion Virginia Cavalry Mosby's Command*. Lynchburg, Virginia: H. E. Howard, Inc., 1993.

Longacre, Edward G. *The Cavalry at Gettysburg*. Lincoln, Nebraska: University of Nebraska Press, 1986.

Lord, Francis A. *Civil War Sutlers and Their Wares.* Cranbury, New Jersey: Thomas Yoseloff Ltd., 1969.

Maier, Larry B. *Rough and Regular, A History of Philadelphia's 119th Regiment of Pennsylvania Volunteer Infantry, The Gray Reserves.* Shippensburg, Pennsylvania: Burd Street Press, 1997.

Matter, William D. *If It Takes All Summer: The Battle of Spotsylvania.* Chapel Hill, North Carolina: University of North Carolina Press, 1988.

McPherson, James M. *Battle Cry of Freedom, The Civil War Era.* New York: Ballantine Books, 1989.

Naisawald, L. BanLoan. *Grape and Canister: The Story of the Field Artillery of the Army of the Potomac, 1861-1865, 2d Edition.* Mechanicsburg, Pennsylvania: Stackpole Books, 1999.

Nye, Wilbur Sturtevant. *Here Come the Rebels.* Dayton, Ohio: Morningside House, Inc., 1988.

Pfanz, Donald C. *Richard S. Ewell: A Soldier's Life.* Chapel Hill, North Carolina: University of North Carolina Press, 1998.

Pfanz, Harry W. *Gettysburg: Kulp's Hill and Cemetery Hill.* Chapel Hill, North Carolina: University of North Carolina Press, 1993.

Ramage, James A. *Gray Ghost: The Life of Col. John Singleton Mosby.* Lexington, Kentucky: University Press of Kentucky, 1999.

Sauers, Richard. *Advance the Colors: Pennsylvania Civil War Battle Flags.* Vol. 2. Harrisburg, Pennsylvania: Capitol Preservation Committee, 1991.

Sears, Stephen W. *To the Gates of Richmond: The Peninsular Campaign.* New York: Ticknor & Fields, 1992.

Starr, Stephen Z. *The Union Cavalry in the Civil War.* Vols. 1 and 3. Baton Rouge, Louisiana: Louisiana State University Press, 1981.

Stephens, Ann S. *Pictorial History of the War for the Union. A Complete and Reliable History of the War from its Commencement to its Close: Volume 1.* Cincinnati: James R. Hawley, 1862.

Summers, Festus. *The Baltimore and Ohio in the Civil War.* Gettysburg, Pennsylvania: Stan Clark Military Books, 1993.

Tanner, Robert G. *Stonewall in the Valley: Thomas J. "Stonewall" Jackson's Shenandoah Valley Campaign, Spring 1862.* Mechanicsburg, Pa.: Stackpole Books, 1996.

Taylor, Frank H. *Philadelphia in the Civil War.* Philadelphia, Pennsylvania: The City, 1913. Reprint, J. M. Santarelli, 1991.

Thomas, Dean S. *Cannons: An Introduction to Civil War Artillery.* Gettysburg, Pennsylvania: Thomas Publications, 1985.

Wert, Jeffry D. *General James Longstreet, The Confederacy's Most Controversial Soldier.* New York: Simon and Schuster, 1993.

--------. *Mosby's Rangers.* New York: A Touchstone Book, 1990.

Wills, Brian Steel. *A Battle From the Start: The Life of Nathan Bedford Forrest.* New York: Harper Collins, 1992.

NEWSPAPERS -- Primary Sources

"As to Milroy" *National Tribune*, September 16, 1909.

Averill, S. R. "About the Running." *National Tribune*, June 6, 1895.

Brachwell, I. G. "Capture of Winchester, Virginia, and Milroy's Army in June 1863." *Confederate Veteran*, (30), p. 330.

Casner, John N. "On the Scout." *National Tribune*, December 15, 1898.

Cramer, George W. "A Few Recollections." *National Tribune*, January 17, 1901.

"Death Notice of Captain William I. Raisin." *Confederate Veteran* (24) (10-1916), p. 466.

Erskine, Charles M. "The Battle of Winchester." *Grand Army Scout and Soldier's Mail*, March 14, 1885.

Griffith, J. M. "Milroy at Winchester." *National Tribune*, February 11, 1909.

Gutelius, H. E. *Mifflinburg Telegraph*, November 17, 1862; May 5, 1863; and May 26, 1863.

Hammer, George H. *Pennsylvania Daily Telegraph*, October 12, 1863.

Hertzog, A. J. "Milroy at Close Range." *National Tribune*, March 31, 1910.

Linn, S. T. "The Cavalry at Winchester." *National Tribune*, March 31, 1910.

Kilhool, Denis. "Winchester Battle and Something of the Last Days at Raleigh Under Sherman." *National Tribune*, September 17, 1890.

McElhenny, R. H. "Milroy at Winchester." *National Tribune*, May 20, 1909.

Philadelphia Inquirer, September 1, 1862.

Powell, D. *National Tribune*, May 16, 1889.

Sawyer, J. H. *National Tribune*, October 23, 1913.

Titus, Addison R. *The Warren Mail*, May 28, 1862; June 7, 1862.

Valentine, Malden. *National Tribune*, November 19, 1908.

NEWSPAPERS -- Secondary Sources

New York Herald, June 22, 1863.
Philadelphia Inquirer, June 24, 1863.
The New York Times, Vol. 7, No. 3660, June 17, 1863.

INDEX

Abraham's Creek 148, 166
Adams, Alonzo W. 96, 159, 163, 252, 266
Alabama Infantry
  15th Regiment 111
Alexander, Frederic W. 202
Alexander's Baltimore
  Battery 159, 256
Allegheny Mountain 23
Apple Pie Ridge 181
Arckenoe, Frederick H. 182, 196

Bailey, Ezra H. 84
Baker, James C. 188
Ball, William H. 192
Barrett, Donald xii
Bate, William B. 310
Bath, West Virginia 267
Belle Island, Virginia 261
Benham, Henry W. 20
Black, John H. 206, 274
Blenker, Louis 108
Bloody Run, Pennsylvania 269, 271, 272
Bower's Hill 171
Boyd, William H. 96, 160
Boyd, William H., Jr. 158, 214, 275
Brewer, Melvin 130
Bruder, W. H. 174, 257
Buffalo Gap 25
Bull Pasture Mountain 27
Bull Pasture River 26
Bunker Hill 164
Bunker Hill, West Virginia 164
Byrne, Edward 79

Cafferty, Milton 276
Carlin, John 149, 166
Carpenter's Battery 222
Carrington, James M. 188
Castle Thunder, Virginia 263
Cedar Creek Road 142
Cedar Creek Turnpike 187
Cedar Mountain 36
Cedarville, Virginia 135
Cheat Mountain 22
Clarksburg, West Virginia 89
Cluseret, G. P. 55, 74
Cochise 106
Coleman, R. T. 217
Connecticut Infantry
  18th Regiment 98, 119, 120, 143, 172, 178, 184, 185, 234, 236, 239, 241, 256, 265
Couch, Darius N. 270, 277, 279
Cravens, John O. 137
Cross Keys 33
Cunningham's Crossroads 277

Dance, Willard 188
Daniel, Junius 135
Dement's Battery 221
Dumont, Ebenezer 19

Early, Jubal A. 112, 143, 151, 187, 195
Elliott, Washington L. 85, 87, 126, 148, 167, 182, 224, 229
Ely, William G. 126, 143, 239
Ewell, Richard S. 104, 143, 181, 182, 204, 217

Fisher's Hill, Virginia	87	Irwin, David A.	86, 91, 279
Forrest, Nathan Bedford	310		
Fort Rosecrans, Tenn.	310	Jackson, Thomas J.	32
Frame, A. B.	165	James, Edward	209
Franklin, Western Virginia	32	Jamison, Alfred	180
Free, Peter	234	Janelew, West Virginia	90
Fremont, John C.	25, 108	Jenkins, Albert G.	157, 207, 208
Frey, Lewis	180	Jessie Scouts	129
Frick, B. F.	180	Johnson, Edward	23, 28, 113, 143,
Front Royal Road	131, 143		217, 218, 221, 230
Funsten, O. R.	79	Jones, Abram	76, 96, 277, 279
		Jones, John M.	147
Galligher, James A.	268	Jones, William E.	75, 89
Garnett, Robert S.	19		
Georgia Infantry		Keifer, J. Warren	63, 149,
12th Regiment	29		182, 229-231
13th Regiment	154	Kelley, Benjamin F.	18
31st Regiment	154	Kernstown, Virginia	150, 151
Gilmor, Harry	132, 133	Kerwin, Michael	78, 94, 247
Golding, Sylvester	237	Klinedinst, L. J.	237
Gordon, John B.	152	Klunk, John B.	155, 192, 272
Gough, Ben	177		
Green River	23	Lambie, William T.	145
Griffin's Baltimore Horse Art.	149	Lang, Theodore	42
Gutelius, Henry E.	86	Latham, G. R.	55
		Leary, Peter, Jr.	203
Halleck, Henry W.	54, 115	Lemon, John	165
Hammer, Graves B.	261	Lincoln, Abraham	54, 214, 280,
Hancock, Maryland	267		307, 309
Hanson, J. B.	147	Lost Creek	90
Harrison, Montgomery S.	171	Lost River	87
Harvey, John V.	214	Louisiana Infantry	
Hays, Harry T.	152, 195, 216	2nd Regiment	249
Hedgeman's River	39	5th Regiment	195
Hendrich, Friedrich	140	6th Regiment	195
Hertzog, A. J.	129	7th Regiment	195
Hertzog, Robert H.	77	8th Regiment	195
Hoffman, John C.	237	9th Regiment	152, 176, 195
Hotchkiss, Jedediah	102	10th Regiment	249
Humphrey, John D.	214	Louisiana Tigers	195
		Lupton House	187
Imboden, John D.	89, 269		
Indiana Infantry		Martindale, Franklin G.	83, 159
9th Regiment	18, 22		

Maryland Artillery (U.S.A.)
  Baltimore Battery   160, 202
Maryland Cavalry (C.S.A.)
  1st Regiment   133
  2nd Regiment   95
Maryland Infantry (C.S.A.)
  2nd Regiment   149
Maryland Infantry (U.S.A.)
  5th Regiment   143, 242, 256
  6th Regiment   159, 160, 245, 248,
                         251, 256, 265
Massachusetts Artillery
  14th [1st] Heavy Regiment   128,
                              147, 256
Maulsby's Battery   207, 210
McClellan, George B.   19
McConnellsburg, Pa.   270, 274
McDonald, Brenda   xii
McDowell, Western Virginia   25
McGee, J. Lowry   231
McReynolds, Andrew T.   127, 158,
                              244, 245
Michigan Cavalry
  1st Regiment   130
Middletown, Virginia   139
Milroy, Robert H.   120, 129, 143,
        149, 171, 175, 179, 191, 203,
            214, 220, 234, 244, 270
  biographical sketch   14
Milroy, Samuel   14
Monterey, Western Virginia   25
Morgan, Charles B.   186
Morris, Thomas A.   19
Morris, W. T.   164
Mosby, John S.   75, 96
Mosby's Partisan Rangers   91, 96
Moss, Joseph L.   86, 131, 135, 149,
                              222, 273
Myers, S. B.   85

Nadenbousch, J. Q. A.   146
New York Cavalry
  1st Regiment   74-78, 82, 84, 91,
        96, 140, 157, 159, 160, 214,

        245, 251, 256, 266, 268, 272,
                   273, 274, 277
New York Infantry
  106th Regiment   207, 209
Newton, James W.   184
Newtown, Virginia   133
North Carolina Infantry
  1st Regiment   221
  3rd Regiment   221
  54th Regiment   187

O'Neal, Edward A.   158
Ohio Infantry
  25th Regiment   28
  28th Regiment   90
  32nd Regiment   25, 28, 30
  75th Regiment   28
  82nd Regiment   28, 30, 41
  110th Regiment   55, 84, 142, 148,
       149, 182, 194, 224, 226, 229,
                              256, 265
  116th Regiment   55, 81, 85, 87,
       150, 164, 182, 194, 196, 200,
            242, 254, 256, 265, 266
  122nd Regiment   55, 84, 178,
            192, 200, 201, 224
            230, 234, 256, 265
  123rd Regiment   55, 81, 85, 87,
       148, 150, 156, 167, 174, 176
       192, 201, 224, 236, 241, 256
  126th Regiment   207, 210

Orr, John   198

Palmer, F. A.   232
Passegger, Franz   78
Peale, Henry   178
Penn, D. H.   176
Pennsylvania Cavalry
  12th Regiment   80, 85, 87, 89,
       90, 135, 142, 149, 173, 185,
       206, 220-222, 256, 265, 267,
                   270, 273, 277

13th Regiment   75, 76, 78, 84, 85, 87, 88, 94, 131, 139, 142, 143, 148, 173, 245, 247, 256, 264, 265
Pennsylvania Infantry
   67th Regiment   81, 91, 245, 249, 256, 262
   87th Regiment   55, 75, 87, 88, 120, 131, 143, 145, 164, 168, 179, 200, 234, 238, 256, 262, 264, 265, 268
Petersburg, Western Virginia   57
Piatt, Donn   271
Pierce, Lewis B.   186, 270-272, 276, 277, 279
Pitman, George   214
Pleasonton, Alfred   113
Potomac Home Brigade Cavalry   207
Pritchard's Hill   151, 152
Pughtown Road   186
Pughtown, Virginia   185

Quinn, Timothy   163, 253

Raine's Battery   222
Raisin, William   133, 134
Randolph, Wallace F.   146, 182
Reed, Thomas B.   170
Renssellaer, Indiana   16
Rich Mountain, Western Virginia   19
Rihl, William H.   276
Roberts, B. S.   89
Rodes, Robert E.   112, 135, 143, 208
Romney Road   186, 187
Rousseau, Lovell H.   310

Schall, John W.   131, 132, 234
Schenck, Robert C.   28, 47, 116, 117, 213
Seymour, William J.   194
Shaw's Ridge   26
Shenandoah Mountain   26
Sigel, Franz   35
Sir John's Run   267

Smith, Benjamin F.   207
Spooner, Edmund D.   144, 145, 247
Stafford, L. A.   152
Stanton, Edwin W.   54
Star Fort   166, 173, 181
Staunton, F. J.   91
Stephenson's Depot   217
Steuart, George H.   147, 217
Stiles, Robert   203
Stonewall Brigade   238, 241
Strasburg Road   142
Strasburg, Virginia   85, 88
Sweeney, J. W.   159

Taliaferro, William B.   30
Theaker, Lieutenant   149
Titus, Darius   186, 271
Trimble, Isaac   110
Tyler, Daniel   207

Union Mills   148
United States Artillery
   5th Regiment, Battery L   81, 131, 143, 182, 256
Utt, James R.   95

Valentine, Malden   223, 257
Valley Turnpike   131, 132, 148
Vermylia, Isaac D.   96
Virginia Cavalry
   4th Regiment   82
   7th Regiment   79, 85
   11th Regiment   79
   14th Regiment   133, 275
Virginia Infantry
   2nd Regiment   146, 147, 238, 241
   5th Regiment   184, 185, 238, 241
   10th Regiment   221
   44th Regiment   29
   52nd Regiment   29
   58th Regiment   29, 258
   Richmond Home Guard   261
   Stonewall Brigade   264

Wade, Mary Virginia   180
Walker, James A.   147, 217, 241
Wardensville, Virginia   87
Washburn, James   56, 243, 266-268
West Virginia Artillery
  1st Light Battery   256
  1st Regiment, Battery D   85,
                             148, 166
West Virginia Cavalry
  1st Regiment   90, 256
  3rd Regiment   90, 95, 256
West Virginia Infantry
  2nd Regiment   42, 55
  3rd Regiment   28, 30, 42, 45, 55
  4th Regiment   55
  5th Regiment   39, 42, 55
  8th Regiment   55
  9th Regiment   75, 87, 88
  10th Regiment   55
  12th Regiment   55, 73, 75, 120,
        148, 150, 151, 154, 167, 177,
    192, 201, 242, 254, 256, 266, 267
West Virginia Light Artillery
  Battery D   149
Wild, Frederick W.   203
Williams, J. M.   147, 217, 249
Wilson, J. W.   275
Woodruff, Charles   82
Woodstock, Virginia   85

Yonley, Alma   196
Yonley, Lizzie   196
Young, Charles   83

Zimmerman, Charles E.   180